S0-CAW-968

THIS BOOK BELONGS TO

_____

FROM

_____

DATE

_____

366 devotions on how to **find** **Jesus** in real-life situations

Skateboards, Scooters and Scripture

Anne McFarlane

CHRISTIAN ART PUBLISHERS

Published by CHRISTIAN ART PUBLISHERS
PO Box 1599, Vereeniging, 1930

© 2002
First edition 2002

Cover designed by Christian Art Publishers

Scripture quotations taken from the *Holy Bible*, New International Version®.
NIV® Copyright © 1973, 1978, 1984 by International Bible Society.
Used by permission of Zondervan Publishing House. All rights reserved.

Set in 12 on 14 pt Weidemann Book by Christian Art Publishers

Printed and bound by Paarl Print, Oosterland Street, Paarl, South Africa

ISBN 1-86852-906-1

© All rights reserved. No part of this book may be reproduced in any
form without permission in writing from the publisher, except in the
case of brief quotations embodied in critical articles or reviews.

02 03 04 05 06 07 08 09 10 11 – 11 10 9 8 7 6 5 4 3 2 1

Acknowledgements

- Thanks to my family and friends who passed on stories to me, and who faithfully prayed for me. I value your support.
- Thanks to my husband, Theo, whose encouragement and understanding are precious to me.
- Thanks to all the writers, preachers and storytellers from whom I borrowed plots and plans.
- Thanks to Sua du Plessis at Christian Art Publishers who motivated and advised me so enthusiastically.
- Thanks to the Lord who gave me this opportunity and provided all that was needed for the project.

This book is dedicated to all my grandchildren.

Foreword

This is a book of stories and anecdotes. Many of the stories are true, some are made-up and others are Bible stories, but each reflects a biblical truth. Some of the stories are for 8 to 10-year-olds, while others will interest slightly older readers. There are even stories that will appeal to teens and adults, which makes this an excellent book to use for family devotions. I hope that those who use this devotional will find it simple, concrete, direct and practical!

I trust that parents and teachers who are concerned about establishing Christian values and norms in the lives of children will find this book useful. Educators have long been aware of the special responsibility we have towards young children. Foundations for life, good or bad, are laid while children are young and impressionable. But these days, parents have sleepless nights over the ogres of street thugs peddling drugs in school grounds and the Internet streaming its dangers into homes. Concerned adults are desperately seeking ways for godly influence to speak more loudly than the cries of the world. I trust that this book will be of great value to them. The Dutch educationalist, Waterink, said, "Education is not what your child learns, but what he retains from what he learns." May this book cultivate a lifestyle of dedication and commitment to God and His Word.

God bless you. May parents experience that special joy of seeing their children come to a personal faith in Christ through His Holy Spirit.

Kids: If you are between the ages of 8 and 12, this book is just for you! You can use it to develop your own quiet time each day. But it can also be fun to read it together with your parents. Then you can chat about the stories.
Have fun!

JANUARY

Remember to remember

How many times a day do you think about God? Does it sometimes happen that a whole day passes in which you haven't even given Him a thought? It can easily happen, you know! Because things that are visible can take up all our attention. And then there's no time left for thoughts about the invisible God.

That is why it is a very good idea to start a few habits that will remind you of God. He wants you to remember Him. Aren't you the same? Don't you also like knowing that people you love think about you often?

A good idea is to talk to God before you jump out of bed in the morning. Invite Him to join you in everything that you plan to do that day. You can put up a bright poster to help you to remember to do this. Picture in your mind how He accompanies you to school, to the sports field and back home. Some kids wear a WWJD wristband to remind them of Jesus. Others have a sticker on their schoolbag. Every time they see these reminders, they can rejoice that they belong to God and that He will never forget them.

During World War II the biggest clock in the world, the Big Ben in London, had a special pealing of bells at 6 in the evening to remind the people of England to pray for peace.

We should also remind ourselves to keep a regular appointment with God. I hope this book will help you to remember God.

See what David said in Psalm 132:2-5. We can also prepare a dwelling for the Lord in our hearts.

1 January

Follow my leader

You probably know the inspiring hymn: "Guide me O Thou great Jehovah, pilgrim through this barren land. Let the fiery, cloudy pillar, lead me all my journey through." At the beginning of a new year we all feel the need for God to guide and protect us. He is the One who knows the way ahead and who can protect us along the way. He is our Shepherd and we follow Him, as John 10:4 puts it: *"He goes on ahead of them, and his sheep follow him because they know his voice."*

If we follow in the footsteps of Jesus, we can also show others the way. There's an interesting custom in North Africa that can help us to remember this truth. People who travel through the desert often lose their way and then they do not know where to find water. But camels know exactly where all the oases are. That is why the owners sometimes let a camel loose to walk out in front. The group cannot move as fast as the loose camel and they do not want to lose track of him. So, when the camel in front goes over the furthest sand dune, another camel is set free. This camel will follow the leader and just before the travelers lose sight of him, a third camel and later a fourth one is set free. In this way the animals follow the leader and each other so that you often find a string of camels walking in the desert, all on their way in the same direction, moving towards water and towards home!

Paul said in 1 Corinthians 11:1, *"Follow my example as I follow the example of Christ."* In this way we can be part of a whole chain of believers on our way to our heavenly home!

Ask God to help you to follow Him faithfully during this year, so that others can learn from your example.

2 January

Do you love Jesus?

There once was a king who was looking for a wife for his son. You see, in those days a prince was not allowed to choose his own wife. So, his father, the king, sent servants all over his kingdom to look for a suitable wife for his son. They had to look for somebody who could marry the prince and who would one day be a good queen. After searching all over the country, the king's agents brought three special young girls to the palace. One by one they were brought before the king so that he could get to know them better. To each one he put the question, "Why would you like to marry my son?"

The first girl answered, "Because I would like to be famous. I want my photo to appear on front pages, so that people can know about me."

The second one said, "I want to marry the prince, because my parents will be glad if I do."

But the last one said, "It will give me great joy to marry the prince, because I know him and I love him."

Can you guess which one of these girls became the prince's bride?

Jesus also wants us to follow Him because we love Him. It is not good enough if we go to church or Sunday school or to a youth club just to please our parents or to impress our friends. Jesus wants friends who know Him and love Him.

We read in 1 John 4:19, *"We love him, because he first loved us."*

Read in John 21:15-17 how Peter got the opportunity to tell Jesus that he loved Him. Then write a letter to Jesus, telling Him how you feel about Him. Keep it in your Bible.

3 January

New spectacles

Have you noticed how different the world appears through sunglasses? Have you ever tried to put on Grandpa or Grandma's spectacles? Wow! Everything sure looked different, didn't it?

When we start to follow Jesus, things around us also start to look remarkably different. We ourselves look different. We realize that we used to be sin-stained, but now we are clean and pure, because we have asked Jesus to forgive our sins.

All of a sudden, other people also look different. The boy or girl at school who seemed ugly, now looks beautiful to us, because we realize that God sees him or her as precious. With our new eyes we can also see how enormous problems have shrunk miraculously, just because Jesus is in the picture. The tests that we face at school seem less difficult, because we trust Jesus to help us.

On top of it all, the whole world looks lovelier than ever! We notice the colorful flowers, the swaying tree-tops, the blue mountains and we praise God for giving us such a marvelous world to live in. We cherish it so much, that we try to fight pollution and take care of the environment whenever we have a chance.

But the best feature of our new pair of glasses is that we can now see Jesus in our mind's eye. We know that He is with us, walking with us, listening to us and helping us.

Many people cannot see God's will, presence and power in everything that happens in their lives. When they have problems, they do not realize how near God is. We must tell other people what we are seeing. We can give them a new pair of glasses!

Read the Bible story in 2 Kings 6:8-17. Elisha saw things that his servant could not see.

4 January

The King's highway!

First read Matthew 7:13, 14: *"Enter through the narrow gate. For wide is the gate and broad is the road that leads to destruction, and many may enter through it. But small is the gate and narrow the road that leads to life, and only a few find it."*

Jesus says that life is like a highway. And somewhere along the way we will get to a crossing where we will have to choose between two roads. How do we go about making this choice? Do we choose the road that seems broad and easy? No, of course not! We should take the road that will lead us to the place where we want to go. Surely it will be silly to choose a pleasant road to one place if we actually want to go to another place!

Would you like to go to heaven one day? Then you must choose the road that will take you there. Unfortunately, it is a narrow road and often very difficult. But this road will eventually bring you to a place where you will be happy for ever and ever. Some people call this road the King's way, because it belongs to King Jesus.

The other road is broad and comfortable. That is why so many people choose it. But it will bring you to a dreadful place. The Bible calls it a place of destruction. It is a place where God will not be found. Would you ever want to be in a place without God? It must surely be the most devastating place imaginable! If you choose to travel along the King's highway, you will never regret it. Have you made the choice yet?

Why don't you tell Jesus that you want to travel along the King's highway, even though it might be a difficult journey.

5 January

Open the door!

Read Revelation 3:20. Jesus says, *"Here I am! I stand at the door and knock. If anyone hears my voice and opens the door, I will come in and eat with him, and he with me."*

Jesus loves you very, very much and He wants to be with you all the time. He actually wants to come and live with you! But He does not rush into your life and ask, "Where's my room?" Oh no, He stands at the door and knocks while He softly calls your name.

Maybe you can hear His voice in the quiet of the night. Maybe you hear Him while reading your Bible. You can also be aware of His call while at Sunday school or in church. Some people say that they were outside in the beauty of nature when they first felt an aching longing for God. Afterwards they realized that it was a visit from Jesus.

When you hear Him calling, you can invite Him to come and stay with you and He will do it! It will be a joyous occasion! And in heaven there will be a party, because the Bible says that the angels rejoice over each one of God's children who turn to Him.

Corrie ten Boom, a woman who traveled to more than 64 countries all over the world to tell people about her experiences with Christ, met thousands of Christians on her travels. Yet she never came across anybody who regretted the day on which he had opened his life to Christ. That really makes one think, doesn't it?

Do you want Jesus to be your Friend? A Friend who will always be with you, even though you cannot see Him? You can be sure that He is standing at the door of your heart, knocking. Why not open the door now and invite Him to come and stay with you?

6 January

Who may travel on the King's highway?

Do you want to travel on the King's highway? In other words, do you want to be a Christian? You will be more than welcome! God wants everyone to choose His way, because it leads to the Heavenly City.

But wishing to be a child of God is not enough. In Matthew 7:21 we read, *"Not everyone who says to me: 'Lord, Lord' will enter the Kingdom of heaven."* So, who will be allowed to travel on this special road to heaven?

"He who has clean hands," says David in Psalm 24:4. It means, "Only people without any sin." It is like a traffic officer looming up in front of us saying, "Stop! Let me see your I.D." And when he looks at it, he shakes his head and says, "Sorry. You cannot travel on this road. You do not love the King enough! You have been telling lies and you were rude to some people and on top of that you were disobedient to your parents."

Oh dear! What can we do? It seems as if we will never be allowed to travel on the King's highway, because we are too sinful.

But in 1 John 1:9 we find good news! It says that if we confess our sins, God will forgive us. Jesus then appears on the scene with a stamp that has been steeped in His blood and He stamps all over our record of sin: `Paid in full`

Our lives can never be good enough to pay for the right to go to heaven. But Jesus has paid for our passage!

Find the Scripture verses mentioned in today's devotion and underline them in your Bible.

7 January

We have an enemy!

There is one thing that you will soon notice when you are traveling on the King's highway: there are lots of turn-offs!

The devil will do his best to lure you away from the narrow road that you have chosen. He always tries to get God's children on a side track. Right at the beginning of the Bible we see how he went about convincing Adam and Eve that God's way wasn't the best way. He told them a bunch of lies! He said, "Eat the forbidden fruit and then you will become like God Himself." But when they did that, they got into severe trouble. The Bible is full of similar stories about people who listened to Satan's advice and who were eventually very disappointed.

Satan is still alive today, trying to make us do things to make us lose our way. He says things like, "Take the money that fell from the old lady's purse! You can buy ice cream or sweets with it!" Or, "The Bible isn't true. It's just a boring book." Or, "Praying is a waste of time. There are many more exciting things to do!" He might also say, "Why not watch a video that's supposed to be for grown-ups! You'll enjoy it!"

Yes, all such things will be whispered into your ear. Satan wants to persuade us to follow him instead of Jesus. He tells us that we will be much happier if we do not obey God. But do not listen to him. Watch out for him and resist him.

Remember, Jesus paid an enormous price to earn you the right to be God's child. Do not take a turn-off that will lead to disaster.

Read Genesis 3:1-9 to see how Satan tempted Adam and Eve and then read verse 23 to discover the terrible consequences of their wrong choices!

8 January

A new page

Adrian did something very irresponsible! He borrowed Fred's bicycle to go to a shop nearby for a new ballpoint pen. There he went into the store without locking the bike. "This won't take long," he reckoned.

But when he came back, the bike was gone! "What can I do?" he wondered. Fred would be so upset, his father would be furious and he could hardly forgive himself for being so careless. He didn't have enough money in the bank to buy another bike and the chances were that the police wouldn't find the thief.

Adrian walked home, his mind in a spin. He tried to fight back the tears and kept asking himself, "Why did I do such a dumb thing?" He realized that he had to tell his mother about the theft, but it was so embarrassing!

Adrian's mother listened attentively while he told her everything. Then she dried his tears with a kitchen towel. "We all make mistakes," she said reassuringly. "You shouldn't have borrowed the bike and you should've locked it. You need to look after other people's property better than your own. But, seeing that this has happened, there are three things you should do:

"First: tell Jesus about it. He already knows everything, but He wants you to ask for His help and counsel. Then you can go to Fred and ask his forgiveness for your negligence. After that, we can decide how you are going to raise money to buy a new bike."

Later, when Adrian was on his way to Fred's house, things seemed a little less hopeless. Jesus had forgiven him. It felt as if he had received a clean page to write on with his new ballpoint pen.

Read in Psalm 51:3-15 what David said to the Lord after he had committed a serious sin.

9 January

Going to church

It was Sunday morning and it was cold outside. Jane's mother called, "You will have to hurry up, dear, otherwise you'll be late for church!" Jane snuggled a little deeper into her cozy bed. She didn't feel like going to church today. A lot of kids don't go to church during school holidays anyway.

Her mother opened the door. "You're still in bed!" she gasped. "Yes," Jane replied obstinately. "I don't think I'll go to church today." Her mom moved closer and sat down on the edge of the bed. She asked, "Are you glad that we have a home that can shelter us from the icy cold weather? Are you grateful for having warm clothes to wear, enough food to eat and a comfy bed to sleep in?" "Of course!" said Jane. Then her mom asked, "And do you remember who gave us all these things?" Jane knew that it was God who provided all the comforts that she enjoyed. Although her father bought the things, God provided him work and the strength to do it. "I know that God is good to us, but church will be boring and I probably won't understand the sermon, as usual," Jane complained.

Her mother became very serious, "Jane, we do not only go to church to get something for ourselves. We go there to thank God for all that He has done for us."

An hour later Jane and her family walked down the church aisle. The people were singing, "Give thanks, with a grateful heart!" Jane joined in and couldn't help feeling glad that she could be amongst people who loved the Lord and who wanted to praise Him for His loving kindness. Jane knew she would have enough opportunities to sleep a little later during the rest of the school holidays.

Sing a song of worship or read Psalm 84:1-8.

10 January

What does "holy" mean?

In Revelation 4:8 we read, *"Holy, holy, holy, is the Lord God Almighty!"* What does it mean?

"Holy" means that God is very different from us. He is so much higher and bigger and more wonderful, that we should honor and respect Him above all else. The Bible says that He is so holy that even angels cover their eyes when they bow before Him.

Long ago people treated God and all His things as 'radio-active'. For instance, nobody except the high priest was allowed in the inner sanctuary of the temple. And ordinary people were not allowed to even touch the ark of the covenant. Those who did, immediately fell to the ground and died. Yes, in days gone by, people took God's holiness very seriously. They often shook with fear before His holiness.

When Jewish scribes copied the books of the Old Testament by hand, they used to wash their hands out of respect each time they had to write the name of God.

But since Jesus came, we can think differently about God. We can now talk to Him as a Friend and we can call Him Father. We can even imagine sitting on His lap. But we should still respect and honor Him. It is wrong to make jokes about God and it is a sin to use His name in vain. It is also inappropriate to try to be silly in church. In church we should listen to God's Word and try our very best not to distract people's attention from the important things that need to be done to God's glory.

Remember, He is the King of kings and the only true God!

Read how John described our holy God in Revelation 4:2-11. You can read verse 11 as a prayer.

11 January

Choices

"**W**hy do you make so many wrong choices?" Nico's father asked when he got home. Nico, who had had a bad cold for weeks was soaking wet. His mother had warned him about the weather and told him to take his raincoat, but he hadn't felt like carrying a load of stuff with him.

Nico always found the wrong thing so much easier to do than the right things. It was much easier to copy someone else's homework than to do it himself. Watching TV was much more fun than doing sums. Hanging out with the bad boys was much less effort than being with the good guys. Why was it so difficult for him to make the right choices?

The reason was that Nico, like all of us, has a sinful nature that likes to take the easy way out. But wrong choices have bad consequences. Nico chose to ignore his mother's advice and so he will probably end up with bad flu. He will have to stay in bed and lose his position in the soccer team. If he had listened to his mom, things could have worked out so much better.

Good choices may be difficult, but they have good consequences. Choosing the right friends will help us make good choices. Working hard at schoolwork will help us in tests. And making good choices also gives us the boldness to ask God to help us. With His aid tough things become much easier.

In Proverbs 13:13 Solomon warns his son, *"He who scorns instruction will pay for it, but he who respects a command is rewarded."*

Thank the Lord for parents and other grown-ups who can guide you in making the right choices.

12 January

A shining light

"Do you want to stay Mommy's little baby forever?" Don could hear his friends' mocking voices as he walked away from them. They were smoking behind the fence near the tennis courts. Although he hated being mocked by the gang, he knew that staying with them today would be wrong. He had made a decision never to smoke and he wanted to stay clear of temptation. He decided to go to the library to find a good book to read. But he couldn't help feeling a bit lonely.

We are all like Don, aren't we? We don't want to be mocked. If everybody is wearing baggies, who wants to wear shorts? And if everyone's hair is cut short, who wants to have a pony-tail? There is nothing wrong about feeling this way. All of us want to be accepted by the people we hang out with and none of us wants to be without any friends!

But this desire to be like the crowd around you, might become a problem if you are a Christian. If you land up in a group where Christ is not honored, things might crop up that will put you in a real tight spot. What will happen if your friends start acting the way Don's friends did? Or what if they start sniffing glue or skipping school?

Jesus told His followers, "Be holy, because I am holy." "Holy" means "different." In Matthew 5:16 He said, *"Let your light shine before men, that they may see your good deeds and praise your Father in heaven."*

Don't be afraid to be different. Jesus will help you! He wants you to shine like a light in a sinful world.

Write down the names of friends who love the Lord. Ask God to help all of you to be shining lights for Him.

13 January

Every day is a gift

Let's play a game called "What if?" What if you learn that today is your last day on earth? What would you do? I know what I would do! First of all, I would go to all the people I love, to hug them and to make sure that they know how much they mean to me.

Then I would spend a lot of time outside. I would like to walk along a seashore or in a garden, where I can enjoy all the beauty around me. I would also like to listen to good music and to praise God for all the good times that I had on earth.

Do you know that each day has one and a half thousand minutes in it? This is a precious gift from God! He wants us to make full use of each minute. That does not mean that we must work all day and have no time to play. But it does mean that we must appreciate each day. We should call out like David in Psalm 118:24, *"This is the day the Lord has made, let us rejoice and be glad in it."*

If you are a child of God, all your time belongs to Him. Sometimes He expects you to work hard, but at other times He wants you to play and relax. Even Jesus took time off to relax. You can read about it in Mark 6:30-32.

Some people think that you need thrilling entertainment at luxurious holiday resorts to be able to enjoy yourself. But these people are seriously mistaken. They have probably never tried baking apples in an open fire or hiking in the woods. Swimming in a dam, playing with one's dog or fishing in a mountain stream can be just as exciting as the most expensive outing!

Learn John 10:10 by heart. These words mean that God wants us to enjoy the very best things in life.

14 January

Waiting

Waiting is difficult, isn't it? If you want to go for a swim, but your mom is taking her time dressing your baby sister, it can be most frustrating. And it can really be irritating if you want to play soccer outside, but the rain keeps pouring down. Not to mention the times when your family has to drive to faraway places. How many times do you say, "When will we ever get there?"

But do you know that God expects His children to be patient? The Bible teaches us that we must be able to wait. 1 Thessalonians 5:14 says, *"Be patient with everyone."*

God wants us to have patience, because impatience makes everybody unhappy. If you become moody when you do not get what you want, the people around you suffer with you. And anyway, it is a good habit to wait patiently! It will help you in your walk with the Lord. God does not always supply the things that we ask from Him straight away! He knows when it is the best time to give us the things that we ask for.

There are quite a few people in the Bible who discovered this truth. But they also found out that waiting on the Lord was never in vain! Abraham and his wife Sarah waited for 40 years before they could have a baby. Joseph had to wait many years before he was released from prison. And David, although he was told that he would one day become the King of Israel, had to wait years and years before this came about!

Is there something that you have been praying for for a long time? Does it seem as if God is not listening to your plea? Wait a little longer! Maybe there is a surprise for you around the next corner, just because you waited patiently!

Read Psalm 27:14. Why not memorize it?

15 January

Winners and losers

Many people think that you have to be richer or cleverer or better than others to be a winner. But God has a different idea of winners and losers. We learn this through the lives of many people in the Bible.

Jeremiah is a good example of a winner who might have been regarded as a loser by the people around him. At his funeral by-standers could easily have thought, "Today we are burying a real loser: he was a poor man all his life and although he preached a lot, nobody ever listened to him. Poor guy, he didn't even have a wife. Part of his life was spent in prison, at one stage he was banished from his country and he was even thrown into a pit because of his stubbornness!"

Yes, during his lifetime poor Jeremiah was rejected by his family, his friends, the priests and the king. In the eyes of the world he was a complete loser! But in the eyes of the Lord he was one of the most successful people who ever lived! He stands out as somebody who obeyed God. To God, medals and trophies are not important. If people obey God, they are successful in His sight.

When Jeremiah was still very young, God told him, *"Do not say, 'I am only a child.' You must go to everyone I send you to and say whatever I command you"* (Jer. 1:7). And that was exactly what Jeremiah did.

It must have been a glorious day when he eventually entered heaven! Surely joyful shouts met his ears, because during his whole life he did not work for the applause of men, but for the smile of approval from God.

Read in Revelation 2:26 about the reward that awaits a faithful Christian when he enters heaven.

16 January

Does a cockroach have a soul?

"Dad, what does it mean that we are created in God's image? Our Sunday school teacher says that's what is written in the Bible. Does it mean that we look like God?" John asked this question just after church one Sunday morning. He had often tried to picture God in his mind's eye.

"Oh no!" his dad answered. "To be created in God's image does not mean that God has hair, fingers and ears like us. It means that He made us very special, quite different from other creatures. God is Spirit and He has given each of us a spirit too. That's why the Bible says that we were made in God's image. The Bible often talks about God's eyes and ears and arms, but that's only so that we can understand Him better."

"Does that mean that animals and insects have no souls?" John wanted to know. "We believe they don't," his dad answered. "There are people in India and other parts of the world who believe they do. They say that your spirit can enter into an animal after you die. For that reason they never kill any creature, whether a mosquito or a cockroach. Although we believe that animals do not have a soul, we can learn something from them. We should never kill anything unnecessarily! Precisely because we were created in God's image, we should care about nature, just as God does."

When the family got home, John's father opened his Bible at Genesis 1:27. He showed John a verse that he had underlined with a red pencil. "Come and see for yourself what God says about nature. That is why we must look after it to the best of our ability. God has appointed us to see to it that all His creatures, men and animals alike, live on earth in perfect harmony."

Read the Bible verse to which John's father referred.

17 January

The day God spoke to a little boy

You may know the story about Samuel, the little boy who actually heard the voice of God one night. Do you remember? He was the child who lived with Eli and who helped the old priest with his temple duties.

When he was still very young, Samuel's mother brought him to Eli so that he could learn everything about God from the old priest. And then one night, something very extraordinary happened to this boy. God spoke to him personally! He was in bed already, when he heard, "Samuel, Samuel!" He thought that it must be the old priest calling him. He jumped out of bed and went to Eli. "Here am I!" he said. But Eli said, "What are you doing here? I did not call you. Go to bed again!"

Three times in a row the same thing happened. When Samuel came to Eli for the third time, Eli said, "It must be God calling. Go back to bed and if you hear the voice again, answer like this, 'Speak, for Your servant is listening!'"

When Samuel heard the voice once more, he did exactly as Eli told him. And you know what? God spoke to him in person! He gave the little boy a message to give to the priest. Samuel was obedient to God and he delivered the message the next day.

Now you are probably wondering whether God still speaks to people today. O yes, He still does, but not in the same way. He speaks to us in various other ways, mostly through the Bible. And in the Bible God often has a message especially for us. That is why we must listen very carefully when somebody wants to teach us from the Bible. Because it is God speaking to us. Then we must also say like Samuel, "Speak, for Your servant is listening!"

Read this story in 1 Samuel 3:1-18.

18 January

Do you believe in angels?

"My guardian angel must be tattered and torn tonight," Juanita said when she came home from a hockey practice. "First I was almost run over by a car and then, on the hockey field, I fell and could've broken my neck!" "Do you really believe that soppy junk about angels guarding human beings?" asked her brother, Harry. "To me it's like believing in fairies and dwarfs," he added.

Juanita put her fingers in her ears. She wanted to believe that angels watch over people. In her grandma's house there was a picture of two little girls leaning over a dangerous cliff to pick a flower. Looking at it, you could see how easily their feet could slip and how they could fall to the depths below. But above them there was an angel with wings outspread to protect them. Juanita has always been comforted to know that there are invisible creatures who watch over God's children day and night.

"I believe in angels," her mother said later on. "The Bible is full of stories involving angels. We can look in the Bible concordance to see how many times they are mentioned," she said.

At bedtime they called Harry to have a look at all the discoveries that they had made about angels. These heavenly creatures are mentioned more than 300 times in the Bible. Now Harry seemed interested too. His mom showed him Hebrew 1:14. It said, *"Are not all angels ministering spirits sent to serve those who will inherit salvation?"* "Well I never!" exclaimed Harry. "I really thought all the stuff about angels was just fairy tales. Does that mean that we can count on an invisible task force to come to our rescue when we land in something like a lion's den?" "Of course!" his mom said reassuringly.

Read what is written about angels in Psalm 91:11.

19 January

Forgiving and forgetting

For early morning devotions the principal read from Matthew 6. He repeated verse 14 which says, *"For if you forgive men when they sin against you, your heavenly Father will also forgive you. But if you do not forgive men their sins, your Father will not forgive your sins."*

Lydia bit her lip. She had real bitter feelings about a boy in her class. Grant had been spreading terrible stories about her all over the neighborhood. Even though her teacher made him confess in class that he had been telling a pack of lies, she was still furious.

"One day I might forgive Grant for what he did, but I will never ever forget it!" she told a friend after school.

What do you think of Lydia's words? Will you be able to forgive and forget if somebody does something like that to you? Is it at all possible? Scientists say that the brain is like a very complicated computer. It can store 800 items each second for more than 75 years without getting tired! Nothing that happens to us can really ever be forgotten. Each experience is stored in our memory and can be recalled any time.

Maybe the key to forgiving and forgetting is that when the thought of the wrong that had been done to us surfaces, we should not hold on to it. (Like pulling your hand away from a heated hotplate.) Do not brood over the injustice, but don't deny it either. Just say, "I forgive you, because Christ has forgiven me."

Paul once said, "I am forgetting what is behind and straining toward what is ahead." Think how many people treated him badly!

In 2 Corinthians 11:24-27 you can read about all the things that Paul had to forgive and forget.

20 January

Bad angels

Carol's uncle was very ill. The doctors said that there wasn't anything they could do to make him better. He had developed lung cancer after working in an asbestos mine for many years. During that time a fine dust infiltrated his lungs and really damaged them. "But didn't anybody see what was happening?" Carol asked her dad. He replied, "Unfortunately the dust was not visible to the human eye, and people only realized afterwards how badly it had affected the workers' health."

Yes, there are many things that are invisible to us, that can have a very negative effect on our lives if nobody tells us about them. For instance, the Bible warns us against invisible powers that are trying to harm us. In Ephesians 2:2 we read about the devil and his army who want to lure us away from God and who are trying to get us to be disobedient to Him.

According to the Bible there aren't only good angels who do everything that God wants them to do, but there are also bad ones, called demons. Their leader is Satan. They try their best to get people to sin against God. Bit by bit they can enter your life if you listen to them, until you become spiritually sick. It works the same way as the poison in the asbestos mines.

But although Satan and his demons are enemies of God's children, we must always remember that God is mightier than the devil. In 1 John 4:4 we are assured, *"The one who is in you is greater than the one who is in the world."* We know that God will eventually cast Satan away for ever. Then he will not be able to hurt God's children any more.

In Revelation 20:10 you can read how Satan and his army will one day be defeated.

21 January

Right and wrong

How do you know you've done something wrong when nobody else is around to tell you? A little instrument or voice inside you makes you feel uncomfortable, not so? We call that voice your conscience. It helps you to choose right instead of wrong. If you hurt an animal or if you have been dishonest in a test or if you were rude to a friend, this little instrument starts to grind in your mind. It is as if it squeaks out certain words, "That was a mean thing to do!" "That was a lie!" or "That was ugly!"

Animals do not have this tool. Your dog sometimes knows that he has done something that you do not like, but he cannot tell the difference between right and wrong. Some animals have things that we haven't got, like feathers and fins and horns and tails. But we have something that they don't have, a conscience that tells us when we do something wrong.

You can teach your dog not to chew your mom's shoes, but you will have to punish him if he does, and reward him if he doesn't. Otherwise he will go on chewing! Our parents must also teach us about some things before we realize that they are wrong, but we know pretty well whether most things are good or bad. That is because God made us different from animals.

When Jesus went to heaven, He sent His Holy Spirit to come and help us with our choices in life. That is why somebody who is a Christian has a conscience that is controlled by the Holy Spirit. If you are one of God's children, you have a conscience that guides you and a Spirit that helps you. Isn't that marvelous!

Read in John 14:23 about the special gift that God has given to all of His children.

22 January

The dream

One morning Granny Adams got up with a song in her heart. She had had the most wonderful dream! She had dreamed that the Lord Jesus Himself came to pay her a visit.

"What if it really happened today?" she thought as she started tidying up her little house. She put a bunch of flowers on the table and a saucepan with soup on the stove.

Suddenly there was a knock on the door. When she opened it, there was an old man with ragged clothes. "Madam," he said, "can you please give me matches? I want to make a fire against the cold." She felt so sorry for the poor beggar that she gave him a blanket as well. A little later she heard someone knocking again. This time it was a young man. "Please," he asked, "can you give me a job for a piece of bread?" "All right," she answered, "once the snow has melted, you can come and sweep the patio. But have this cup of soup so long." The man took the mug gratefully.

After a while there was yet another knock. "This time it must be Jesus!" she thought. But a girl stood there and asked, "Please, can I pick one of the daffodils in your garden for my mother? Today is her birthday!" Granny Adams took the flowers on her table and gave them to the girl. "You can have these with pleasure!" she said.

She looked at her watch. "Jesus won't come today," she realized with disappointment. "I will read my Bible and then go to bed." She opened her Bible at Matthew 25:40 and read, *"Whatever you did for one of the least of these brothers of mine, you did for me."* Suddenly she knew that Jesus had come and visited her after all! She smiled as she snuggled into bed.

Read in 2 Corinthians 9:7 what Jesus feels about a generous person.

23 January

Tread lightly!

Angola is one country where people know how important it is to tread lightly. There has been war in that country for many years, and landmines have been hidden all over the countryside. These bombs are buried beneath the soil, and if somebody treds on one by mistake, it causes a huge explosion, hurting and maiming many people. That is why you see so many people on crutches in that country, they have lost their limbs because of the war.

The Bible teaches us that Satan is also fighting a war. He is fighting over us. God wants us to follow Him so that we can one day live in heaven with Him, but Satan wants us to be disobedient to God. That is why he puts temptation in our way like landmines hidden in a field. He tempts us to sin and when we listen to him, great harm can come to us.

Somebody might tell you, "Try this sin once to see what it's all about!" Or, "A little naughtiness can do you no harm!" Don't listen to these people. If you do, you'll be in trouble. And that is just what the devil wants. He loves seeing people getting into trouble and hurting themselves.

In 1 Peter 5:8 we are told that Satan prowls around like a roaring lion looking for someone to devour. That is why Jesus taught us to pray, "Lead us not into temptation." It means something like this, "Please help us not tread on Satan's landmines!" You know that it is foolish to play soccer in a mine field. So why be foolish and listen to friends who invite you to play in Satan's territory?

You will find advice for suitable armor against Satan in Ephesians 6:14-17.

24 January

You have a choice

Abe loved to ask his dad difficult questions. This time his dad had to think hard before he could answer. Abe asked, "Dad, why do I often do wrong stuff, even when I know for a fact that it is wrong?"

"I know what we were taught at Sunday school," his dad replied. "'No man is able in this life to keep the commandments of God perfectly, but daily breaks them in thought, word and deed.' But let me try to explain it more simply: Before you do anything sinful, you are given a choice." Abe nodded his head. He knew about quite a few instances where he had to make difficult choices. Just the other day a shopkeeper gave him too much change. Immediately he had to choose: Should he give back the money that did not belong to him or should he keep it and buy something for himself?

His dad continued, "The devil will always encourage you to make the wrong choice, but your conscience and the Holy Spirit will prompt you to choose the right way. Remember, nobody will force you. The choice remains yours."

That night Abe's dad read to him from Genesis 3, where Adam and Eve made a fatal choice. "You see, ever since that day people have found themselves doing things that they know full well are against God's law. They cannot find enough power in themselves to resist Satan. An ostrich has wings and is free to fly, but lacks the ability. Man is free to choose, but because of his sinful nature he finds it very hard to do the things that please God."

Abe's mother put her arms around his shoulders. "That's why we need Jesus. His Holy Spirit will help you to make good choices. Trust and obey Him."

Can you guess what Abe told God in his prayers that night? Why not say a similar prayer right now!

25 January

Trying things out

Beth peddled like mad. She wanted to get home as soon as possible. She seemed to be fleeing from the devil himself! She had almost done something that she would have regretted for the rest of her life. After basketball practice two of her friends tried to persuade her to try out one of their "smarties". Beth had heard about this drug before; they say it makes you feel as if you are walking in the clouds. "It's good to try things out! Then you will also know what it's all about! One trip can't do you any harm!" they said.

Have you ever been in a similar situation and were you able to resist the temptation like Beth did? It is true that the Bible says, *"Test everything. Hold on to the good."* But some things people try out develop such a hold on them, that they cannot break free. Take drugs, for instance. You can get so addicted that you cannot go without them at all!

In Romans 16:19 we get very good advice, *"Be wise about what is good and innocent about what is evil."* There is no need to fall into sin because you can distinguish between right and wrong. A teller at the bank will immediately spot a false banknote, even if he has never seen one before. Working with genuine money gives him the ability to recognize false money. If we keep ourselves occupied with things that are wholesome and good, we will have no trouble sniffing out what is bad.

It is a good idea to decide beforehand how you will react when temptation comes along. You can even practice it! Say, "Sorry, it's against my principles!" Or, "I don't like that!" And if anybody tells you, "Everybody is doing it!" you could say, "Everybody but me!"

Make a list of ready-made answers that you can use if someone offers you drugs.

26 January

Like a fish in water

One day the fourth grade children found a huge fish tank on Mr. Crouse's table when they arrived for Sunday school. "What can he be up to?" they asked one another. He was always bringing interesting stuff along on a Sunday morning. The children watched him eagerly as he joined them. But he announced something quite disappointing, "Guys, today we are going to talk about God's rules." "Oh no!" they thought.

"Yes," said Mr. Crouse. "We will learn today that we can only be truly free if we obey God's laws."

Chris loved arguing with his teachers. "But Sir, if there are laws to restrict your actions, how can you be free?" "You can!" said Mr. Crouse, pointing to the fish tank. "Just as these fish are free while they are swimming in the water, so we are free while we stay within the boundaries of God's laws. The fish will die if we take them out of the tank. In the same way God's rules protect us. Within the limits of His commandments, we can move about freely. But when we break loose, we are in grave danger and not free at all."

While their teacher was talking, he took a slippery gold fish out of the water and put it back when it started gasping for breath. "We can choose whether we want to stay in the water of God's care or not. God does not force us to stay near to Him. But the moment we choose to jump out of the tank of His protection, we are in danger. We leave the life-giving water for the dangerous territory where Satan rules." He added, "Luckily we can always return to God once we've gone astray. We can admit our stubbornness and ask Him to make us free again."

Read God's rules in Exodus 20. Remember that we can only be free while we obey them.

27 January

The belt of truth

Doreen was cheerfully helping her mother in the kitchen. Her mother smiled. She knew her daughter well enough to see that she was preparing to ask something. And sure enough, after a while, Doreen asked, "Mom, I need a new belt. The one that I'm wearing with my jeans is really old and worn. They have nice ones at the new shop in the mall."

"You can put that on your wish list for the time being," her mom replied while she hung out the dishcloths to dry. "But I think that there's another belt that you need even more." Her mom fetched her Bible from the bedroom and said, "Read Ephesians 6:14. Then you will know what I'm talking about!" Doreen found the place and read out loud, *"Stand firm then, with the belt of truth buckled around your waist."* She gave her mom a puzzled look.

"Were you wearing that belt yesterday when you told me that you had to stay after school?" Her mother looked serious and Doreen blushed. "No. But I was afraid that you would be cross with me if you knew that I was at Jo's place without your permission."

"I don't want my children to hang around with friends after school without my permission, but I am even more disturbed if they do not tell the truth," her mother said sternly.

Now Doreen felt really bad about what had happened. Her lies brought about a lot of unhappiness. And what if her mom didn't trust her again after this? "Mom, I don't need that belt in the shop so badly. But I promise you, whenever I put the old one on, I will remember that I must always wear the belt of truth." Her mom hugged her and said, "You will never be sorry if you do!"

Read Proverbs 12:22 to see how God feels about liars.

28 January

Foul language

David was shocked when he heard what his little sister was saying. She was playing with her dolls and scolding them in the foulest language imaginable. "Dinky," he said with concern, "you shouldn't use those words. Foul language like that must never cross your lips again. Do you hear me?" "But Doris always says them!" said Dinky. Doris was one of her friends at the crèche. "That doesn't matter! Remember what Mom told us, 'If other children do something, it does not mean that it is right!'"

Later that afternoon David was watching a gripping movie on television. Suddenly his mom called from the kitchen, "Dave, please come and take out the trash. The garbage van will soon be here." David said a few nasty swearwords under his breath as he got up. He hated to be disturbed like this. Dinky looked at him with wide eyes. He used the same words that she used that afternoon.

As David took out the trash he felt guilty. He knew that swearing was wrong and that he had set a bad example for his little sister.

That night when his mom came to say good night, he asked her, "Where in the Bible does it say that we are not allowed to swear?" Maybe if I know what the Bible says about it, I will drop the habit of using foul language, he reckoned. After a while his mom returned with a slip of paper with three Bible references on it. "You can look these verses up in your Bible to see whether using bad language is a sin."

After David had read these verses, he knelt beside his bed and prayed, "Lord Jesus, help me never to use foul language again."

Are you curious which verses in the Bible David's mother showed him? You can look them up in 1 John 2:6, Ephesians 4:29 and James 3:10.

29 January

Movies

There was a war raging in the Craigs' house. Ernest wanted to go to a movie with his friends, but his parents would not allow it because of the age restriction on the film. "Oh Dad, why are you so old-fashioned? None of the other parents care." "That's not true," his sister chipped in, "Martin's father also said no."

"Well, give me three good reasons why a thirteen-year-old may not see what a sixteen-year-old may see!" Ernest asked.

His dad replied, "I can think of more than three reasons, but seeing that you want only three, here they are:

"One. At the age of thirteen your knowledge about right and wrong still needs some polishing. Your conscience is like a computer that still has to be fed some important data before the programming is complete. If you see a display of evil stuff that has been dished up as acceptable, all our hard work as parents might be in real danger of being swept aside. One day when you are sixteen-years-old and we have done a good job, your conscience might be a reliable compass that will immediately recognize evil and shun it.

"Two. Some movies contain so much violence that they can disturb you, make you violent or insensitive.

"And three: The Bible says in Philippians 4:8: ' ... *whatever is true, whatever is noble, whatever is right ... think about such things.'* The people who make movies are often not Christians and they do not care if the minds of children become spoiled. But we care and for that reason there are lots of movies that we won't go to either."

Ernest's dad took some money from his wallet and put it into Ernest's pocket. "Think of some other form of fun that you and Martin can have this afternoon," he said with an encouraging smile.

What would you do if you were Ernest?

30 January

Bullying

Do you think it is wrong to hit back when someone hits you? What does the Bible teach us on this subject? Matthew 5:9 says, *"Blessed are the peacemakers, for they will be called sons of God."*

A kids' club came up with a wonderful idea. They put up a STOP sign in the room where they meet. It was there to remind them of what they had learned from the Bible about handling bullies.

S Slowly count to ten.
T Treat him the way Jesus would've treated him.
O Overcome anger.
P Pray.

If you can overcome the urge to hit back and rather talk in a firm but friendly way to a bully, he will be most surprised! He will definitely have something to go and think about. But if you hit back, you will join in a fight that may never end.

Jesus was angry at times, but He was never involved in a fight. There was a day when he took a whip and drove the people from the temple, but that was not out of self-defense. It was because the people did not show respect for His Father's house.

If there is somebody who keeps on bullying or harassing you, you should ask your father or a teacher for advice. But usually a friendly word will put an end to hostility, as Proverbs 15:1 says, *"A gentle answer turns away wrath, but a harsh word stirs up anger."*

Pray for the bully. He is probably a very unhappy person who desperately needs Christ in his life.

You can also make a STOP sign to remind you how to respond to bullies.

31 January

FEBRUARY

When Mom and Dad are fighting

Fiona picked up the local newspaper and turned to the regular column where children can ask advice from a counselor. She was interested immediately. Somebody had asked, "What must I do when my parents fight? I can't take it when they argue all day long." Fiona was eager to see what Amy, the counselor, would advise, because in their home they had exactly the same problem. Her parents could quarrel for days on end and it really was very upsetting. What if they ended up in a divorce court?

The words of the columnist helped a little. "If your parents are quarreling, it does not necessarily mean that they have serious problems. Like children, grown-ups can differ on all sorts of issues. And very often, after a period of strife, they are fonder of each other than before, because they understand each other better. Remember, it is always a good thing to talk about your problems." The writer then gave advice to children who lived in homes where the father sometimes hits his wife. Fiona was very glad that she needn't worry about that. According to Amy, it is then necessary to call in outside help.

Finally, Amy told the child who was asking advice to write a letter to her parents. Fiona decided that she wanted to do that too. On a pretty card she wrote:

Dear Mom and Dad,
I love you both very much and it upsets me when you fight!
I know that it is impossible for you to agree over everything, but I pray that you will never get so cross with each another that you decide to divorce! Lots of love, Fiona.

1 Peter 5:7 says: "Cast all your anxiety on Him, because He cares for you." If these words are a consolation to you, why not learn them by heart?

1 February

To love or to hate

"I hate her!" George said passionately. He was talking to his grandma about his stepmother. Since his dad got married again, George often came to visit his grandmother.

"Yesterday she took Mom's photograph from the mantelpiece and hung it in the passage. I was furious."

Grandma was sorting photos. At first it seemed as if she hadn't heard George. "Just look at this family photo that was taken when you were a toddler," she said. George hardly recognized the people on the old picture. But it brought back sweet memories of all the times their family had spent together. Grandma also showed him a picture that was taken on the first Christmas after his mom's death. That was a miserable day for everyone. They had missed their mom very much. Although his dad had bought them presents, there was no Christmas tree and no real Christmas dinner.

"Now your family is complete again," said Grandma. "It's not nice if there's no mother in a house." George admitted that it was awful to try and cope without a mom. When his father had to look after them on his own, things really got out of hand.

He realized what his grandmother was getting at. "But Granny, how can I love somebody that I hate?" he asked. This time he sounded less aggressive.

"Luke 6:31 says, *'Do to others as you would have them do to you,'*" Grandma quoted. "You want your new mom to be kind to you. Be kind to her and you will be suprised at the results. I will ask Jesus to help you." With these words Grandma gave George a kiss on his forehead. Suddenly he felt a lot better.

Is there anybody in your life that you do not like? Read Matthew 5:43-48.

2 February

Walking with wise guys

Harry's mother smelled something musty when she put his jersey into the washing machine. She looked upset. This wasn't the first time that she smelled tobacco when washing his clothes. Harry's parents were very aware of the dangers of smoking and they had often warned their children. Their grandfather had died of lung cancer and that was a good enough warning to all of them to stay away from tobacco and cigarettes!

When Harry returned from soccer practice, his dad was waiting for him. "Harry," he asked straightaway, "did you smoke?" Harry felt very uncomfortable. He could not lie to his dad. "I just took a few puffs, Dad. But I swear that I have never spent any money on cigarettes."

"Don't you know that smoking is addictive?" His dad was serious. "Do you realize how many people are trying to kick the habit? They try anything to be able to stop smoking because of their health. Doctors and expensive medicine often cost them a fortune. Anybody who starts smoking today must be crazy!"

Harry looked down. He realized a while back that the group of friends who persuaded him to smoke, wasn't such a good crowd to hang around with. Maybe he should leave that crowd. That very morning a teacher had written something on the blackboard that made him think: *"He who walks with the wise grows wise, but a companion of fools suffers harm"* (Prov. 13:20).

Harry felt as if more than a bad smell was clinging to him. "Dad," he said reassuringly, "from today on, I will choose the right friends!"

Have you got friends who lead you into temptation? Read Proverbs 18:24 and think about the type of friends that you would like to have.

3 February

Finders keepers

Heinz was terribly upset. They were on holiday at the seaside and he had phoned a friend from a phone booth. When he got back to the tent, he remembered that he had left his wallet on top of the phone. All his money for the holiday was in that wallet. And the wallet was a special gift from his grandfather. "How could I be so stupid?" he wondered.

"Aren't you going to look for it?" his brother asked with surprise. "Why bother?" Heinz replied. "Do you honestly think that somebody who came across a goldmine like that would think of searching for the owner? Remember: finders, keepers." But eventually he decided to go back anyway. He started walking towards the phone booth. At a turn in the road a young boy on a skateboard suddenly appeared. "Hi!" he said. "You must be the guy who was in the phone booth earlier. You left your wallet there." He took the wallet out of his pocket. "Here it is," he said and added with a chuckle, "I almost kept it!"

Heinz could not believe his ears. "Th-thanks a lot!" he stuttered. "Your parents sure raised you well." The little boy smiled from ear to ear. Before Heinz could say anything else, he was gliding away at top speed on his skateboard. Heinz opened the wallet. All the money was still in it. "And to think that he did not even wait for a reward," he marveled.

He prayed out loud, "Lord, thank You for this little guy's honesty. Help me to do the same if I ever get the chance."

In 2 Corinthians 8:21 we read, "We are taking pains to do right, not only in the eyes of the Lord, but also in the eyes of men." Why not write these words on a card and keep it in your wallet?

4 February

From poverty to wealth

On 25 April 1980 a poor Japanese man, Mr. Unooki, was driving down Ginza Street in Tokyo, collecting old newspapers for recycling. On the sidewalk he spotted a parcel wrapped in cloth. Thinking that it might be old newspapers, he stopped his van and picked it up. When he opened the parcel, he was astonished to find a hundred million Yen in it!

He immediately took it to the nearest police station. In Japan the finder of lost property usually gets the found goods if they are not claimed within six months. After six months he went to the police station to claim the money. He was surprised to to see camera men and photographers all over the place. Journalists and TV interviewers were asking questions, all at the same time. The news about this simple man's honesty spread like a wildfire throughout the country.

He paid a third of the money to tax. "What are you going to do with the rest?" a bystander asked him. "I will build a comfortable home for my family," he said. "Will you be happy now?" another asked. "That I will only know at the end of my life," Mr. Unooki answered.

Years later, when he died, his words were remembered. "Did he find true happiness?" everybody wondered.

This story was published in a Japanese paper. Many people in Japan know nothing about the happiness and joy that can be found through Jesus Christ. Some of them realize that money alone cannot bring them happiness. But do they realize that not even a deed of honesty like that of Mr. Unooki's can secure happiness in the life after death?

Read Jude 1:24, 25.

5 February

If you could do whatever you wanted to

In a school classroom in a big city a teacher once asked the children, "What would you do if you could do whatever you wanted to?" He was shocked at their answers. "I will break as many windows as I can," one twelve-year-old said. "I will watch movies all day long," declared another one. "I will eat and sleep all day," was another reply. The teacher did not expect answers like these from healthy, educated boys and girls. What do you think of their answers? What would you have said?

It sounded as if these kids had nothing to live for. Apparently they had not yet discovered which things in life really make you happy.

Why don't you decide today on your goal in life? "To make people happy," is a good goal. "To make this earth a better place to live in," is also a good resolution. A guy once said, "My aim in life is to make my way to heaven and to take as many people as possible with me." God likes such ideas. If you have a goal like that, you would never waste your time doing nothing and you would not break and ruin other people's property. Always remember that God had a special plan with your life when He created you.

In Judges 21:25 it is said that *"everyone did as he saw fit."* If you read further you will see what terrible things happened to the people of Israel when each one did what he felt like doing, without having any good goal at all. God gave us His rules to live by to help us live meaningful lives. He knew that that is the only way in which we will find happiness.

Finish this sentence: I want to live to ... Do you think that Jesus will like your plan?

6 February

Safety first

Have you ever tried opening a tin of sardines with the little key supplied with the tin? It is a very dangerous operation, as many people have discovered too late. If your hand slips, you can injure yourself very badly.

The people who sell the tinned fish must have thought they invented a good device that allows you to open the tin without a can opener. But using it can have disastrous effects. A well-known pianist in America hurt himself so badly on such a tin that he lost his job as a concert pianist. He took the manufacturers of the tin to court and they had to pay him an enormous amount of money. But his career was ruined.

After this incident, six engineers in Japan set to work to invent a safer tin. It took them five years, but then they came up with a very clever idea. They actually made a tin that can be opened in the same way as the old one, but it could not cut the user. When you start opening the lid, both the lid and the tin start curling inwards. Thus the sharp edges of the tin can do no damage at all. Now isn't that clever!

A lot of inventions make life easier and safer for us. But it often cuts both ways. Take the Internet for example. It is an enormous help to thousands of people, but it can also do a lot of damage. Make sure that you don't visit web pages with information and photos that will damage your mind. In 1 Timothy 5:22 we read, *"Do not share in the sins of others. Keep yourself pure."*

If you're ever tempted to look at bad things, move away! Ask God to protect you from the dangers of such evil.

7 February

Feathers in the wind

Have you heard the story of the woman who gossiped about her next door neighbor? Well, the stories that she told about him spread like wildfire. It wasn't long before the whole town knew what the man had done. Later on she was sorry that she had spread bad rumors about her friend. It wasn't her intention to let the whole world know about his mistakes. She also noticed that he was getting lonely, because nobody wanted to talk to him after they had heard the stories.

She decided to ask her pastor for advice. "What can I do to change the situation?" she asked.

The pastor replied, "Go home and take a pillow. Cut it open and let the feathers out. Then come back to me." It was a strange command, but the woman did exactly what the pastor said. She took a pillow stuffed with feathers and shook it out in her back yard. A fresh breeze took the feathers over the wall and out into the big world outside. The woman went back to report what had happened. "Now go and pick up all those feathers," said the minister. "But that would be impossible!" replied the woman. "Well, it's just as impossible to wipe out all the rumors that you have spread about your neighbor. Go home and ask God's forgiveness for what you have done. You can also ask Him to show you how you can help this man."

We should never speak badly of other people. If we have nothing good to say about them, we should keep quiet. The Bible says that we should not praise God with our tongues and then use them to harm other people. Look this up in James 3:9.

Read more about the poison that can be spread with our tongues in James 3:5-12.

8 February

The ventriloquist

"You worm!" Gertrude shouted to her brother Theo who had hidden her schoolbag. "You're a lousy pig and I hope that everything you own either gets lost or burnt or eaten up by rats!" Just then her mother came in through the back door. "Gertrude, come with me!" she said sternly. Gertrude knew what her mother was going to say. It wouldn't even change things if she told her mother why she had said bad things to Theo. In their home bad language was never allowed.

"I'm sorry, Mom," she said. "But I think the devil made me say those words. Before I knew it, they just came out." Her mom looked serious. "Do you remember the day we went to the school concert? There was a ventriloquist with a funny doll on his knee." "Yes, I remember it well," she said. Why would her mother bring up this event? she wondered. "That man sat there without moving an inch, but he made the doll's mouth move all right!" Gertrude still remembered the funny conversation the man in the clown suit had with the doll. "Well, let me tell you, the devil is no ventriloquist!" her mother continued. "He can prompt you to say ugly things, but he can't force you to say them, because you are not a doll. You can choose whether you want to listen to him or not. You can also ask Jesus to help you fight the urge to say such things. Why don't you pray right now?"

It became quite still in the room while Gertrude knelt next to her mother to talk to Jesus.

In Psalm 19:14 David asked the Lord, "May the words of my mouth and the meditation of my heart be pleasing in Your sight, O Lord, my Rock and my Redeemer!" Why not learn this verse by heart and use it as a prayer?

9 February

Make your choice

Have you ever been to a sushi bar? Sushi is the raw fish dishes that Japanese people prepare so elegantly. All over the world you get sushi lovers and sushi restaurants. Because the dishes must be very fresh, they are usually prepared in front of the customers and often they are put on a conveyer belt. The customers sit at a counter and look at the dishes as they pass by. They can then choose the dish that looks the most appetizing.

It works the other way around in a supermarket, doesn't it? There the people move about and the food stays put. In a sushi bar the people sit in one position and the food moves around.

In the same way that people can choose what they want to eat, they can also choose who they want to serve as their god.

Some people choose money as their god. Money and their possessions are the most important things in their lives. They think about material things all day long and all their energy is spent on getting more. Other people choose sport or a hobby to be the most important thing in their lives. Then they have no time left for God. What would you choose if money, soccer, ballet, surfing, music, television, parties and movies were all put onto a conveyer belt for you to choose from? Once you have made your choice, will God still be the most important part of your life?

In Joshua 24:15 you can read the words of the leader who said to his people, *"Choose for yourselves this day whom you will serve. But as for me and my household, we will serve the Lord."*

Close your eyes and tell God that you choose to love Him above all else.

10 February

Looking for landmines

What is one meter high, weighs 120 kilograms, has six legs and walks like a crab? It is Comet 1. Never heard of it? Well, the people of Cambodia know it very well. It is a robot that was designed to find landmines. Each leg of this robot is about a meter long with a metal detector at the end of it. (The same kind that beachcombers use to find lost jewelry or money in the sand.) As soon as these detectors get near any metal substance like iron or steel, they make a distinct noise.

When Comet 1 detects a bomb that was planted underneath the soil, it squirts a certain liquid which colors the soil nearby and also desensitizes the landmine. Then the landmine cannot explode. It can be dug from the ground and taken away.

Manufacturing this robot was a wonderful achievement, because thousands of people have died through setting off hidden landmines. When Cambodia was at war, the enemy buried these bombs in the soil. After the war the landmines had to be taken away, but nobody knew for sure where they had been buried. So you can imagine how glad the Cambodians were when Comet 1 was made!

The robot moves very slowly, but it can clean up about a 100 square meters per day. People thought that it would take more than 600 years to get rid of all the landmines in Cambodia. But now they hope that they will be removed within a few years.

God must be very sad when people fight and make war. But He is surely proud of His creation when they come up with such an excellent idea to achieve peace.

You can get advice on handling strife in James 3:17-18.

11 February

Fresh air

Do you live on a farm or in a city? In a house or in an apartment? How fresh and clean is the air you inhale every day? If you live far away from factories with smoky chimneys and if you get enough fresh air every day, you are very lucky. In some big cities the smog is so dense that people have to wear masks to keep out the toxic air. There are even places where people are so desperate for a bit of fresh air, that they go to a salon where they can buy it! Instead of asking for a cooldrink or a cup of coffee, they buy a bottle of fresh air. They are then given an easy chair where they can sit and inhale the clean oxygen. People don't mind paying lots of money for these bottles of fresh air, because they say they feel so much better afterwards.

We often forget to thank God for something like fresh air. Only when you hear about people who do not have it, you realize what a privilege it is to get it for free every day!

There are many things that we are often not grateful enough for. You might not notice all the things your mom does for you every day, until you have to cope on your own for a day. You might never thank God for your thumb, until you cut it with a knife. Only then you realize how useful that finger is. Let's not take everything for granted. The best things in life are free and we ought to praise God for them!

In 1 Thessalonians 5:18 Paul said, *"Give thanks in all circumstances, for this is God's will for you in Christ Jesus."*

See how many things you can write down in five minutes that you have never thanked the Lord for. Now spend a few minutes thanking Him for these things.

12 February

Shocking news

"The world has gone crazy!" said Mavis, paging through the weekend newspaper. "Why do you say that?" her mom asked. "Look at this teenager. He got cross with his parents and started hitting innocent people with a hockey stick. And this girl, who was only thirteen, killed herself for not getting good results at school." "Yes," her mom agreed. "It is shocking to hear how people handle their anger and disappointment. I read about a young boy who hit an old man and when they asked him why he did it, he said that he was curious to know how it felt to do such a violent thing."

"Did things like this happen when you were young?" Mavis wanted to know. "Oh yes," her mom replied. "Sinful responses have been around ever since Cain killed his brother Abel. But I do think that violence on television encourages violent behavior. A person who pulls out a revolver or a knife whenever he is frustrated and who attacks someone with his fists if he can't get what he wants, must have learned it somewhere."

"Is that why you are so strict with us about watching TV?" Mavis asked. "Exactly," her mom replied, glad about the insight that her youngest daughter was showing. "People often hurt each other with words, too. There are better ways to solve problems than to use violent language. In real life one has to be patient with the people around you and you can definitely not always get what you want."

"I get uncontrollably angry with Julian," Mavis confessed. "I know," her mother said. "He can be a real teaser! You must pray that God will help you not to react violently." "Will you pray for me?" Mavis asked softly.

Read what God says about anger in Colossians 3:12-15.

13 February

Exam fever

Writing the last exam of your school career is a major event in most countries. But for the pupils in South Korea it is even more of an occasion. On the last day of the exams everything at school is brought to a standstill. The pupils who must write the tests, get chocolate axes and forks from friends and family. The good wishes that accompany these gifts are, "Hit the right answer!" and "Fork out the correct responses!" At school the learners are greeted by the school orchestra and cheering crowds. All workers around the country are allowed to be late for work on that particular day, because of the traffic jams in the cities. Even the landing and departure times of planes are adjusted so that they will not disturb the young people while they write this important examination.

In all the temples right across the country incense is burnt and prayers are offered for family members who are writing exams. One mother became famous by bowing down 2 000 times while praying for her daughter. "If I do my best, it will help my daughter," she said.

People who do not believe in God are often willing to go to a lot of trouble for the gods or spirits in which they believe. They sometimes torture themselves and go without food to gain the favor of their gods. But we only need to close our eyes and speak softly to God, and He will hear us!

In 1 Kings 18 the story is told of the prophets of Baal who went to much trouble to awaken their god. They even slashed themselves with swords and spears. But Elijah just asked God once to light the fire on the altar, and it was done!

Pray especially for people who live in countries where God isn't known. Also pray for missionaries who work there.

14 February

More and more like Jesus

Have you ever seen the painting of the Mona Lisa? It is probably the most famous work of art in the whole world. It was painted by Leonardo da Vinci and it can be seen in an art gallery in France. Most people who visit Paris, the French capital, want to see this painting. But because there are many people who cannot travel to France, the painting has often been taken to distant countries, so that more people can have the privilege of seeing it. It was once taken to Japan, where more than one and a half million people went to have a look at it!

What makes this painting so special? Some people say that the woman who is portrayed has the most beautiful face they have ever seen. Others say that it is the smile on her face that fascinates them. A famous plastic surgeon told the media that a young girl once asked him to change her face to look like Mona Lisa.

If you could change your face, whom would you want to look like? Maybe you would want to look like a film star or a model.

The Bible teaches us that that we will get to look more and more like Jesus if we follow Him closely. We will become friendlier and more loving as we walk with Jesus. Some people say that a husband and wife often resemble each other after years of living together. They learn certain habits and mannerisms from each other.

According to 2 Corinthians 3:18 we, as followers of the Lord, reflect His glory and *"are being transformed into His likeness with ever-increasing glory."* Nasty looks and sulky faces do not suit a child of God. They are like masks that should be removed when we become followers of Jesus.

Look in the mirror and pray that you will become more and more like Jesus.

15 February

Save our planet!

Do you get upset when you see people littering? Beer cans on our beaches, plastic bags in our beautiful rivers and bottles along our hiking trails can upset a person so much that he can hardly appreciate the beauty of the ferns, trees and waves around him. You might feel like getting your hands on the litterbugs and teaching them a lesson!

Recently there was an article in a newspaper that mentioned how much trash can be found on Mount Everest. You probably know that it is the highest mountain in the world, and not many people ever get there. Yet people who couldn't care less left all sorts of rubbish on the snowy slopes of this famous mountain. A few nature lovers decided to clean up the mountainside and they collected one and a half tons of rubbish! They removed empty oxygen cylinders, metal parts of tents and all sorts of other junk.

God must have been glad about their concern. He appointed us to look after His creation. He said that we must work and take care of the earth. You can read about this in Genesis 2:15. The Lord also said, *"Let us make man in our image, in our likeness and let him rule over the fish of the sea and the birds of the air, over the livestock, over all the earth"* (Genesis 1:26).

This means that we must look after the plants and animals in the same way that God would have cared for them. And He will not be satisfied if we made a junk yard out of His beautiful creation!

When you go picnicking or jogging again, see what you can do to make the environment look better.

Get a picture of a beautiful scene in nature to remind you that God wants us to preserve the beauty of His creation.

16 February

To forgive

Do you know what it means to forgive? It means that you do not feel angry towards someone who has done you harm. God expects this from His children. Sometimes it is very difficult to forgive. Actually it is only God who can help us to forgive fully. Neil Verwey, who is a missionary in Japan, once told the following amazing story.

A beautiful girl named Aomori had taken part in a beauty contest and she was selected as the winner. But one of the other contestants was jealous and felt that she should have won first place. She did a terrible thing. She waited for Aomori around a corner and threw acid into her face when she passed by. As a result the beauty queen would have ugly marks on her face for ever. The girl who did this cruel thing was put into jail and Aomori was taken to hospital, where plastic surgeons tried their very best to repair her face.

A pastor who visited the hospital told Aomori about God's immeasurable love for her. "I want to be a child of God," she said, "but I will not be able to forgive the girl who damaged my face." "Then God cannot forgive your sins," the pastor answered.

After a few weeks Aomori decided that she would write a letter to the girl in prison. She had decided to accept Jesus' forgiveness and she was prepared to forgive the prisoner. She wrote, "Christ has forgiven all my sins and therefore I forgive you."

Would you be able to forgive somebody who did such an awful thing to you? In Colossians 3:13 we read, *"Forgive whatever grievances you may have against one another. Forgive as the Lord forgave you."*

Think of someone who had done you harm. Ask Jesus to help you to forgive that person.

17 February

A book about your life

How would you feel if you went into a bookshop and found a book with your name printed on it in bold letters? And how would you react if you opened that book and found that the whole story of your life was written in it? Most likely you would start reading it straight away! And while reading it, you would probably sometimes laugh and sometimes cry about all the experiences that you have had. You might suddenly remember lots of things that you had forgotten about, like gifts that you received, outings with your family, good times spent with friends. Maybe you would also be ashamed of some of the things that you have done. You might want to tear some of the pages out of the book! You would wonder who the author was and how he got to know so much about you.

In Revelation 20:12 John wrote these words, *"And I saw the dead, great and small, standing before the throne, and books were opened. Another book was opened, which is the book of life. The dead were judged according to what they had done as recorded in the books."*

It seems as if we will really see a book about our own lives one day in heaven. Therefore it is important how we live. If you are a child of God, there will be nothing in that book that you will be punished for. Remember, children of God are forgiven because they believe that Christ paid for all their sins. But we will nevertheless be very sad about the things that we have done wrong. We will also be very happy about the things that we had done to gladden our Savior's heart.

Write down what you did today. Will you feel happy if this page were a page in the book of your life?

18 February

The bread of life

How many different kinds of food do you eat each day? Maybe cereal for breakfast, sandwiches for lunch and fish for supper? Then you are very privileged, because in many parts of Africa people have maize morning, noon and night. And in many parts of South America people live on yams, a kind of sweet potato. Only now and then do they add something else to their diet. In Eastern countries rice is the main dish for each meal. ·

Having exactly the same kind of food every day is dangerous, because our bodies need different kinds of food in order to stay healthy. Many children in poor countries of the world are often sick and have swollen tummies because they eat only bread or porridge. That is why your mom wants you to eat vegetables and fruit. She wants you to be healthy and strong.

There is another type of food that we must have, although it cannot be seen. The Bible calls it the Bread of Life. That is the kind of food that feeds our spirit. Just as your body needs nourishment, so your spirit also needs to be fed. In Matthew 4:4 you can read the words spoken by Jesus when Satan asked Him to change a stone into loaves of bread. *"It is written: man does not live on bread alone, but on every word that comes from the mouth of God."*

And where can we find this bread? In the Bible. Therefore it is important for us to know the Bible. Of course you will not understand everything that you read there, but you should be keen to listen to people who want to explain to you what the Bible teaches. In church or at Sunday school or during home devotions you should be eager to receive the Bread of Life.

Ask your mom or dad to read their favorite part of Scripture to you.

19 February

A thousand years from today

In quite a few places on earth people have assembled time capsules. Do you know what that is? It is a rustproof, non-perishable container into which all kinds of interesting things are placed. Then it is sealed and buried. A report is written about the place of burial, the contents and the people involved. The descendants of these people can dig it up one day and have a look at what's inside. They will be able to see which type of radios, telephones, magazines, shoes and all such stuff were fashionable at the time of the burial. Seeds and bulbs are also put into these containers, so that scientists can see what happens to wheat and rice and pine-kernels after they have been lying in the soil for ages.

Osaka is one of the cities in which such a time capsule was buried – five meters underground! More than two thousand items are stored in it. The people who organized this stated in their report that it should be opened again in the year 3000. We wonder, "Will there still be people around to open it?"

Well, nobody knows whether that capsule will still exist a thousand years from now. But we who are children of God, know that we will still be alive then. Jesus once told His friend Martha, *"He who believes in me, will live, even though he dies, and whoever lives and believes in me will never die."* That means that everybody who knows Jesus as Savior and Lord, will still be alive and well a thousand million years from now … even though their bodies may be buried deep under the ground like a time capsule.

Jesus asked Martha, "Do you believe this?" You can find Jesus' question and her answer in John 11:26-27. If He asked you the same question, what would your answer be?

20 February

A new pet

Have you heard about Aibo, the little sausage dog made out of tin? A factory that normally makes television sets, made 3 000 of these toys and they were sold out within 20 minutes!

This little robot dog can do wonderful things. It can gnarl at you if you hit it and wag its tail if you scratch it. If you turn the tin pet over, it can roll back onto its feet and if anyone plays with a colored ball nearby, the doggie will go and fetch it!

Because this pet was so popular, the same firm is now trying to make a lion that will be even more clever. It will be able to respond to any name given to it by the owner. It will be able to understand 50 words, like "Sit!", "Fetch!" and "Come!" It will even take photographs through its eyes if you order it to.

Having a pet like that would be fun, don't you think? Luckily it won't be necessary to feed it or clean its kennel! It will also not eat socks and carry fleas around. But will a pet like that give you the same warmth and love that a real animal can give you?

People can invent amazing things, but nobody can create a human being or a living animal. Only God can do that. In Genesis 1 you can read how God created everything: the earth, stars and planets and all the living creatures in the universe.

There are people who do not believe in God. They must sometimes wonder how it was possible for all the different things in the universe to come into being in such a special way. Surely there must have been an Architect behind it all?

Read Genesis 1:31 and thank God for creating all the marvelous things in nature.

21 February

Beautiful on the inside

In Proverbs 27:19 you can read these words: *"As water reflects a face, so a man's heart reflects a man."* What does this mean? It means that what's on the inside of a person is just as important as what's on the outside.

Women can put on lipstick and mascara and moisturizing creams and powder, but if they have ugly thoughts, they won't be pretty. In the same way a man can spend hours on his beard or moustache or hairstyle, but if his thoughts are not good, he will not look good.

People these days spend a lot of money on stuff to make them more beautiful. Even pre-schoolers spend hours in front of the mirror. According to a newspaper report, some countries find that little girls are buying fewer toys and more cosmetics.

There is nothing wrong with trying to be more beautiful, but it is sad if lots of money is spent on things that can improve the outward appearance, while the inner person is being neglected.

How can we beautify the inner person? The words from Proverbs at the beginning of this passage give the answer. Our hearts and minds should be pure. Then our beautiful thoughts will be reflected in our faces and in our eyes. If all your thoughts center on yourself and you never think of other people with love and affection, then God will not see you as a beautiful person.

When the prophet Samuel had to look for a new king for Israel, God told him, *"The Lord does not look at the things man looks at. Man looks at the outward appearance, but the Lord looks at the heart"* (1 Sam. 16:7).

Look at a picture of yourself and ask God to make you even more beautiful on the inside.

22 February

The talking walking stick

Have you ever heard of a walking stick that can talk? Yes, believe it or not, clever people who want to help blind folk, are making sticks like that! They will mainly be used on big railway stations. Try to think what it must be like to be blind and to have to find your way around in a big railway station. Lots of people rush past you and you have to find your way to the right platform. Of course, you have to catch the right train as well! You will probably be scared, because you might miss your train or you might even fall off the platform.

Some blind people have a friend or a dog that can help them. But blind people might one of these days be able to get along on their own. They will have little speakers in their ears to catch signals coming from the tip of their special walking sticks. As the person moves about, the sender on the stick will give him messages like, "Turn to your left," or "Walk straight ahead for five steps and then turn to your right." It can also say, "We have come to a flight of stairs going up (or going down)."

Isn't that amazing! Or maybe something like that would be useful for finding your way around an unknown shopping mall. Wouldn't you also like a little voice to tell you when you are entering a danger zone?

In Isaiah 30:21 we find a wonderful promise for every child of God: *"Whether you turn to the right or to the left, your ears will hear a voice behind you, saying, 'This is the way, walk in it.'"*

Ask the Lord to help you to hear His voice clearly, so that you will not do wrong things.

23 February

Big brother

In many supermarkets and shops there are security cameras which film everything that is happening in the shop. Even people who are moving about behind high shelves can be watched carefully. This enables the shopkeeper to see if somebody is trying to steal something.

There is a TV program that some people love watching. Everything that is happening in a certain house is shown on TV. Each room in the house has a camera eye that records everything in that room and then other people can see everything that happens on their own television screen. The people in that house can do nothing in private. Each word and each deed is recorded and broadcast all over the country. The name of the program is *Big Brother.*

Would you like a camera to be focused on you all the time? It must be weird not to be able to do anything away from the eyes of curious onlookers!

But do you realize that the eyes of the Lord are watching you all the time? There are at least two verses in the Bible that say that. In Proverbs 15:3 it says, *"The eyes of the Lord are everywhere, keeping watch on the wicked and the good."* And 2 Chronicles 16:9 states, *"For the eyes of the Lord range throughout the earth to strengthen those whose hearts are fully committed to Him."*

That means that the Lord can see all of us at the same time. Nothing can happen that He does not know about. He can see when you are good and He knows when you need help. He also sees the evil things that people do and that makes Him sad.

Do you have something which you are ashamed of? Ask God to forgive you. Is there anything that makes you unhappy? Talk to Him about it!

24 February

A true story

Krishna was a little girl who lived in Nepal. Until she was seven years old, she lived happily with her family on a farm on the mountainside. One night, while as she was helping in the kitchen, her mom saw a white spot on the golden skin of her daughter's arm. She shouted in alarm, "You have leprosy!" Immediately everything changed for Krishna. She wasn't allowed to stay with her brothers and sisters in the same house any more, because her parents were scared that they might also get sick. She had to stay in a room outside and nobody was allowed to play with her. The white spots on her skin became little sores that spread all over her body.

Early one morning her dad called, "Krishna, come with me! I am taking you to a hospital." Krishna cried. She didn't want to stay with strange people in a strange place.

But when they reached the hospital after traveling all day long, she discovered that the people at the hospital were very kind indeed. They didn't mind touching her and they gave her medicine and put ointment on all the sore spots. "Leprosy isn't as contagious as people say," one of the friendly doctors told her. "If you cooperate with us, you will soon be able to go back to your family." And that is exactly what happened. After six months Krishna went back to the farm.

Krishna's dad had taken her to a missionary hospital, where all the workers were Christians who went to Nepal especially to tell the people of that faraway country about Jesus. They wanted them to know that God loves them and that He can help them.

You can read in Mark 1:40-42 how Jesus healed a leper.

Pray for doctors and nurses who are being used by God to heal people and to let them know about His love for them.

25 February

The rebel

Galileo Galilei was a student who lived 400 years ago. His classmates called him "the rebel", because he didn't simply accept everything his teachers told him. He asked many questions and sometimes argued with his professors. Later he taught at a university and there he made the first telescope; a huge magnifying glass with which one could see the moon and stars more clearly. Then he saw that a lot of things that he had learned at school were not true at all. The moon was not smooth and shiny as they had taught him and the sun did not rotate around the earth, although that was what was written in his school textbooks. In fact, it was the earth that rotated around the sun!

He wrote all these new discoveries in a book and that really got people talking. Not everyone was very happy with the things he wrote. How could he insist that what everybody had believed for so long was wrong? Even the people of the church were mad at him. They said that he was disagreeing with the Bible (even though nowhere does the Bible say that the sun rotates around the earth).

Do you know what the people did? They put Galileo under house arrest. That means that he could never again leave his house. But many people read Galileo's book and today everybody knows that he was right all along.

When we see that something is wrong, we should be brave enough to say so, even if people are mad at us for doing so. The Lord is always on the side of the person who speaks the truth.

Read in John 9:13-34 about someone who was also brave enough to persist with what he believed in, even though people hated him for it.

26 February

Say thank you

Greta was in a bad mood by the time she got to school. She didn't like being woken up early every morning. If she didn't have to make her own bed, she could sleep much later. And then there was porridge for breakfast. She hated porridge. On top of all this, her dad left earlier than usual and she had to walk to school. "Everything is going wrong today," she thought.

After lunch they had English with Miss Small. Everybody had to select a piece of paper and then speak about the topic on the paper. Setina had to go first. She came from a neighborhood outside of town. On her piece of paper was written: "What I have to do every morning before I go to school".

Greta listened curiously. She had often wondered what happened in the township next to the main road. Setina explained how she had to get up very early every morning to make the fire so that her mother could make coffee for the family. She also had to fetch water from a tap quite far away. Before she left for school, she had to take her baby brother to a house on the other side of the river where an aunt looked after him until their mom came home from work at night. Then Setina had to walk to school every morning, whether it was raining or not.

Greta felt quite ashamed. She thought of how unhappy she was that morning just because she had to make her own bed, eat porridge and walk three blocks.

One of the very first Scripture verses that she had learnt at Sunday school jumped to her mind: *"Be thankful!"* It came from Colossians 3:15. "Thank You, Lord!" she whispered softly.

Do you know of a family who is having a hard time? How can you help them?

27 February

Wow!

John 14:14 says, *"You may ask me for anything in my name, and I will do it."* Many people have found these words to be absolutely true. There are many stories of answered prayer. Tom Dawson was a missionary in Central Africa. One day he was swimming in a river when he saw a crocodile. He fled, but encountered a lion in the dense vegetation on the river bank. "Please help me, God," he prayed and ducked when the lion jumped at him. And where did the lion land? In the wide open mouth of the crocodile!

The missionary Bannerij from Tibet also had a remarkable experience. One night during one of his travels, he had to sleep in a cave as a snow storm was raging. He was scared of freezing to death, but in answer to his prayers, God sent a snow leopard to the same cave. The two of them kept each other warm throughout the night.

On another mission field Dan Crawford and his team reached a river that had to be crossed. There was no boat or bridge to make it possible. They prayed and that night God sent a strong wind which caused an enormous tree to fall across the river, a perfect bridge across the stream!

At Feba, the radio station that broadcasts the gospel from the Seychelles, the engineers needed tons of building sand for the erection of the broadcasting tower. They prayed about it, and God sent a storm that caused enormous floods to bring the needed sand right to the building site.

Through all these events God is glorified! We can also ask God for miraculous relief in cases of need, so that His name can be magnified throughout the world.

Underline John 14:14 in your Bible.

28 February

The secret

Graham was playing with his brother's catapult in the backyard of their home. Every now and then he took a pebble, put it in the leather sling and pulled it backwards. At first he wasn't too successful at hitting the object at which he aimed, but after a while he was proud that he could aim and hit his target so successfully. Then something awful happened! The neighbor's dog came round the corner, wagging his tail. He often came to play with Graham. "Today I am going to give Smokey the fright of his life," Graham thought. He was aiming to hit the corrugated iron fence just above Smokey's head. But oh dear! The pebble hit the poor little dog on the back of the neck. He ran yelping back home with his tail between his legs.

Graham quickly put the catapult back in his brother's room and started doing all sorts of odd jobs in the garden, whistling a tune as if nothing had happened. But he felt awful. "It was a mean thing to do," he said to himself.

That night Graham didn't sleep well. When his mother called him for breakfast the next morning, she could see that something was wrong. "What's wrong?" she asked. Graham started crying and his mom put her hand on his shoulder. Then he told her everything. "I feel awful about what happened," he sobbed. "God knows that you are sorry, Graham. Ask Him to forgive you and you will feel much better," his mom said kindly.

When his mom left the room, Graham knelt at a chair and asked God to forgive him. All the terrible feelings of guilt vanished while he was praying. On his way to school he passed Smokey a piece of sausage through the neighbor's fence.

Read in Psalm 103:12 how far God removes our sins from us if we ask Him to forgive us.

29 February

MARCH

A child like you

Have you ever thought about the fact that Jesus was once a child just like you? He grew up in an ordinary family in an ordinary place. Nazareth was a small village with white-plastered, flat-roofed houses against a hill. Jesus probably raced with some of His friends among the fig trees and olive trees that lined the streets. He worked for His dad in the carpenter's shop and He might even have swept the house for His mother. He also attended classes in the synagogue, where He learned to read and write and memorized parts of the Old Testament, like all the other Jewish children His age.

Yes, His childhood was a lot like yours. He played with friends, helped His parents and went to school. And yet He was different from anybody else who ever lived, because He never committed any sin. That doesn't mean that His life was easier than yours. Oh no! He had to obey His parents whether He felt like it or not. And maybe He even sometimes thought that they were treating Him unfairly. Remember, He had many brothers and sisters and you can be sure that they sometimes teased Him and fought with one another. But Jesus loved His heavenly Father too much to ever do anything wrong.

Another reason why Jesus always did the right thing was because He loved you! Yes, He knew that you would often do sinful things that you ought to be punished for. But because He Himself never ever sinned, He can stand between you and God's punishment. So when God looks at you, He sees only Jesus, the One without any sin and the One who paid for all your sins on the cross.

Read Hebrews 4:15 to see whether what has been written in this passage is true. Then tell Jesus how you feel about it.

1 March

The rock

One day, long ago, a king told his workers to place a huge rock in the middle of the road that led up to his castle. Many people had to travel along that road on their way to the king. The rock would be a hindrance for horse-drawn wagons and coaches traveling that way.

When the rock was in place, the king sent the workers home and he hid himself behind the shrubs along the road to see what would happen. The first traveler who came along was a rich friend of the king. He looked at the rock, but ignored it. He walked around it as if nothing was wrong. Then the king's gardener came along. He was furious that somebody had placed a rock in the road. He shouted and swerved to avoid the rock, but also did nothing about the problem. Quite a few people did exactly what the king's friend and the gardener had done. They moved on without doing anything about the rock that was blocking the way.

Eventually a farmer with a wheelbarrow full of vegetables came along. When he saw the rock, he left his wheelbarrow and tried to move the obstacle. He groaned and struggled and sweated, but he did not give up until the rock was removed from the road. Then he took up his wheelbarrow again to walk further. But, to his surprise, he saw that there was something lying in the road where the rock had been. It was a letter from the king! In golden letters the king had written, "To the person who moves this rock: Come and see me at my palace. I want to make you the chief minister in my government."

Jesus also told a story about a king and his servants. Read it in Luke 19:11-24.

2 March

Taking the blame

Ivan lived on a farm near Swellendam. His family was very poor and Ivan often went to pick berries to help his parents pay for his schooling.

One day he started too late, the sun was setting and his bucket wasn't even half-full. Ivan knew that he wasn't allowed to pick berries on the other side of the fence, because those belonged to the owner of the farm. He could only take those growing along the road.

That evening Ivan took a chance and climbed through the fence to fill up his bucket from Mr. Dowling's orchard. But oh dear! Jo, one of the workers, saw him. "What are you doing, young man?" he asked sternly. Jo took the bucket from Ivan and started walking towards the farmhouse. Ivan tried to explain why he had done such a terrible thing. Suddenly a car stopped right next to them. It was Mr. Dowling himself.

"Jo!" the farmer sounded really annoyed. "How dare you pick berries for yourself on my property! I did not expect that from you." Ivan was waiting for Jo to tell the owner that he was innocent and that Ivan was the culprit. But Jo said nothing to defend himself. "I will take this matter further," the farmer said and drove off.

"Why did you take the blame?" Ivan asked with amazement. "Because Jesus took all the blame for my sin upon Him," Jo said, as he gave Ivan the bucket full of berries. "Take this. But don't ever again take anything that does not belong to you. And when you pray tonight, tell God that you are sorry for what you have done. Then thank Him for taking the blame for all your sins."

That night Ivan did exactly what Jo had told him to do. He also thanked God for a friend like Jo.

Read in Matthew 27:27-31 what Jesus was prepared to do for you.

3 March

Miracles

Do you believe in miracles? A miracle is something extraordinary, something that happens unexpectedly and cannot really be explained. Miracles happen when God intervenes in the natural course of events in order to help people. The Bible is full of stories about miracles. Do you remember how a prophet multiplied the oil in the poor widow's jug so that she could sell it and make a living? In the Old Testament we also read about sticks that became snakes, an axe that could float upon the water and many other miraculous things. In the New Testament there are stories about blind people who could suddenly see, deaf people who could suddenly hear, even dead people who became alive again.

Some people do not believe in miracles and things that they cannot explain. Such people even find it difficult to believe in God. That is a pity, because you needn't understand everything before you can believe it. For instance, who knows how the very first living cell came into being? And who can explain why two people fall in love? But that doesn't mean that we do not believe in living cells and falling in love, does it?

God is big enough and mighty enough to make miracles happen. Whether we understand them or can explain them, makes no difference. We confidently believe that He loves us and that He can help us when we need Him.

Thousands of Christians over hundreds of years have witnessed God doing miraculous things in their lives. May you also know the God who still works miracles, even today.

Read Psalm 105:5 and ask your parents whether they have ever experienced a miracle during their lifetime.

4 March

Barnabas

On 21 July 2000 a 71-year-old Japanese man decided to sail around the world in a yacht all on his own. He started the voyage in spite of gusty weather and a stormy sea. That was something even experienced yachtsmen were scared to do. More than 80 000 people followed his journey on the Internet and he completed it within nine months.

Journalists asked him, "Why did you do it?" They probably expected answers like, "Because I wanted to be famous," or "So that people can remember me," or "To prove myself." But that was not his answer. He said, "I wanted to encourage people of my age. I want them to realize that you can still do a lot of things after you've turned seventy!"

Isn't it refreshing to hear of somebody who is doing his best to encourage other people?

In the Bible we also read about someone who was an excellent encourager. He was so good at it, that his friends changed his name from Joseph to Barnabas, which means "encourager". He was one of Paul's helpers and when you read about their journeys together, you wonder how Paul would have survived without Barnabas. God had given Paul an extremely difficult task. He was the first missionary to heathen nations and he had to endure much suffering. People often beat him and he was often hungry, tired and disheartened. But God gave him a friend to encourage him on the way.

God also wants to use you to encourage other people. In Hebrews 10:24 we read, *"And let us consider how we may spur one another on toward love and good deeds."*

Think of someone who needs encouragement this week and decide what you can do to help him or cheer him up!

5 March

The wedding

There is a legend about a wedding that reminds us of Jesus' parable in Matthew 22:11-14. Why not read the parable first and then read this story? What lesson do we learn from this parable? Yes, it teaches us that we cannot live any way we like and then expect to be welcomed into heaven one day!

Remember that a parable is a story with a lesson. A legend is a story that isn't true, but parents have told it to their children and these children have passed it on to their children and thus this story had never been forgotten.

Here is a legend that has the same message as the parable that you have just read.

Once upon a time there was a prince who lived on an island. When he turned thirty, he got onto a ship to go and find himself a bride. When he found a girl to marry, he sent invitations to all the inhabitants of the island. Together with the invitation cards, he also sent a white garment for each of the guests to wear to the wedding.

On the island there was a tailor and a dressmaker who were very disappointed about this arrangement. They were keen to make luxurious outfits for all the guests and thus become rich overnight. They persuaded some of the people on the island to ignore the prince's wishes and to have stylish outfits made for the wedding.

On the day of the wedding the people with the expensive clothing had a shocking experience. When they entered the reception hall, their clothes turned into tattered rags. But the garments that were supplied by the prince turned into shimmering gold!

We must make sure that we do not live any way we like, but that we are living the way God wants us to.

Paste the words of Revelation 3:5 on your wardrobe.

6 March

God's gift

"**H**appy birthday to you!" Carina's family was singing to her while they handed her a big parcel. And what did she find inside? A beautiful multi-colored parrot! "Hello!" the bird said as he reshuffled his feathers and looked at everybody, holding his head a little bit askew. It had been really stuffy in the box!

Carina was very excited about the gift. She had always wanted a parrot and now she had one that could even talk! She immediately decided to use her savings to buy the bird a nice cage.

"I don't think that Polly would like a cage," her dad said. "He will be much happier in the aviary in the garden." But Carina wanted to keep her parrot in a cage in her room. She bought an expensive cage and put Polly into it.

But when her friends arrived for her birthday party, Polly was sitting in a corner of the cage, looking sad and forlorn. He wouldn't talk and he didn't eat a thing. He hated being cooped up like that! Only when Carina let him out of the cage, did he become his own chirpy self again.

The following Sunday at Sunday school Carina's teacher told them that it was Pentecost. "At Pentecost God gave us a very special Gift," he said. "He gave us the Holy Spirit to help us and guide us. But if we do not listen to Him, we can quench the voice of the Spirit in our lives, as 1 Thessalonians 5:19 says. We should not coop up the Holy Spirit, but give Him free range in our lives."

Carina thought of Polly in the cage and immediately understood what her teacher was telling them.

Praise God for the gift of the Holy Spirit. Tell Him that you want Him to inhabit your whole being so that He can have a say in all the things in your life.

7 March

Surprise! Surprise!

Mrs. Smith was very upset. Somebody was removing things from their garden at night. She had gorgeous little figurines in her rock garden, but every now and then she found that one was missing. First the frog disappeared, then the rabbit and then the tortoise. She called her husband. "Alex," she said, "we will have to put up a fence. This can't go on for ever!"

"I'm sorry darling," he said. "I can attend to it later, but at the moment I am too busy." The next morning Mrs. Smith was almost in tears. Now the little duck was also gone. "I promise you that I will do something about it tomorrow," her husband said and put his arm around her to comfort her.

The next day was Mrs. Smith's birthday. Early in the morning the family brought her breakfast in bed. When she had finished drinking her coffee, her husband said, "Put on your gown. I want to show you something outside." Excitedly everyone crowded around outside. What did they find in the early morning light? All the figurines were back, painted sparkling white, looking like new! Mrs. Smith was very glad for the double gift that she received on her birthday. Her darling statues were back in place and they each had a new coat!

This story can help us to understand a deep spiritual truth. Sometimes God takes away certain things in our lives, but then He puts something better in its place. Have your parents forbidden you to go certain places or watch certain programs? Maybe there is something else that you can do instead, something that will give you the double joy of being obedient and gaining something worthwhile.

Read how David was disappointed at first, but later danced with joy in Psalm 30:5-12!

8 March

Who is God?

Louise often heard about God in her home. As long as she can remember, she had believed in God.

One day Awd, a school friend, came to visit her. The Plerns were immigrants and Awd had difficulty understanding English. Louise felt sorry for Awd, because the children at school didn't bother to make her feel welcome.

Above Louise's bed Awd saw a large poster. On it was a Scripture verse of the stars in the milky way. The heavens declare the glory of God (Ps. 19:1). "Who is God?" Awd wanted to know. "Don't you know?" Louise asked. "God is the One who made everything. Yes, everything that you can see around you He made, the sun and the moon, the mountains and the plants, the animals and the people … everything!" "Some things were made by people," Awd said. "Like buildings and cars and cups and saucers." "Yes," Louise agreed, "but people made them from stuff which God had made; sand, stone, iron and water."

The little girl with the beautiful black hair and lovely skin looked at the picture for a long time before she started to ask questions about their homework.

That night Louise asked, "How can it be possible that no one has ever told Awd about God?" "Well, Awd comes from Thailand and the people there are mainly Buddhists. They do not believe in God. But we can tell her about God and we can be kind and loving towards her so that she can get to know God's loving kindness through us." Louise's father said, "Let's pray that the Plern family will also get to know Him."

You can pray for the millions of Buddhists around the world who do not know God.

9 March

The rainbow

"Come and look!" Sarah shouted when she opened the front door. Her mom followed her and soon discovered why she was so excited. A beautiful rainbow spanned the heavens after the rain. "Our teacher says that it is only drops of water that reflect the sunlight," Sarah told her mother. "The light of the sun breaks it up into all those colors."

"Yes, that's true," her mom agreed. "But a rainbow is more than just a display of colors. It is a symbol of God's faithfulness."

While they were still marveling at the glorious sight in the sky, her mom went on talking. "After God had sent a flood over the earth in Noah's time, He promised that the earth will never again be flooded by so much water. And He said that the rainbow will remind us of His promise. Now, whenever we marvel at a rainbow, we can also be glad about the faithfulness of God, who keeps His promises forever."

Sarah went back into the house reluctantly. She still had to make her bed and get ready for school. Her mom was listening to the early morning news on the radio in the kitchen. All the bad news was very depressing.

When Sarah sat down for breakfast, her mom had left a little note on her side plate. It said, *"I am making everything new." Signed: God. (The One who had made the rainbow) Revelation 21:5.* Sarah was glad that her mom reminded her of the message of the rainbow. God is faithful and He will keep all His promises. One day all the bad news will be something of the past, just as Noah's flood is history today.

Draw a rainbow and put it in your Bible to remind you that God is completely trustworthy.

10 March

Chocolates for God's kingdom!

Who doesn't like chocolates? Do you know how a particular famous brand of chocolate got started?

It all began in the city of Blackpool when two brothers, George and Richard Cadbury, took over a cocoa factory from their parents. But the business wasn't doing very well. The two brothers worked hard and did not overspend, but after three years of toiling, they realized that something drastic had to be done to save the business from bankruptcy.

They tried to figure out why people did not buy more of their cocoa. "Maybe it isn't such a good product," they said to each other. For years they had mixed the cocoa with potato flour and sugar. Now they decided to market pure cocoa powder. Of course it would be much more expensive, but it would also have more flavor. Their plan succeeded. Slowly but surely their sales improved and they had one of the most successful businesses in England.

But George Cadbury never became a rich man. He was a true child of God who believed that he was not placed on earth just to build a kingdom for himself, but to help build God's kingdom. He gave a huge part of his income for God's work. He gave money for missions, churches, hospitals and schools. He knew that when he died, he would not be able to take anything with him. Only what was given to God, would one day go with him to heaven.

Read what Revelation 14:13 says about this truth. It says that our good deeds will follow us to heaven. We needn't meet Jesus empty-handed one day when we die. We can take with us all the things that we have done for Him!

Decide how much of your pocket money you will give for God's work.

11 March

The race

Imagine sitting on the grandstand at the Olympics watching the 10 000 meter marathon. The race is very exciting, because two of the athletes have been running neck and neck from the start. But suddenly Mark, the smaller one, breaks away and starts leaving David behind. The crowd is cheering like mad. Today a record will surely be broken! Mark reaches the home stretch and the spectators urge him on. But then he stops. Yes, you heard correctly. Mark just stopped! Nobody can believe what they see. He smiles at his coach and waves at the spectators. Then he turns to David, his friend, who has caught up with him. He grabs his hand and they cross the winning line together!

Now the spectators cheer like crazy. They have never experienced anything like this. Mark wanted to share his moment of glory with his best friend David!

Don't you think this is a delightful story? But can you imagine what a sad ending this story would have had if David had refused to take the hand of his friend? People would have thought that he was crazy. And Mark would have been very disappointed indeed.

Of course one normally competes in a race to win. It is good to try one's best. It is not selfish. This story just illustrates how two good friends share victory.

In Hebrews 12:1-2 the Bible says that life is like a race and that Jesus, the Victor, wants to help us to the winning line. But some people do not want to take Jesus' outstretched hand. They want to do everything on their own. They never ask Jesus to help them and so they lose the fight against sin and death and never reach the winning line. You wouldn't be that silly, would you?

Read 1 Corinthians 15:55-56.

12 March

A pleasant aroma

Winnie loved to make people smile. Whenever she saw some-one who was looking down-hearted, she did her best to brighten up that person's day. She would do nice things for people without letting them know that she was the one who did it. It gave her a lot of satisfaction.

For Valentine's day she made a potpourri sachet for the girl in her class who had the fewest friends. She dried leaves of thyme, rosemary and lavender from her mother's garden and put a few drops of aromatic oil on them. Then she made a small sachet, put everything inside, and fastened it with a red ribbon. It had a lovely aroma! She carefully wrote "Jesus loves you!" on a card.

On Valentine's day she went to school a little earlier and asked permission from the caretaker to go into the classroom. She took the sachet from her pocket and put it in Ellen's desk. She smiled when she came outside. Nobody would know why their classroom smelled so good, she thought.

After assembly all the children went to their classrooms. They were excited about the Valentine cards which were going to be dis-tributed among them. Ellen didn't get a card. But when she lifted her desk-top and found the gift inside her face lit up. She looked straight at Winnie and smiled gratefully. "How did she know?" Winnie asked herself. Then she suddenly realized that her blouse had given her away. She was smelling just as sweet as the bag of potpourri which she had made for Ellen. You cannot distribute perfume without catching some of the fragrance yourself!

Read 2 Corinthians 2:14-17. We must be a pleasant fragrance for the Lord.

13 March

The small woman (Part 1)

"Sorry, Miss! You are too old. You will not be able to learn the language." That was what the committee in England decided when Gladys Aylward applied to be a missionary to China. But Gladys had a very strong desire to go to China to tell the millions of people who live there about God's love for them.

When she heard of a woman in Yangcheng who was looking for a helper, she started saving money to go there. Going by ship would cost too much, so she decided to travel by train across Europe and through Russia to get to China. Everybody who heard about her plans tried to discourage her. It was a very long journey that included icy cold Siberia. On top of it all, there was a war raging between Russia and China, which made the journey very dangerous indeed. But she strongly believed that the Lord had called her for the work in China, and so she set off on the journey with two suitcases and very little money in her purse.

For ten days the train rattled on until it suddenly came to a halt in the middle of a snowy place. They could not travel any further, because of the war. But Gladys wasn't discouraged. She started walking back along the railroad until she reached a harbor from where she could travel by ship to Japan. From Japan she traveled by ship, by bus and by donkey, until at last she reached Yangcheng, where Mrs. Lawson lived.

They worked together for twenty years and Gladys had many exciting adventures in that strange country. She led hundreds of people to Jesus Christ. Wouldn't it have been a pity if she had been put off by all the trouble that she had in the beginning?

Read the Scripture verse that motivated Gladys to go to China: Matthew 28:19.

14 March

The small woman (Part 2)

Gladys Aylward arrived in China after many hardships. She was eager to tell the people of Yangcheng about Jesus. But the Chinese people she met were not interested in her story at all. They even threw mud at her and at her friend, Mrs. Lawson, calling them "strange demons"! Then Gladys thought of a way in which she could make friends with her neighbors. Many of them owned mules that were used as pack-animals. Gladys started to befriend the mules. She attracted them to their guesthouse and gave them fodder. Soon the owners of the mules came to meet her. Everybody was treated kindly and eventually their guesthouse was a popular gathering place for the whole neighborhood. It became known as "The Inn of the Sixth Happiness". Many of the guests learned about Jesus at that inn and some of them became His faithful followers.

One day Gladys bought a neglected orphan from a trader and it wasn't long before she had changed their home into an orphanage where she looked after a hundred little orphans.

During the Second World War she became famous when she fled from China with all of these children. They had to travel by foot over mountains and through rivers, but she brought them all to safety.

A book, *The Small Woman*, was written about her life and a film was made about her adventures. It was called *The Inn of the Sixth Happiness*. But she was not somebody who was looking for fame. To her it was important to be obedient to God's calling. When missionaries weren't allowed to go to China any longer, she started working in Formosa which is today known as Taiwan. She never grew tired of telling people the good news about Jesus.

Will you go to a strange country if God asks you to go?

Read Psalm 96.

15 March

The story of two kings

This bit of history comes from 2 Chronicles 18:1-19:3. Would you like to read it in your Bible first?

What a story! Two kings decided that they wanted to work together. The one was King Jehoshaphat of Judah and the other one was King Ahab of Israel. There was a big difference between the two kings; the king of Judah wanted to do what was pleasing to God, while the King of Israel wanted to do what pleased him.

Ahab wanted to start a war with the Cyrians. But Jehoshaphat first wanted to ask God for guidance. So Ahab sent for his prophets, who were trained to say exactly what Ahab wanted them to say. "Oh yes," they said, "go ahead with your plans. God will give you the victory!" But Jehoshaphat wasn't so sure that these people were truly God's messengers. "Is there no other prophet?" he asked. Now Micaiah was brought before the two kings. He was a true messenger of God who didn't care what the king wanted to hear. And what did he say? "These so-called prophets are lying," he said.

Ahab was furious and Micaiah was put in jail. Ahab then convinced Jehoshaphat that the other prophets were right all along, and both their armies started a war against the Cyrians. You can probably guess what happened. Yes, the soldiers had to flee and Ahab was killed during the fight. Jehoshaphat learned a great lesson that day. He would never again listen to false prophets.

This story also has a lesson for us. God wants to guide us in all the choices that we make. He speaks to us in various ways. If we do not keep contact with Him through prayer and Bible study, we will never be able to distinguish between the advice of God's messengers and that of false friends. The result can be disastrous.

Ask God to help you enjoy His Word, the Bible.

16 March

God's protection

One day a hiker was resting under a tree when he heard a noisy twittering in the branches above him. When he got up to investigate, he saw a dangerous snake heading straight for a bird's nest in the tree next to him. A little bird was doing its best to frighten off the snake by flapping its wings frantically. She wanted to protect her chicks from the dangerous onslaught.

Just at that moment her mate came flying back to the nest. He saw what was going on, turned around and soon came back with a twig in his beak. He placed it on top of the nest next to the little hen and her chicks. Then he took position in a tree nearby to see what would happen.

By this time the snake had already slithered up the tree and was starting along a side branch in the direction of the nest. But all of a sudden he stopped, turned back and slinked away from the nest!

The hiker was very curious. Why did the snake change its mind all of a sudden? He took the twig to a friend who knew a lot about plants. He learned that the twig came from a plant that was very poisonous to snakes.

How did the male bird know how to protect his family? God made him in such a special way that he instinctively knew what to do. God cares about the tiniest bird, as Matthew 10:29 teaches us.

In the Bible the devil is sometimes described as a poisonous snake that is trying to harm us. If we try to scare him off, we might not succeed. Therefore we must call upon Jesus to help us against him. If we hide behind Jesus, the devil will soon turn around and leave us alone.

See what good advice James 4:7 offers.

17 March

God made everything

Conrad was doing his homework when his mom called him for supper. As was the custom in their home, his dad first read a passage from the Bible. Conrad was still thinking about all the things that he had just been reading in his textbook; how mountains and rivers and deserts had been formed through the ages. And now his father was reading Psalm 104:24, *"How many are your works, O Lord! In wisdom you made them all."*

Conrad said, "Dad, Mr. Fox says that there is no God that created the universe." "Yes," his dad replied calmly, "there will always be people who do not want to believe in God. If you do not believe in Him, you needn't obey Him. But there are others who genuinely try to believe in an invisible Being, but don't really understand the Bible. Maybe Mr. Fox is one of them. I find it easier to believe in God than not to believe in Him. It is odd to believe that everything was made so perfectly without a Designer behind it all. Albert Einstein, one of the greatest scientists who ever lived, once said, 'Through all my studies of nature, I learn more about the Creator!'"

Now Conrad's mother spoke up, "I agree with him. When I realize how planets move about in the universe without bumping into one another, when I watch bees making honey, or the waves of the ocean breaking against the rocks, or trees growing from tiny seeds, then I am amazed. And then I can't help saying, 'How great God must be to have created all of this! Surely it could not have happened by chance.'"

After that, Conrad's dad said a prayer. He thanked God for making such a wonderful world.

Do you also know of someone who does not believe in God? Why not pray that he might get to know the Lord.

18 March

Where does God live?

Monica was all muddled up. The thought of where God lived had never really bothered her before, but now her little sister had asked her about it. And she really didn't know what to tell her. They were in the kitchen and Monica was doing her biology homework. Nell was looking through Monica's textbook and came to a picture of the heart. "Does my heart also look like that?" Nell wanted to know. "Sure," was the answer. "So how does Jesus get into it?" This question wasn't so easy to answer. Monica thought for a while. "I know that Jesus lives in my heart, but He is also in heaven. Oh dear, we'll have to ask Mom," she replied.

Just then their mom came into the kitchen. She had heard Monica's words. She explained, "God is everywhere. But He does not live everywhere. He only lives in people who allow Him to live there. If somebody tells you that God is in his heart, it does not mean that He is living in a particular part of that person's body. It means that you love Him dearly and that He helps you love all the things that He loves."

"But why does the Bible say that God lives in heaven?" Monica wanted to know. After some thought her mom replied, "You can't confine God to one place. He is completely different from anything or anybody that we know. He can be everywhere at the same time."

The children's mother went to fetch her Bible. She read Psalm 139:8-9. "I'm so glad that God is everywhere!" little Nell said and clapped her hands.

Read the Psalm that Monica and Nell's mother showed them.

19 March

Renewed friends

Gordon had two special friends, his brother Paul and his dog Pinks. But now his brother was furious at him. No wonder, because Gordon had damaged Paul's computer programs. He had been trying to find the picture of the roaring lion that Paul used as a screen-saver, but then something went wrong!

After that, Paul put up a huge sign on his door, which said: NO ENTRY . He didn't even want to speak to his brother. Gordon was really sorry about what had happened. He went to sit in the backyard, while Pinks was playing around. He thought about every-thing. It was almost like the story about Adam and Eve in the Bible. They had been banned from Paradise because of sin, he thought.

Gordon closed his eyes and prayed, "Please God, help me to get things straight between Paul and me." And as it often happens when one asks God something, He gave Gordon a magnificent plan.

First Gordon made a nice card with a message to Paul. Then he fastened it to Pinks's collar. And finally he knocked on Paul's door.

"What do you want?" Paul asked when he opened the door. Gordon spoke with a small voice, "You can have Pinks," he said. Paul was very surprised. He knew how much Gordon loved his dog. "Do you actually want to give your best friend to me?" he asked. "Yes, if that will stop you from being mad at me," Gordon answered. Now Paul's frown turned into a smile. Pinks stood nearby with head askew, watching the two brothers wrestle and giggle as if nothing at all had been the matter!

Read in 1 John 2:2 what Jesus did to renew the friendship between God and man after Adam and Eve spoilt everything and were driven from Paradise.

20 March

Wild geese can teach us a lesson

Today's story comes from a book by Albert Schweitzer. He was a famous doctor who did missionary work in Central Africa long ago. He had great respect for God's creation and always pointed out how we can learn lessons from nature. This is one of his stories.

One day a flock of wild geese came to rest on the water of a big dam at a homestead in Africa. They were taking a break on their long flight to Europe. Each year they flew thousands of kilometers to get away from the cold when winter came, and then in the spring, they returned again.

A gardener who was working nearby, saw the flock and caught one of the geese. He cut its wings, because he was curious to see what would happen when the others flew away. (He probably thought that he could keep this bird for himself afterwards.)

When the other wild geese got ready to leave, the one with the snipped wings tried very hard to join them, but it couldn't get off the water. The other geese encouraged their mate with their hoarse cries, but it was all in vain. He simply could not fly with them!

What would the others do? Although the urge to fly further was very strong indeed, they did not leave the disabled bird behind. They all came back and stayed with him on the dam. They waited there for a few days, until his feathers had grown again, and then they all departed together.

The gardener was ashamed of what he had done and he was also glad when he saw the whole flock fly away together. He decided never again to do such a cruel thing. And he also decided to be more considerate towards his fellow human beings.

Read 1 Peter 4:8-11 to see how we should treat one another.

21 March

Crumpled notes

The church caretaker was amazed when he found yet another crumpled piece of paper in the third pew on the left side of the church. For months now, he found the same thing on a Monday morning when he cleaned the church. It was a blue sheet of writing paper with notes scribbled on it and then crumpled up and left on the same seat. He started collecting these bits of paper. "Celia, math; Mary headaches; Car breakdown; Harold, rent". These were the type of messages written on the scraps of paper.

The caretaker decided to find out who sat there on Sunday mornings. He discovered that it was a friendly lady who always came on her own and was active in the service. Eventually he told the pastor about her. The following Sunday, the pastor went up to the lady and showed her the small stack of paper. "Does this mean anything to you?" he asked. "Oh yes!" she said, blushing. "I used to worry a lot about things. Then my mom, who is a true believer, told me to take my worries to God and leave them with Him. So I started to write down all the things that bothered me on a sheet from my writing pad. Afterwards I crumple it into a small ball and leave it in God's house on a Sunday. I can then walk home without a care in the world."

"That's a marvelous idea!" the pastor said. "I am preparing a sermon on Philippians 4:6-7 for next week. Can I tell the congregation about your plan?"

The lady smiled. "You had better ask the caretaker first!" she said.

Write down your cares on a slip of paper and put them into a box called SOMETHING FOR GOD TO TAKE CARE OF.

22 March

The shoemaker who became a missionary

There was a time in the history of the church when people did not believe in missionary work. But there was a young man in England who knew his Bible very well. He spent a lot of time thinking about certain verses like Acts 1:8 where Jesus said that His followers will be His witnesses to the ends of the earth.

One day he came across a book on the voyages of Captain Cook. The more he read about all the places that this famous seafarer had visited, the more interested he became. When he read about all the strange idols that people in faraway places served, he felt an urge to go there and tell them about the true God. His name was William Carey and he was a shoemaker. In his shop he had a huge piece of leather on which he had burnt out the map of the world. While he was making shoes, he prayed to God to make it possible for him to go to the ends of the earth with the Good News about Jesus.

His prayers were eventually answered. One day he and his wife and two children boarded a ship that would take them to India.

The voyage took five months. Once in India he started working in a factory where he could learn the language of the people around him. Later he started to translate the Bible into Hindi.

Today many people in India know and love Jesus. They can read the Bible and serve God, all because missionaries like William Carey were obedient to God's calling. They were prepared to leave their home countries and live among strange people to tell them about God's love.

Look on a world map to see how far William Carey had to travel to get to India.

23 March

True friends

In Mark 2:1-11 you can read the story of four men who helped a friend in a very special way. Their friend had been paralyzed for years. One day they heard that Jesus was in the neighborhood. They knew that He would be able to help their friend. They decided to carry him to Jesus on his mattress. But when they arrived at the house where Jesus was, they couldn't get near Him. Lots of people were crowding around the house to see and to hear Jesus.

Suddenly they had a splendid idea. They carried their friend up the stairs onto the roof of the house. Then they made a hole in the roof. Yes, in those days you could do that! They just had to take away a few pieces of wood and mud, and that was that. Carefully they lowered the man through the hole with ropes until his mattress rested at Jesus' feet.

Everybody was amazed. Where had the patient come from? But Jesus looked at the man with a friendly smile. He probably also smiled at the four faces peeping through the hole in the roof. "Your sins are forgiven," He said to the man on the mattress. "Get up, take your bed and walk."

To everybody's astonishment, the man first sat up straight, then struggled to his feet. And then he stood there on both legs, the same legs that were paralyzed before! He then took his mattress and started walking home.

And his friends? They must've fixed the roof in two ticks so that they could go home with their friend. They sure had a lot to tell everybody along the way.

Do you know of someone who is ill? With your prayers you can take that person to Jesus. He will know exactly what to do.

24 March

You and your enemies

Few people in the world know the story of André Trocmé. But in France everybody knows about him. He was a French minister who allowed people to hide from the enemy in his church during World War II. People still honor his memory for what he meant to those fugitives. But there are some other very interesting things about this remarkable man.

When he was a young boy, war broke out in his country. German soldiers took over their village and some Germans moved into their homes. Food became very scarce and there were times when André and his family were really hungry. Luckily André had some friends who loved the Lord and this group of friends gathered in the attic of their church regularly to talk and to pray. They often told one another how much they hated the Germans.

One day André bumped into a German soldier in their home. To his surprise the man smiled at him and offered him a piece of potato-bread. But André refused to accept anything from the enemy. The man put the bread back in his pocket. "I'm not as vicious as you think," the soldier said. "I am a Christian. Look, I'm not even carrying a gun. My job is to send telegrams."

André listened with interest to the soldier's story. "My friends and I have a meeting tonight," he said. "You can join us if you like."

When his friends saw the German, they were very scared. But André told them everything that he had heard from the soldier, and it wasn't long before they all prayed and sang Christian hymns together. God was helping them to love their enemy, as is commanded in Matthew 5:43-48.

You can pray for countries where there is war. You can also pray for people you regard as your enemies.

25 March

Trouble!

Theo was in serious trouble. His teacher had asked for volunteers to decorate the wall surrounding their school. When Theo arrived, he found that a lot of kids were using aerosol spray paint. They were excited and acted quite strangely. He soon discovered the reason for their weird behavior. They were spraying the paint into a paper bag and then sniffing the fumes.

"Just try it," Ulrich said to him. "You'll feel great!" But all of a sudden Ulrich's nose started to bleed. The other boys were shocked and scared and ran away. "If you tell anybody you're dead!" Ulrich threatened. Theo was torn between two feelings; he did not want to tell on his classmates, but he had heard that sniffing could be really dangerous. He had even read about a kid who died after sniffing too much glue.

Eventually he decided not to tell anybody, because it was none of his business and he didn't want to be known as a telltale.

But the next morning the principal called Theo to his office. He seemed distressed. "Theo," he said, "Ulrich was taken to hospital last night. He is seriously ill. His liver and kidneys have been affected. His parents told me that you persuaded him to inhale the fumes from the spray paint that you used yesterday."

Then Theo told the whole story. The headmaster listened attentively and then spoke to him with concern, "Theo, it is more important to save lives than to be popular with your friends. In Ezekiel 3:18-20 God said that we must warn people who are destroying their own lives. Will you remember that in future?" Theo nodded.

Do you have a friend who needs to be warned about something serious? Ask God to help you to do it!

26 March

Vandals!

Do you know what a vandal is? It is someone who willfully destroys an object of beauty. The name comes from history: a tribe known as the Vandals was at war with Rome. They destroyed all the beautiful works of art that they could lay their hands on. Since then such destructiveness has been called "vandalism".

People who study human behavior say that vandals are people who regard themselves as no good and they want to destroy everything that is good, so that their own worthlessness is not noticed. Isn't that terrible? That is why some people ruin gravestones, destroy lovely plants and break well-made wooden benches in parks.

Every now and then you hear of a vandal who has broken a beautiful statue or ruined a costly painting in an art museum. In the British Museum in London something like that once happened. The Portland vase was exhibited in a glass case. It was more than two thousand years old and people from all over the world came to see it. It was made of fine porcelain and it was a miracle that it was still undamaged after all those years.

But then one day a visitor to the museum broke the glass case, lifted the vase high above his head, and threw it onto the floor. Of course it broke into a thousand pieces. It took years and years of careful workmanship to put it together again.

Have you ever wondered why people wanted to kill Jesus? He was the loveliest, kindest, most wonderful Person who ever lived and He shared His love with everybody. And yet people whipped Him and nailed Him to a cross. They could not bear the thought of having somebody so flawless around. Their own sinfulness showed up too clearly in His presence.

You can read about Jesus' crucifixion in Matthew 27:32-44.

27 March

Celebrating Easter

It was the Wednesday before Easter and Helen and Cora were sitting under the old oak tree in front of their school. They opened their lunchboxes. Cora had an Easter egg in her box. "My mom says that we eat chocolate eggs at Easter because new life comes out of an egg. It is to remind us about Jesus who rose from the dead to give us new life."

"We have a different way of celebrating that," Helen said. "My dad made a wooden cross that we put up each Easter, just like a Christmas tree." "Wow! That's a good idea! Do you put lights on it and everything?" "No, my mom sticks cards with Scripture verses on the cross. We can take them off, learn them by heart and write our names on them. Next to the cross is a box where we put the cards when we know the verse." "That's great!" Cora exclaimed. "Does your mom check on you?" "O yes, on Easter Sunday we recite the verses and if we know them by heart and can also give the Bible reference, we get a token. It is the first clue to a treasure hunt. In the end each one of us receives a great book to read."

"I'd never receive a book if I was part of your family," Cora said. "I can't remember Scripture verses." "Why, it's easy!" said Helen. "Just make a song out of it. Then you can remember it zap-zap!" She started singing, "Proverbs 20:11, *'Even a child is known by his actions, by whether his conduct is pure and right.'*"

Cora was very impressed. "You could become a rap artist!" she exclaimed. She gave Helen a piece of her Easter egg. "Thanks," said Helen, "I'll lend you my book once I've finished reading it."

Why not start a similar tradition in your home?

28 March

Passover and Easter

It was almost midnight and it was quiet throughout the land of Egypt. In the Jewish slave quarters, however, mysterious activity was going on. In every little mud house a lamb was being slaughtered and its blood was painted above the front door, just as God had ordered. You could smell the meat being grilled and see herbs and bread on the table. People were standing around ready to leave.

At midnight a shadow passed through the streets. It was the angel of death. He went from door to door. He entered every home that was not marked by the blood of a lamb.

Pharaoh, the king of Egypt, could not sleep. He tossed and turned in his bed. "These bothersome Jews with their fanatical leader, Moses," he thought. "They want to leave Egypt, but how can I allow such a thing? Who will then build my cities?" He got up and went over to where the crown prince was sleeping. He stroked his hair lovingly. But the child was cold and still ... he was dead! Pharaoh cried out in sorrow and all over Egypt people woke up to find that their first-born children were dead. There was crying throughout the city. Only in the homes where the lamb had been slaughtered, everybody was still alive.

The king called Moses. "Tell your people to go, before we all die," he said. And so at last after hundreds of years of slavery the Israelites left Egypt.

Jewish people still celebrate Passover. Each year they remember the night of their deliverance so long ago. We Christians celebrate Easter at the same time because Jesus, our Lamb, was crucified during Passover. He provided the blood that keeps the angel of spiritual death away from us.

Read this story in Exodus 12:21-33.

29 March

God will provide

Vera and her twin sister were chatting as they usually did every night before they went to sleep. But tonight their discussion was more serious than ever before.

"What will happen to us now?" Vera asked. She was always the one who was scared. But tonight even Wilma's voice was shaky. "God will take care of us," she said. That afternoon the children had heard the bad news that their parents were getting divorced. They both cried bitterly, but their aunt said it wasn't the end of the world. This kind of thing happened to lots of families and they would get over this crisis like everyone else did. But her words did not help them one bit and they could see that their mom's eyes were red from crying too.

"Will we still get pocket money?" Vera asked. "That's the least of our worries," Wilma answered. "Do you realize that we will have to spend some weekends with Dad's new wife? And poor Mom will have to see to everything on her own; the car, the garden, the plumbing! I hate that woman and I hate Dad! How can he do this to us?"

Vera tried to calm her sister, "You know Mom always says that God can't help us if we have bitterness in our hearts. We still have a lot to be thankful for. Betty's parents are also divorced and she has no one to talk to. She told me that she takes all her sadness to a secret place where she locks it away. The other day she told me that her secret place was almost full. At least we have each other."

"And God!" Wilma said as she turned over for the night.

Read Philippians 4:19. Do you think that these words could be a comfort to the twins and to Betty?

30 March

Easter eggs

Why do people eat chocolate eggs wrapped in shiny colorful paper at Easter time? Many imaginative stories try to explain this custom. Here are two stories that are certainly thoughtful, but are not true.

One story explains that a bird made a nest just above the grave where Jesus was buried. When Jesus rose from the dead, the eggs in the nest turned the most beautiful colors. One turned red to symbolize Jesus' blood which had flowed on the cross. One became white to show how clean we could be washed in the blood of Jesus. One became blue. Blue is the color of hope and it reminds us of the hope that we have in our hearts for eternal life. The fourth one turned into gold, because one day in heaven we will inherit great treasures.

Another story says that Mary, after she had seen the risen Christ, ran home to tell everybody what she had seen. When she met a friend along the way and told her about her experience, the woman would not believe her. She had a basket full of eggs with her. Mary said, "If what I told you is the truth, the eggs in your basket will change color!" And immediately the eggs in her basket became a colorful witness to the truth of Mary's story.

Christians do not believe stories like this. Some people even say that we should not buy Easter eggs, because it makes us forget the true reason why we have Easter. But if you get an Easter egg from somebody this year, think about this: just as a little new-born chick comes forth from an egg, so Jesus came out of the grave and He can give new life to everybody who believes in Him.

You can read in Matthew 28:1-10 how Jesus was resurrected from the dead and came out of the tomb.

31 March

APRIL

Why did Jesus have to die?

Dan and his parents were touring a foreign country. He had never seen so many crucifixes before. A crucifix is a cross with Jesus on it. Their tour guide showed them the beautiful churches and monasteries which had very vivid displays of Jesus' crucifixion.

One night back at the hotel Dan asked his parents, "Why did Jesus have to die?" "He died as a sacrifice for all our sins," his mom answered. "But why did anybody have to make any sacrifice at all?" he asked again. "I hate the parts in the Old Testament where innocent animals had to be slaughtered for God."

Now Dan's father spoke. "You see, sin is a serious offence against God. And people have been sinning ever since Adam and Eve first disobeyed God. God wanted to convince people of the seriousness of their sinful deeds. He said that they had to pay for their sins with blood. They could bring their best lamb or a dove to the temple to be slaughtered. Many, many animals were killed for the sins of mankind, because the sacrifices had to be repeated again and again, as men and women kept on doing what was wrong.

"But then God announced a better plan. He sent Jesus to the world. Jesus never sinned and when He was nailed to the cross, He was the perfect Lamb who could pay for all the sins of every person, once and for all.

"Because of Jesus' crucifixion nobody needs to pay for his sins with the blood of animals anymore. People who believe in Jesus can confess their sins, repent and ask Jesus' forgiveness."

Dan remembered an engraving that he had seen that day: "For the transgressions of my people He was stricken." He understood it much better now.

Look up this verse in Isaiah 53:8.

1 April

Good Friday

"**S**ome things are hard to understand!" Peter said as they were leaving church on Good Friday. "Jesus was such a kind person and He did so many good things. Why did people want to kill Him? You would think everybody would have loved Him."

"Yes," his younger sister Ronel added, "I was wondering about the same thing. Last week our Sunday school teacher told us how everybody waved branches from palm trees at Jesus while He was riding on a donkey. They were singing and praising Him. Why did they change their minds and start yelling 'Crucify Him!' only a week later?"

As the family got into the car, their dad said, "People often do strange things. Although Jesus was the best person who has ever lived, there were some people who hated Him. He said things that they did not want to hear. He preached against sin and they weren't prepared to stop living sinful lives. So they must have felt guilty and uncomfortable when He was around. Then they started making plans to get rid of Him."

"And they nailed him to a cross even though He had done nothing wrong," Peter's mom added.

"That must've been the worst thing that has ever happened on earth," Ronel said. "Yes, but it was also the best," her dad replied. "Do you remember what our pastor said today? We call this day a *good* day, because Jesus paid for all our sins. After Jesus had died God said that our sins are paid for. Satan thought that He had won when Jesus died on the cross. But he was mistaken. Jesus was the Victor! He completed the task that God had given Him to do."

Read the Scripture verses that the pastor read on Good Friday: Colossians 2:14-15.

2 April

Easter

"**H**e lives! He lives! Christ Jesus lives today! He walks with me and He talks with me along life's narrow way!" Steph loved this song and she was thrilled when the choir sang it in church on Easter Sunday. It had really been a very special service. A wooden cross with wire netting around it was put in the foyer. People were invited to bring flowers to church to put on the cross to thank God for raising Jesus from the grave.

While little girls in white dresses brought in the cross and put it in front of the pulpit, the congregation sang, "If we died with Him, we shall also live with Him!"

"Dad," Steph asked when they were having hot-cross buns with their tea later on, "how was it possible for Jesus to be alive again after He had already died?"

"Well," her dad replied, "Jesus was stronger than death. He could break the chains of death. God did not intervene when Jesus died, but He did not allow Jesus to be dead forever. With the power of God, Jesus could rise from death after three days. Then God sent angels to move the stone that was put in front of the grave, so that Jesus could walk out into the world again, strong and free!"

Now Tommy had something to say, "The soldiers didn't know about it, because they were fast asleep." That was the part of the story that he liked best. "Imagine how puzzled they were when they saw that the big stone had been moved." He grinned.

"Yes," their dad said, "the people who wanted to hush Jesus up for ever, discovered on that day that it is not possible!"

Make an Easter greeting card and write Acts 3:15 on it. You can send it to someone you love as an encouragement.

3 April

Was Jesus really resurrected?

"**M**om, do we have to believe that Jesus rose from the dead?" Richard asked his mother. "I do," she answered, "but what makes you doubt it?" "Well, the Muslim children at school say that He never even died. And Henry said that many Christians don't believe in the resurrection either."

"I believe that Jesus died on the cross," Richard's sister Wendy said. "The soldiers who took Him from the cross wouldn't have made such a mistake. My Sunday school teacher said that they were so sure about His death that they did not even take the trouble to break His bones, as was customary."

Their mom continued, "I know that there have always been people who denied the fact that Jesus rose from the dead. They even paid the soldiers to say that His body was stolen. But there's enough evidence to convince me that He came out of that grave alive. First there were the men and women who saw the empty grave. Then there was Mary Magdalene who spoke to Jesus at the grave. Jesus appeared to the disciples on that same evening. He showed them His hands and feet with the marks of the nails in them and also the wound in His side where He was pierced with a sword. A week later Thomas, who at first did not believe that Christ had risen, saw Him and said, 'My Lord and my God!' On another day Jesus appeared to 500 people at the same time. Would all of these people be liars? And would the disciples go around telling lies and be willing to be martyred and killed for a hoax? I don't think so! Jesus really was crucified, buried in the tomb and rose three days later. This is the basis of our Christian faith," Mom said earnestly.

Read in 1 Corinthians 15:1-15 what Paul had to say about the resurrection of Christ.

4 April

Disobedience

William lit a cigarette rather clumsily. He wasn't very good at it yet, but at least he didn't choke and cough as much as he had at first.

Suddenly the back door opened and his father appeared on the porch. There was no chance to run away, so William quickly hid the cigarette behind his back and just hoped his father didn't see or smell anything. "Dad," he said quickly, trying to divert his father's attention, "can I go swimming with Stephen and the others tomorrow?" His father looked him straight in the eyes. "William," he said, and each word was clearly meted out, "don't ask me for favors when you are hiding your disobedience behind your back!"

William quenched the cigarette in the bird-bath and threw the stub in the dustbin. He felt very embarrassed now. He wished his father would give him a hiding rather than a lecture. "I am sorry, Dad, I won't do it again," he said, meaning every word. He knew that smoking was a waste of money and bad for his health.

"We've talked about the dangers of smoking many times before," his father said. "Today I want you to think of something else. How do you feel towards God when you do things like this?" William's face turned red. He had been having difficulty praying recently, almost as though there was a wall between him and God. "I will fix it, Dad," he answered.

"There is in fact a Bible text about this," his father replied. "I will show it to you tonight. And I trust that you won't do such a stupid thing again." His father roughed his son's hair the way he always did when he had just told him something important.

Read in Psalm 66:18 what William's father showed him that evening.

5 April

It makes you numb

Today there is some good news and some bad news. First the bad news. Thousands of young people in our country and all over the world are addicted to drugs. Criminals often sell them to children who later cannot live without them, because of their addictive effect. This means that the user's body becomes so used to the drug that he almost gets sick if he cannot get hold of it. That is why addicts eventually do not care what they do, as long as they can get hold of drugs. Children even steal their own parents' money just to buy marijuana, cocaine, ecstasy or mandrax-tablets. Criminals get richer and richer while the drugs ruin the lives of the people who use them.

The good news is that you can say no to drugs. You should say no, because drugs can harm your body and because you can very quickly become a drug addict. You shouldn't even try it once. Even taking a drug once can make your body start craving for more. You might do something which you will regret forever, because you cannot completely control what you are doing while the drug is in your system. And above all, you will not learn to handle life with its ups and downs. You will become dependent on drugs to help you cope with everyday situations.

Drug addicts cannot handle the crises of life, because they escape to a world where everything seems easy, until the effect of the drug wears off, of course.

Paul wrote in 1 Corinthians 6:12, *"Everything is permissible for me – but I will not be mastered by anything."* That should also be your resolution.

Stick this motto inside your schoolbag:

USING DRUGS IS DUMB BECAUSE THEY MAKE YOU NUMB.

6 April

Talk about it!

"**I** wish I could talk to someone about this whole business," Sandra thought as she was walking home from school. A lady had talked about children's rights to them that day. It was the first time that she had heard the word "molested", but she knew immediately what the woman was talking about when she said that some grown-ups misuse children. She thought that nobody else ever experienced anything like it, but it seemed that it happened quite often.

"Mom," she said as soon she got home, "there is something that I need to tell you." She poured out the whole story. "Uncle Albert did something horrible to me." Her mom got such a fright that she left what she was doing and came to sit next to Sandra. "Tell me everything," her mother prompted.

Sandra cried as she told her mother how her uncle had taken her on a boatride once when they were on holiday. And when they were on the other side of the island, he started touching her body. "I started yelling and then he stopped doing it. But I still feel terrible about it. I have even prayed about it, but the bad feelings won't go away."

"I am glad that you told me. You shouldn't have tried to carry this load alone." Her mom hugged her and said, "Try not to think about it any more. Daddy and I know what to do. But remember you must always be careful. Unfortunately there are people with sick minds who want to misuse children. Don't ever go alone anywhere with someone you don't know or you don't trust completely. And if anything upsets you, come and tell us about it."

Has anything like this ever happened to you? Read Matthew 11:28 and talk about it to your parents or to any other Christian you can trust.

7 April

Big sins and small sins

"Mom, are some sins bigger than others?" Tilly asked while she was helping her mother to peel the potatoes. "Why do you ask?" her mom wanted to know. "Our Sunday school teacher said that we must think about it this week." "Well, and what do you think?" her mom asked.

"I think that some sins are big and others are small. Surely the drunken driver who caused the accident in which Mr. Miller was killed, committed a bigger sin than Pete who only stole sweets from the grocer's shop." Her mother disagreed, "The truth is that all types of sin are equally bad. When you sin, you are breaking God's law. Your sinful deed says that you will not listen to Him and that you are your own boss. The man who got drunk and caused the accident ignored Ephesians 5:18 and his sin had terrible consequences. But Pete's sin also had an ugly outcome." "How?" Tilly asked. "When our elder invited the owner of the grocer's shop to come to church, he said, 'Why would I want to visit your church? The children from your congregation are dishonest and give me more trouble than I can handle.' Maybe Mr. Abrahams will never go to church and never hear God's Word, all because of a tiny little sin. And won't that also be a terrible thing?"

"Anyway," her mother continued, "an unfriendly word may look like a small sin, but it can do a lot of harm. And selfishness and lies may be regarded as small transgressions, but they can really cause a lot of damage."

Tilly sure had something to go and think about. She now realized that all sins, big or small, have severe consequences. They dishonor the name of God and can hurt other people.

See what Romans 14:7-13 has to say about this topic.

8 April

The accident

Mrs. Bradley called her three sons to her room. "Boys," she said with tears in her eyes, "I have wonderful news. Mr. Stone has become a Christian." They all sat dead quiet. They were thinking of the day when they heard that a careless driver had knocked their dad over as he was crossing the street. He died in the ambulance on the way to the hospital. It was a terrible day and they had had a really difficult time during the two years since then. They missed their dad so much.

"Did Uncle Peter tell you about it?" Robert asked. He was the eldest. He knew that his uncle had talked with the driver of the truck. "Yes," replied his mom, "since Uncle Peter visited Mr. Stone, God has worked in his life. Now he has become a follower of Jesus. He is sorry about what happened and God has forgiven him. We must too."

"I won't," said Adam, the youngest. "Whatever he says can't bring Dad back!" "I know," his mom said softly, "but Jesus could forgive His murderers and He can help us to do the same. Anyway, it is wonderful news that Mr. Stone is now a child of God." Now John spoke, "You can't say that Dad had to die so that this man could be saved!" "Of course not," his mom replied, "but Jesus died so that we could be saved and He has a plan with our lives. Even out of a tragedy like this He can bring something good."

The next day Mrs. Bradley found a letter in John's Bible. It said, "I have forgiven Mr. Stone." She pressed it to her heart and prayed, "Please God, help us all to do the same."

Read Romans 8:28 to see where Mrs. Bradley found out that good things can come out of our worst experiences.

9 April

Go for gold!

Marion Jones was born in America in 1976. When she was eight years old, she attended the opening ceremony of the Olympic Games in her hometown, Los Angeles. She was so impressed, that she wrote on a blackboard in her room,

> I will be an Olympic champion!

She trained hard and never lost sight of her goal. In the 2000 Olympics in Australia, she became the first woman to win five medals during one Olympic session. She won gold medals for the 100 meter and 200 meter sprints, as well as a bronze medal for long jump and two medals for relays.

Do you think that Marion regretted all the hard training? Or do you think that she was upset that she missed some parties or movies or ice-creams with her friends because she was practicing? No, she did not mind, because the gold medals were worth much more to her.

Her success story reminds me of 1 Corinthians 9:24, *"Do you know that in a race all the runners run, but only one gets the prize? Run in such a way as to get the prize. Everyone who competes in the games goes into strict training. They do it to get a crown that will not last; but we do it to get a crown that will last forever."*

We should be ready to make certain sacrifices to reach our goals in life. As Christians our goal is to be more and more like Jesus. Therefore we should be keen to help other people and to please God. Jesus is standing at the finish line and we will one day receive a prize from Him that will be much more precious than a gold medal!

Also read Philippians 3:14.

10 April

Why not?

Tess and her mom were washing wine glasses after a party at their home. "Why don't you ever have a glass of wine like everyone else?" Tess asked her mom. "You are the daughter of a wine farmer after all!" Her mom smiled. She thought for a while and then said, "The Bible doesn't say that we shouldn't drink wine. But somebody who took the trouble to investigate, discovered that there are 75 Scripture verses that warn about drunkenness."

"Surely one glass of wine won't make you drunk," Tess objected. "No, but I find that I can't think clearly after I've had a glass of wine. And I know that Satan is very shrewd. I'd rather be wide awake all the time in case he wants to lead me astray."

"How will he do that?" Tess asked out of curiosity. "Well, he might convince me to have a second and a third glass of wine and before I know it, I could be really drunk."

"Some high school children say that a party without alcohol isn't fun." "What rubbish!" her mom said. "I love being with friends and we always have a lot of fun together. But I have never needed alcohol to make me happy. It is such a pity that teenagers do not take note of all the warnings against drinking when they're young. It has been proven that the chance of getting addicted to alcohol is much greater if you start drinking as a teenager."

Tess took a glass of leftover red wine and pretended to gulp it down, just to tease her mom. "It sure tastes good," she joked. "That's the problem!" her mom said seriously.

Read the description of a drunkard in Proverbs 23:29-35.

11 April

The two brothers

In Matthew 21:28-30 there's a good story that Jesus once told His followers. There was a man who had two sons. He went to the first and said, "Son, go and work in the vineyard today." "I will not," he answered, but later he changed his mind and went. Then the father went to the other son and said the same thing. He answered, "I will, sir," but he did not go. And then Jesus asked the people who were listening to the story, "Which of the two did as their father wanted?" What would you say? Yes, obviously the first brother was the hero of the story.

Which of the two sons do you resemble? Have you told Jesus that you want to obey Him, but in the mean time you are doing just what you want? It is no use going to church and wearing a F.R.O.G. wristband and pretending that you are a child of God if you disobey Him most of the time. People should be able to see by your actions that you love the Lord. Otherwise you are like the son who said, "Okay, Dad, I'll do want you want," but carried on with his life as usual.

Or maybe you are someone who has never decided to follow Jesus. You have perhaps never had the courage to say "Yes!" to the call of Jesus, who wants you to be His follower. Maybe you can even recall a time when you refused point blank to do what He was asking of you. Why not follow the example of the first son, who felt sorry about his reaction and eventually did what his dad wanted him to do. You can admit your mistake on your knees and ask God to make you obedient.

What does James 1:22 say is more important: What you say or what you do?

12 April

Making good choices

A pastor once had two visitors on the same afternoon. First a young man who had just been released from prison came to his office. He was looking for a job. Although he sounded sad and needy, he wasn't really keen to find work. He actually wanted the church to give him some money and a place to stay. "How did you land up in jail?" the pastor asked. "Well," the young man said, "my father was an alcoholic and my mother couldn't find work so I never had any chances in life."

Later that afternoon another young man visited the pastor. He wanted to donate a large sum of money to the church to be used for charity. "You see, sir," he said, "I come from a home where my mom was a drug addict and my father was in jail. I knew that if I didn't get out and do something for myself, I wouldn't get anywhere. Now God has been so good to me that I have enough to give to the poor."

The next Sunday the pastor had something interesting to share with his congregation. He told them about two children who had both grown up in homes where they had really had a hard time. But they turned out completely different. "What made the difference?" he asked. The one child chose to feel sorry for himself and did bad things. But the other decided to learn from his parents' mistakes and to trust God.

Have you got serious problems to deal with in your home? Is your mom or dad a difficult person? Are they too busy to pay attention to your needs? Do they often fight? Is there a drug or drinking problem? Remember, God wants to be a parent to you. Ephesians 6:10 says, *"Be strong in the Lord and in his mighty power."*

Choose to trust God.

13 April

Where is the church?

It was Sunday morning and three boys were standing at a bus stop, waiting for different buses to take them to church. They started chatting. "How many people come to your church?" one asked. "About two hundred," came the first reply. "Our church can take only twenty people, but my dad says that where he came from in Ireland, there's a tiny church built for only two people." "Must look like a doll's church!" said the third guy.

Then a friendly man in a suit who was also waiting for the bus, started talking, "You know what?" he said. "A church isn't a building. It is a group of people who serve the Lord. People who know Greek and who have translated the Bible, will tell you that Jesus never had a building in mind when He spoke of His church. You'll never find anybody saying, 'Let's go to church,' in the Bible."

"Well, what would you call the building over there?" one of the boys inquired, pointing to a tall steeple a little further on. "That is a building where the church is gathering. But they could just as well get together in a house or under a tree. They will still be the church of Jesus Christ if they sincerely believe in His redemption and serve God."

"Are you also on your way to a church?" another one of the boys asked. "Yes," the man answered, "I used to think that I could be a Christian on my own, but I have found that I need to be with fellow Christians. Now I love attending church where I can pray and sing together with other Christians."

"So we all actually belong to the same church?" asked the boy who started the conversation. "Yes, if you are also serving Christ with your whole heart, then all of us belong to His invisible church."

Read Hebrews 11:25.

14 April

Who says it's true?

"How do you know that the Bible is true?" John asked his father out of the blue on a Saturday afternoon. He still had to do his Sunday school homework and he didn't really feel like it. Lately he had been very confused about the Bible. At school a teacher had said that the Bible isn't the only Holy Book. Muslims believe that the Koran was written by God Himself and the Jews say that only the Old Testament is true.

William's dad put down the newspaper. He spoke with confidence. "I believe that the Bible is true and that it is God's Word. If it wasn't, it would have been destroyed ages ago. Many people have been trying for many years to wipe every bit of the Bible from the face of the earth. In many countries people aren't even allowed to read the Bible." William's father fetched a map of the world. "Some governments ordered officials to burn all Bibles," he said as he pointed to England, Russia and China. "But the Bibles were hidden and smuggled away by faithful Christians and today millions of people are still reading this remarkable Book."

William and his dad went back to the lounge while his dad continued, "There have always been people who criticized or ridiculed the Bible and many have tried to prove that it wasn't true. But they couldn't succeed and never will. Others are desperate to get hold of it and that is why it has already been translated into more than a thousand languages. And you know what? It is still the world's best-selling book!"

William suddenly felt different about the Bible study that he had to complete for Sunday school. Who wouldn't be curious to know more about the world's most popular book?

Underline the last 4 words of John 17:17 in your Bible.

15 April

Are you selfish?

The kids at the Children's League were having lots of fun. Miss Peggy was giving out chocolates so that everybody got a piece. But she did it in an unusual way, which got everyone thinking.

She took a huge slab of chocolate and gave three blocks to Wayne. Then she told him, "You can do whatever you want to with these blocks." Wayne had no problem with the decision. He put all of it in his mouth, chewing it with sheer delight.

"Shame on you," Ronald said. He had hoped to get a bit of it! Now Miss Peggy gave three blocks to Melissa. Again she said, "You can do what you like with it." Melissa kept one square for herself and gave the others to her two best friends. The kids got really excited. "Miss! Miss! Give me a chance!" they all shouted. Miss Peggy gave away the whole chocolate in the same way. Most of the kids kept one piece of chocolate for themselves and gave away the rest. Little Amy decided to give her share to the children who didn't get any and she was full of smiles about it!

Now Miss Peggy started to talk earnestly to the kids. "Children," she said, "if you keep everything that you get just for yourself, you are building a kingdom called I-me-mine-myself! Many people on earth are doing just that; building a kingdom for Number One, who happens to be themselves. They gather stuff for themselves and hardly ever give anything to others. They forget that you can't take any-thing with you when you die."

Some Christians give a lot of money for the Lord's work or to needy people. When they die, they may leave very little money and property behind, but they have invested their money in God's Kingdom. "Now go and chew on that one," she said.

Read Proverbs 11:24-25.

16 April

Spread a little sunshine!

Ingrid slammed her bedroom door closed. Everybody in the house could hear her shouting. "Wow! Ingrid is in a bad mood again," her brother Hugh said. "She is so difficult to please and she disagrees with everything you say. It must be because she is a teenager!"

"Well, all I know is that we can't put up with that kind of behavior for the next seven years," her dad said. He went to her room to talk to her, but when he came back, he looked upset.

The next minute Paula burst into the kitchen. She was Ingrid's elder sister, also in her teens, but she was always in a good mood. Nobody could be glum when she was around. She gave her father a hug and asked, "What's wrong, Dad? Have you had a bad day? I'll make you some coffee."

Soon everyone was in a good mood and even Ingrid came out of her room to join them. She seemed a bit more relaxed now. That night after supper their father read his favorite, Psalm 19. But this time he started at verse 8 and when he came to verse 14, he asked Ingrid to read it. She blushed while reading, *"May the words of my mouth and the meditation of my heart be pleasing in your sight, O Lord, my Rock and my Redeemer."*

"I'm sorry about this afternoon," she blurted out. "I don't know how Paula always manages to brighten up the atmosphere. I only seem to spread bad vibes wherever I go."

"It needn't be like that," her mom said. "Even though we all have different personalities, we can decide whether we are going to spread sunshine or gloom. And we can ask God to help us."

Ingrid knew that her mom was right.

Try and see how many people you can cheer up today.

17 April

The circus

When last did you go to a circus? What did you think was the most exciting part of all? Maybe the man who put his head right into the lion's mouth? Or the clowns who had everyone roaring with laughter?

Many children find the performance of the acrobats by far the most spectacular. How the acrobats can walk and jump on a rope so high above the ground, is truly amazing! People in the audience are often heard saying things like, "Wow! Just look at that acrobat! Isn't he brave? Isn't that awesome?"

Once an interviewer asked one of the trapeze artists from a famous circus company, "Aren't you scared while you're up there?" The man answered, "When it's time for me to let go of the trapeze, I trust my partner to catch me. And if he should fail to do it, then I still know that there is a net underneath that will break my fall."

Do you know that the life of a Christian has a lot in common with the performance of the trapeze artists? Lots of people are watching us Christians everyday and they are talking about how we act. Your life should be remarkable, so that your friends can say, "Look at the guy. He is so brave. He's not scared to say no to temptation." Then you can say, "It's because I'm a Christian." And if someone should ask, "But aren't you afraid that your friends will let you down?" Then you can say, "But there's a net underneath. If I make a mistake or if somebody should let me down, then God will be there to catch me and help me."

In Deuteronomy 33:27 you will find these reassuring words, *"The eternal God is your refuge and underneath are everlasting arms."*

You can also read Matthew 10:28 for encouragement.

18 April

Special prayers

A crane is a bird with long slender legs, a long neck and powerful wings. In Japan it is considered a holy bird. If somebody from Japan sends you a picture of a crane, it means that he wishes you a long life. The Japanese are very good at folding paper. Children are taught from an early age to fold paper artistically so that it can resemble all kinds of things. Almost anybody in Japan can fold a square piece of paper to look like a crane. That's because they believe that it will bring good luck. They believe that the more cranes they can produce while they are praying, the more likely their prayers will be answered.

Some people believe that if they can make a thousand paper cranes, the gods will be so pleased that their wishes will be granted immediately. Tourists to Japan are always amazed to see all the paper cranes in the trees near the country's temples. These birds appear all over the place especially during exam times to ensure good results for students.

Neil Verwey, who works as a missionary in Japan, said that the children of Hiroshima once made twenty thousand paper cranes. They placed them at a monument in the city and prayed that there will never again be a war in their country.

We as Christians do not believe in superstitions like these. We admire the art of folding paper into interesting forms, but we know that it cannot bring happiness to anybody. We trust in God alone. Jesus opened the way to God's heart for us when He died on the cross. Now we can be sure that our prayers go to God straightaway and that He listens to them. He will never ignore our needs.

Try to fold a bird out of paper and write Jeremiah 17:7-8 on its wings.

19 April

Back home!

Billy woke up with a terrible headache. "Where am I?" he wondered. There were white beds all around and he was covered in bandages. He tried to remember what had happened. O yes, there had been an accident! He was on his bike and a car smashed into him from behind. That's all he could remember ... But now a worried look came upon his face. What happened to Topsy, his dog? He was running next to the bicycle when the accident happened.

When Billy's parents came to visit him in hospital, he didn't want to talk about his injuries. He just wanted to know about Topsy. His mom said, "We have also been wondering what could have happened to him. We have searched the whole neighborhood, but we haven't found him yet." Before his parents left the hospital, Billy's father prayed. He praised God for saving Billy's life and he asked Him to make Billy strong again. Then he also prayed that Topsy would be safe and that they would soon find him.

Billy had to stay in hospital for a week and he had to use crutches when he went home. He immediately started looking for Topsy.

He went up and down the streets, calling Topsy's name. The little dog had got completely lost after his master's accident. He was scared and sought food in trash cans. He already looked thin and neglected. One afternoon he heard a familiar voice calling his name. He rushed out from behind the hedge where he was hiding and almost caused the little boy on crutches to lose his balance. They were so glad to see each other again!

In Luke 15 there are three stories that tell us about things that had been lost and then were found again. Can you see how glad God is when somebody who has become estranged from Him, is found again?

20 April

Everyone deserves to hear

A missionary couple from Peru came to church to share some of their experiences. The Greens live up in the mountains among the Quecha people. They had to learn the difficult language and live in a mud house, just like the inhabitants of Inkawasi. They have to carry water to their home and they have no electricity and no telephone. They sacrificed the luxuries of their home because they want the people of that region to hear about Jesus. God loves the Quechas just as much as He loves us, and gave Henry and Ruth the desire to go to Peru to spread the gospel there.

A woman in church asked, "Why must you go so far? Surely there's enough work to be done here in our country." Henry took a box of sweets from his pocket. He gave one to each of the people in the first pew. Then he started again and gave them each yet another one. When he was about to do this for the third time, one of the children at the back of the church asked, "What about us?"

Henry smiled. He was waiting for that request. "We in our country hear the gospel over and over. But there are many people in the world who have never even heard the name of Jesus. It's not fair that only the people in the front row get sweets and it's not fair if only some people hear the good news."

Everybody in church could then understand why some people are called to go to places far from home to spread the message about God's love. They thanked God that the Green family was obedient to God's calling.

See if you can find Peru on a map of the world and then read what Psalm 22:27 has to say about the people who are living there.

21 April

Too precious

Today's true story comes from Malaysia. In that country you will find the Chefoo school, where missionaries to the East often send their children for schooling. One day a few pupils at the school had to clean their classroom. They also had to unpack a cupboard full of bits and pieces. Among the junk they found a Bible that was written in the Malaysian language.

"Surely this is too precious to throw away," they said to one another. So they decided to give it to Mr. Nathan. He often took his motorcycle and visited villages in the surrounding area to tell them about Jesus. "Thank you," he said. "I am actually planning to visit the Orang Asli people this weekend. They live deep in the jungle. They do not know the Bible or the message that it contains."

That Saturday Mr. Nathan took a long ride on a dirt track through the dense vegetation. Eventually he reached an opening in the forest where there was a group of houses with thatched roofs on stilts. He took some sweets from his pocket and offered them to the children that were playing there. "Where is the chief?" he asked them. He showed their chief the Bible and told him about the important message that was in it. He left the Bible with the Chief Counselor of the Orang Asli.

Can you guess the outcome of this story? A lot of the people of that village became Christians and they eventually built their own church on stilts. You can imagine how glad the children at the Chefoo school were when they heard this news! It made them think of the words of Psalm 119:72. Can you guess why?

Your Bible is also too precious to lie around in a cupboard! Why not take it out and read from it right now. See how much of Psalm 119 you can get through.

22 April

Blankets needed!

It was freezing cold in Cape Town and the Kregel family sat in front of a heater in their sitting room.

They were watching a television news broadcast. Suddenly they all gasped at what they saw; a slum area on the Cape flats, completely flooded! The houses of the poor people who lived there were surrounded by muddy water. Celia shivered. "I'm glad that I don't have to fish around for my school books like that little boy! And where will they get dry clothes to put on?" Her little sister Dawn started crying. "Who is going to help them, Mommy?" she asked. As if her question had been heard somewhere, the cameras now focused on a church in Langa where the people whose homes had been flooded, could go for shelter. Kind people at the church were dishing out soup and bread. Then the announcer said that people in the vicinity who would like to donate clothing, blankets or food, could contact a certain number.

Mr. Kregel took down the telephone number and phoned straight away. "I can drop our contribution off at a receiving depot on my way to work tomorrow," he said. "It'll mean that I have to get up a little earlier tomorrow morning," he added. Mrs. Kregel said, "I'm going to make a nice pot of soup tonight." The children all went to their rooms to see what clothing they could get together. And because each of them got a new duvet set for Christmas, they could also load blankets and sheets into their dad's car.

When Celia wiggled into her warm bed that night, she prayed, "Please God, help those poor people to get settled again. And forgive us for often being so ungrateful for all our blessings."

Read Matthew 22:39 and think about how you can help people in need.

23 April

How many pages in your Bible?

On the front page of a local newspaper there once was an unusual report. CHAPLAIN TEARS UP BIBLE was the caption. The report said that the pastor at the military base in town had torn some of the pages out of his Bible in front of everybody at church that day. People were shocked, because ever since their childhood they had been taught to treat the Bible with respect and reverence.

But the minister used this extraordinary act to convey a special message. He was concerned about the way the young recruits in the army behaved. They got drunk, they used foul language, they had fights with one another and they made friends with bad women. They really lived as if they did not believe what the Bible taught.

So then the chaplain tore out Exodus 20 from his Bible. "You call yourselves Christians," he said, "but you do not believe God's Word. You have ignored the commandment that forbids you to use the Lord's name in vain. You also act as if the Bible does not condemn drunkenness. So I'm tearing out Ephesians 5:18." To everybody's amazement he also removed 1 Corinthians 13, the chapter on love and several other parts of the Bible. He crumpled up the pages as if they were worth nothing.

The young army boys and the rest of the congregation, as well as the people who read the news in the paper, had something to think about. "How seriously do I take the contents of my Bible?" they asked themselves. They now realized that it was dangerous to ignore the parts of Scripture that don't suit you. You could end up with a Bible that is so thin that God's message is left out completely!

See what Jesus had to say in John 8:47 about people who did not take the words of Scripture seriously.

24 April

A letter to the world

There is one sermon that Erica will never forget. She was still a little girl when Reverend Linden asked her to help him in one of his sermons. They first practiced and then, during the service, she was asked to come to the front. A big red mailbox was put in front of the pulpit. Reverend Linden read a passage from 2 Corinthians 3. Then he repeated verse 2, *"You yourselves are our letter, written on our hearts, known and read by everybody."*

Then he took away the top part of the mailbox and put Erica into it. Whap! He closed it again. It was dark inside. Only a little bit of light came through the opening into which the letters were normally put. But Erica wasn't scared, because she knew that the minister would take her out of the mailbox again after his sermon. She could hear everything that he was saying.

He told the people that every Christian was a letter from God to the world. People who do not believe in God look at our lives and then decide what to think of Him. If God's children are full of loving kindness, they can read in our lives that God is loving and kind. But if we are selfish and sinful, they think that God isn't special. His followers are behaving just like other people, so why would they want to know Him?

Then Reverend Linden asked, "What kind of a letter are you? Do people see godly behavior when they look at your life?" After that Erica was lifted out of the mailbox again. Each person in church could then softly ask God to let him or her be a beautiful letter to the world. Erica also did that.

Put a stamp on your hand and leave it there for a whole day to remind you that you are a letter from God to the world.

25 April

The gift

Once upon a time there were two brothers and a sister. In their country a prince was born and everybody in the kingdom wanted to take a present to the baby. The eldest son made a baseball bat for the little boy and the younger one made him a pair of booties. But their sister decided to write him a prayer. She put it in a little box and when her brothers started on their journey to deliver the gifts, she went with them.

But the two brothers were ashamed of their sister's gift, so they decided to run away from her in order to get to the palace before she did. The queen was glad about the baseball bat and the shoes and she put them with all the other toys and clothing that had been given to the baby.

Much later that day the little girl reached the palace. Her brothers were hiding to see what would happen when she gave the prayer to the queen. To their amazement the queen said, "Nobody has ever brought me such a precious present!" She took the box with the written prayer in it, and placed it in the crib with the baby. "I will read it every night before we go to bed," she said.

This story has a lesson for all of us. If somebody tells you that he or she is praying for you, it is the best gift that anybody can give you. James 5:16 says, *"Pray for each other."* God is waiting for our prayers so that He can give people the good things that they need.

Pray for somebody whom you love.

26 April

Perseverance

"Trrrrrrrrrring!" went the door bell. "I'm sure it's Fran again!" Greta said with a sigh. She opened the door and there was their neighbor's little girl, just as she had predicted. "Will you go ice-skating with me over the weekend?" she begged. "I'll let you know," Greta said, closing the door quickly. "Dear me, but this girl is determined!" she said as she went to the dining room. "What's determined?" asked her young brother. "It is someone who can keep on and on and on!" Greta replied. "I'll have to go with her this weekend, otherwise she'll come here every Friday with the same request."

"In the Bible there was a very similar case," her mom said from where she was sitting. "Jesus told a story about a man who was just as much of a nuisance at his neighbor's house." "And what did Jesus say about that?" Greta asked. "He said that we must pray with the same perseverance," came her mom's reply.

"Where in the Bible do you find that story?" Greta wanted to know. She was really interested, because there was something that she had been praying about for a very long time. So far she had received no answer. Her mom took the Bible from the bookshelf and paged through it. "Here it is," she said. "It's in Luke 11:5-13."

"Does that mean God will give me what I ask if I keep on nagging Him about it?" Greta asked. "No, but it means that the Lord doesn't want us to get discouraged too soon. We must keep on telling Him about our needs and wait for an answer."

Is there something which you have been praying for for a very long time? Don't give up too soon. God will most definitely answer your prayer. Maybe He will give you something even better than what you are asking!

27 April

Earning trust

Arnold loved it when his elder brother came home for the weekend. Frank was much older than Arnold, but they had always been the best of friends. Arnold wanted to ask his brother something important. One Saturday afternoon they took the dogs for a run, and then he took his chance. "Man, how can I get Mom and Dad to trust me?" he asked. "Don't they trust you?" his brother asked. "No. Since that day when I told them a lie about the football match, they suspect me of being dishonest."

"Well, you can't blame them, can you? How can they know that you're not cheating again?" Frank still remembered how shocked his parents were when they discovered that Arnold had been to a movie after he had asked permission to go to a football match. "You will have to work hard to gain their confidence again," Frank said. "See that you keep your promises. Finish all the jobs that you start and don't waste money on trivial things. After a while Mom and Dad will start thinking of you as responsible."

"It sounds as if you know what you're talking about," Arnold said. "Yes, Dad once caught me copying somebody's homework. It took a long time before he trusted me again. Even though I said that I was sorry and promised not to do it again, he watched my every movement for a very long time." The two boys kept running to keep up with the dogs. Then Frank said, "You know, we should be grateful that our parents still worry about our behavior. There are a lot of kids whose folks couldn't care less!"

"That must be awful," Arnold admitted, while getting a better grip on his dog's lead.

Read Proverbs 1:8-10.

28 April

The best lavender

When Miriam got home after school, her mom could see that she had been crying. "What's wrong?" she asked. "I'll never be as smart as the other kids at school," she said. There had been an annual prize giving ceremony at school and Miriam didn't get any awards.

"Let me tell you a story," her mom said.

"A king once went for a walk in his garden. How disappointed he was when he found that many of his trees and shrubs were dying! He went up to an oak tree and asked with concern, "What is the matter?" "I am shriveling away, because I will never be as tall as the pine tree," the oak answered. But the pine tree was also wilted. "What happened to you?" the king asked. "I'm giving up," the pine tree said. "I'll never be able to bear fruit like the apple tree." But when the king saw the apple tree it said, "I'm not interested in surviving. I can't produce beautiful roses like the rose tree."

The king was very upset and started to walk back to his castle. But suddenly he smelled a beautiful fragrance. To his surprise he found a little lavender bush growing cheerfully beside the garden path. "And why, may I ask, are you looking so well while all the other plants are dying?" "You see, Your Majesty," the little lavender bush explained, "I thought to myself, when you planted me, you wanted a lavender bush. You would not come looking for acorns or apples or roses on me. So I reckoned that I'll just be the best lavender bush that I can possibly be!" "And what did the king say?" Miriam asked. "He was thrilled to bits! And God is also glad when you try to be the best that you can be."

Read Psalm 147:10-11.

29 April

A message from prison

Grant was a young prisoner. When he was still a teenager, he was arrested for shoplifting. He was sentenced to go to a special school for young people who had committed a crime. There he made friends with boys who introduced him to drugs, and when he came out of the reformatory, he tried to steal pills from a doctor's surgery. He was caught by a security guard and Grant stabbed the man with a knife. The man died. This time Grant was sentenced to prison.

You can imagine how his parents felt! But they were constantly praying for him. And so it happened that an evangelist who visited the prisoners to tell them of God's love, one day led Grant to Christ.

The principal of the school that Grant had attended before his conviction, heard about his conversion. He asked the authorities whether Grant could visit the school and share with the pupils what he had learned about the serious consequences of wrong friendships and drugs. Do you know what Grant told the children during that meeting?

"I wish I had known Jesus Christ as my Savior when I was your age," he said. "Then my life would not have been such a mess today." The headmaster asked, "Is there anything you want to tell the students about drugs?" Grant replied, "Well, I can only say that it isn't enough to decide that you will say no. I knew all along that it was bad for me, but I wasn't strong enough to refuse it. You need God's power to be able to resist the devil."

After the talk at the school Grant had to go back to his prison cell. But although he was behind bars, he was truly free. Jesus had released him from the power of Satan.

Ask God to give you the power to live a life of victory, as is described in Psalm 18:33-35.

30 April

MAY

Whitsunday

Most Christians know why we celebrate Christmas and Easter. But few people know what Whitsunday is all about. You will find the story in Acts 2.

Forty days after Jesus had risen from the grave, He and His friends were together on the Mount of Olives. There Jesus said goodbye to His disciples and He was taken up into heaven. They could actually see how He ascended from the earth, up, up into the sky!

But before He left, He asked His friends to make sure that people will not forget Him. He asked them to go all over the world to tell all the nations about Him.

Peter must have thought, "Will I be able to witness for Jesus? There was a time when I was too shy to even admit to a young servant girl that I was a friend of His." But Jesus promised His disciples that He would not leave them alone. He promised to send them His Spirit, who would help them to tell everyone about Him.

After this, all Jesus' followers went into a house where they waited for His Spirit to come. They prayed and sang songs of praise and talked about Jesus and waited. And after ten days the Holy Spirit came. First they heard the sound of a soft breeze. Then the wind became fiercer and small tongues of fire appeared above the heads of all the people gathered together. This was how the Spirit moved into their lives. The Holy Spirit helped them to do all the things that Jesus taught them.

Peter realized that he now had a Helper! He was not afraid of people any more. He walked out into the street and started telling everybody about Jesus, the Savior of the world.

Do you want to have Jesus' Spirit in your life? Ask Him for it!

1 May

A new Counselor

Peter was one of Jesus' best friends. He really loved Jesus and one day he said to Him, "Even if all the others leave You, I never will." But one dreadful night in the garden of Gethsemane some soldiers came to take Jesus into captivity. They pushed Him around, hit Him in the face and made fun of Him. All the disciples ran away, because they were scared of the soldiers. Peter followed the procession from a distance.

He saw how they beat Him and how He was taken to court. But he remained on the outskirts of the crowd. One of the onlookers said, "You are also one of this man's followers!" A small voice prompted Peter to say, "No, I'm not." Somebody else made the same accusation, "You have also been with Jesus!" The same small voice said, "Don't admit it. If you do, you might be tortured like Jesus." So Peter said, "I don't even know him!" Then a servant girl came up to him. She said, "You have the same accent as Jesus when you speak. Are you not one of his men?" Peter became very angry. He swore and said, "I told you that I don't know this man!"

Then Jesus turned around and looked at Peter. Peter started crying. He felt so ashamed because he had disowned the Lord. All these things had happened because he was listening to the voice that was giving him bad advice. Luckily Jesus forgave Peter, who was very sorry for what he had done.

Two months later something happened to Peter that helped him to ignore the bad advice that was often whispered to him. A new voice started to speak in his heart! From then on he was brave and eager to admit to everybody that he was a follower of Jesus.

Are you curious to know where the new voice came from? Read about it in Acts 2:14.

2 May

The Good Spirit

Do you know where Papua New Guinea is? It is an island close to Australia. Today we will read a true story about a little boy, Olehofa, who was born there. The people on that island didn't know anything about God. They only believed in evil spirits. When they fell ill, they went to a witchdoctor who slaughtered a little animal and gave the sick person its blood to drink. Olehofa was very scared of the witchdoctor and all the evil spirits.

Sometimes, when Olehofa looked at all the beautiful trees and flowers and multi-colored birds around him, he wondered who had made everything. He wished that there was a good spirit instead of a lot of evil spirits. Sometimes he even pretended that there was a good spirit somewhere and then he would tell this spirit that he wanted to learn more about him.

One day his wish came true. A man from Australia came to their island with a big black book in his hand. He started telling the people that there is a God in heaven who made everything and who loves everyone. He also told them that God sent His Son Jesus to the world so that He could teach people about God. And when Jesus went away, He left His Holy Spirit behind to live inside the people who believe in God.

Olehofa jumped with joy. Then there was Someone who had made everything all along – and a good Spirit, too! Olehofa wanted to know everything about this Spirit and became a Christian. Years later, when the missionary went back to his own country, Olehofa himself started to teach his people about God and the Good Spirit.

Read what Jesus said about the Holy Spirit in John 14:25-26.

3 May

Not even one!

Every day Clint's mom saw him coming from school, walking all by himself. The other kids walked in groups or pairs. She felt sorry for him, because she knew that he loved company.

Then one day she saw him busy with scissors, paper, glue and crayons. "What are you doing?" she asked. "I'm making a card for each child in my class, tomorrow is Valentine's day," he said. His mother winced at the thought. Would anyone give him a card? she wondered.

The next day he went to school whistling away. But his mom fretted the whole morning wondering if any of the children in his class would give him a card. Eventually she decided to bake his favorite cookies. If he came home feeling sad, that would cheer him up, she thought. She was still busy, when she heard the front door opening. "Not even one," Clint said and repeated, "not even one." "Oh no!" his mom thought. But then she saw his face. He was beaming with joy. "I didn't skip one person," he said, "not even one!"

This story makes one think, doesn't it? What would you have done if you were in Clint's shoes? Do you also like to do things for people without getting any reward for it?

The Bible teaches us that our left hand shouldn't know what our right hand is doing. That means that we must be prepared to do kind deeds without expecting anything in return. That's not easy! But Jesus said in Matthew 6:1, *"Be careful not to do your acts of righteousness before men, to be seen by them. If you do, you will have no reward from your Father in heaven."* So let's rather work for the reward that God has in store for us.

Try and do a kind deed without letting anybody know about it!

4 May

If clay could talk

On Monday afternoon, the children at the church Children's League each got a piece of clay to work with. Their teacher told them to make a flower pot for their moms for Mother's day. The kids were really enjoying themselves.

While they were busy, Miss Peggy spoke to them. "If the clay could feel and talk like we do, I'm sure it would have complained about all the modeling and pinching that you have been doing," she said. "What do you think the clay would say?" "Leave me alone," said Sydney. "I don't like this! Stop!" said the other children. "However, if you want to make a pretty piece of pottery, you have to carry on regardless, not so?" Miss Peggy asked. They agreed.

When they exhibited all their works of art on a big table in the hall, Miss Peggy started to talk seriously. "Children, your parents received you as a little bundle from God and He asked them to bring you up for Him. It's not an easy job, because you don't always like the methods your parents choose to teach you and discipline you. You often complain like the make-believe clay voices we heard earlier. If your parents did not interfere with your lives to teach you about right and wrong, you might become ugly, selfish people who meant just as little as shapeless balls of clay. If you allow your parents to shape and discipline you, you could become beautiful, useful people one day."

After that, one of the girls read the Scripture for the day. *"Children, obey your parents in everything, for this pleases the Lord"* (Colossians 3:20). Then they prayed, "Dear Lord, thank You for parents who want to shape us and teach us Your ways. Amen."

Make something for your mom for Mother's day. How about a clay flower pot?

5 May

A hole in the blanket

The Murray family had a lot of magnets on their fridge. They held the photos of seven missionary families in place. They also stuck a world map to the kitchen door. Every night Mrs. Murray took one photo from the fridge door and put it on the table. When the family prayed together before supper, they also prayed for the people in the photo. All the children knew exactly where France, Thailand, India, Peru, Mozambique, Malawi and Zimbabwe were. Those were the countries where the missionaries worked.

One weekend a friend came to stay. She wanted to know about all the photos. Michelle eagerly told her about the work for God that was being done in those different countries.

"But what good is it to pray for them?" asked the visitor. Michelle answered, "My mom says that when we pray for them, it is as if beams of power go to them. If they're tired, they get new strength and if they're feeling down, they get new inspiration." "Yes," Adele, her older sister said, "and God also uses our prayers to bring light to dark countries where Jesus isn't known yet." "How can that happen?" asked the newcomer. "Well, as I see it, there is a blanket of ignorance covering many countries. The people who live there worship idols and don't believe in God. But every prayer that is offered for that country, makes a hole in the blanket. And one day the light will burst through the darkness!"

The girl who was visiting had never thought of it in that way. She decided that she also wanted to adopt a missionary to pray for regularly. Don't you think that that's an excellent idea?

Read how Paul asks other Christians to pray for him in Colossians 4:2-4.

6 May

The jigsaw puzzle

There once was a father who had to go overseas for a long time. He bought a jigsaw puzzle and gave it to his family to complete while he was away. He thought that it would keep them busy and out of mischief until he returned. "If you have successfully completed the puzzle when I come back, we can all go to a steakhouse to celebrate," he said. But on his return he was most surprised to find that they had only completed a small part of the puzzle. Why was that? It certainly wasn't because the reward wasn't good enough. It turned out that a mistake had been made with the packaging of the puzzle. On the box was a picture of a castle in a lovely garden, but inside they found pieces of a puzzle showing parts of a plane. What a blunder!

God has a blueprint for your life. It is like the picture on the outside of that box. And each day you put pieces of your life together. If we take God's Word, the Bible, as our guide, we will find a lot of tips on how to build a meaningful life. But if we do whatever we want to and ignore God's will and follow our own plans, then our lives will be just as meaningless as the puzzle pieces in the wrong box.

In 1 John 3:2 the Bible says that we will be like Jesus when He comes again. That is the picture that we must keep in mind while we are constructing our lives. We must strive to be more and more like Jesus!

Read Revelation 19:9. It tells us where we will eventually find ourselves if we put our lives together according to God's plan. It will be a feast, far better than a visit to a steakhouse!

7 May

The bodyguard

In Westbank Trinity Church, Whitsunday was being celebrated with flair. Beautiful flower arrangements adorned the church and a joyous crowd filled the building to capacity.

They were commemorating the first Pentecost, when the Holy Spirit descended upon God's followers in tongues of fire. A number of people were asked to witness about what the Holy Spirit meant to them in their lives.

First Mr. Niklaus told the congregation about an experience he once had when he was planning a dishonest business transaction. The Holy Spirit kept him awake for two nights in a row, until he decided to cancel the deal. Then Mrs. Miller had a turn. After her husband had died, she experienced the consolation that came from the Holy Spirit. "I know now why He is called 'The Comforter,'" she added. Solly Carpenter was next. "I find that the Holy Spirit gives me the strength to do my job every day and He also gives me the power to say no to temptation. Sometimes I still fall into sin and make serious mistakes, then I tend to doubt whether I am really a child of God. However, the Holy Spirit reminds me about passages in Scripture that ensure me that nothing can separate me from God's love. So I confess my sin and then God gives me a fresh start."

More people shared with the congregation what the Holy Spirit meant to them. He comforted them when they were feeling lonely and He helped them to understand the Bible better. Then the pastor read John 14:16 and praised God for giving us the Holy Spirit to guard and guide us on life's journey. Then the congregation sang with great joy: "Glory be to the Father and to the Son and to the Holy Ghost."

Thank God for giving you the Holy Spirit as a bodyguard.

8 May

Lucky charms

Are you wearing a lucky charm around your neck or do you have mascots or a talisman that you think will bring you good luck? There are people who do nothing without their charms and amulets. They believe that things will go wrong if they don't have their mascot close by.

God does not want us to be superstitious and trust in such things. If you believe that a black cat on a wall brings bad luck or that walking under a ladder is a bad omen, or that your teddy bear helps you win contests, then you are making the Lord very sad. Because that means that you do not trust Him to look after you.

Do you know that there are people who believe if a Friday comes on the thirteenth of the month the day will be unlucky? These folks say that thirteen is an unlucky number and they don't even want to stay in a hotel room that has a number thirteen on the door. There are also people who say that red and white flowers should never be put together, because it will bring death to your family. What rubbish!

The Lord says in Exodus 20:3, *"You shall have no other gods before me"* and in Exodus 23:2, *"Do not follow the crowd in what is wrong."* Therefore, even if all your friends believe that a dream catcher or a fortune fairy or a cross around your neck can bring you good luck, you ought to say, *"My help comes from the Lord."* This is what Psalm 121:2 says. The fish on your dad's car or the "What Would Jesus Do?" wristband around your arm won't bring you good luck. They should only be there to remind you of God's care and to witness to the world of your commitment to God, not so?

Make sure that you have no superstitious beliefs.

9 May

The victor

The crowds on the pavilion were cheering and shouting. The high school football team had beaten their opponents from a neighboring city. Children ran onto the field to be in the procession that was carrying the captain on their shoulders off the field. Some of the players had been injured; the captain's eye was swollen, another player had a head-bandage and two others were limping. The first aid staff were quite busy during the match. They used lots of icepacks and band-aid, it sure had been a tough match!

Scenes like this remind us of the day when Jesus went back to His home in heaven. After His disciples had said good-bye to Him, He ascended into heaven. At His homecoming there must have been great rejoicing in heaven, because Jesus returned home as the Victor. The marks of the nails could still be seen in His hands and feet, but He took the seat of honor at the right hand of God, as we read in Hebrews 1:1-3.

When Jesus sat down on that throne, Satan was completely defeated. He couldn't accuse the children of God of their sins any more. The Savior paid for all our transgressions!

And what is Jesus doing all day long on that throne right next to the Father? The Bible says that He is interceding for us. That means that He is praying for us. He sees when we are struggling or when the devil is tempting us. Then He prays that we will not give in to Satan and that we will have power to fight our battles on earth, so that we can also one day be welcomed into heaven as Victors.

Read Psalm 24:21. It is a song of praise, the same kind that the angels must have sung when Jesus returned to heaven.

10 May

The story of Billy Moore

Billy Moore was a criminal who was a prisoner in one of the biggest prisons in America. He had committed a serious crime. While under the influence of marijuana, he shot a man with his pistol. Then he stole five and a half thousand dollars from the man.

While he was in prison, Christians visited him and told him that Jesus loved him and that all his sins could be forgiven. The Holy Spirit convinced him of these truths and he became a Christian. After this, Billy's life changed drastically. He admitted that he had committed murder and he received the death penalty. But he started to read the Bible and he worked through 32 Bible study books. He also started witnessing amongst his fellow prisoners and he led some of them to Christ.

His execution was scheduled for 22 August 1990. On that day he would have died in the electric chair. But something wonderful happened. The family of the old man who was murdered asked the authorities to rethink the penalty. They had heard about Billy's conversion and said that they had forgiven him for what he had done. His case was opened again in court and the judge ruled that he could go free because of good conduct and also because of his good influence in jail. When this sentence was announced, all the Christians in the court room got up and sang *Amazing Grace*.

Yes, Jesus can change a person's life completely. We must never forget that. Our God is a God of love and grace and new beginnings. He wants to give people a second chance and He does it because of the high price that Jesus paid for the sins of the world.

Read about the difference between an old life and a new one in 2 Corinthians 5:17.

11 May

The other one

You have probably heard of Mahatma Ghandi. He was an Indian leader who fought against injustice. He led a remarkable life and many books have been written about him. There is also a movie called *Ghandi* that portrays his whole life.

Today's story is about him. Once, while he was traveling through India, he and his friends had to change trains at a certain railway station. They had to move fast, because the train which they had to board left only a few minutes after their arrival.

As Ghandi was boarding the second train, his foot got hooked on the steps. One of his shoes fell between the train and the platform, onto the railway line. There was no time to try and get hold of the missing shoe, because the locomotive was already slowly moving forward. Ghandi sat down on a seat near the window, wondering how he would manage without one of his shoes. Suddenly he jumped up, pulled off the other shoe and threw it through the window. "What are you doing? Are you crazy?" his friends asked in amazement. "Well, I can do nothing with one shoe and the person who picks up the lost one will be very glad if he found its mate."

Would you have thought of such a plan? Only people who are extremely unselfish and kind would come up with such a bright idea.

The Bible teaches us, *"Nobody should seek his own good, but the good of others."* You will find that in 1 Corinthians 10:24. Ghandi wasn't even a Christian and he managed to live an unselfish life. We should be loving and caring, after all, we have God's Holy Spirit to help us to live such an exemplary life.

Also read Philippians 2:4.

12 May

The best doctor

Once upon a time there was a doctor in Palestine who could heal people without pills, medicine, ointment or an operation. To tell you the truth, he could be miles away from a sick person and heal him with one word from his mouth. Does that sound like magic to you? Well, this doctor did not use magic power to bring about a miracle. He used His own power, because the Man of whom we are talking was the One who helped to create heaven and earth and everything in it: Jesus Christ, the Lord!

When He was still on earth, a man once came up to Him in great distress. He fell on His knees before Him and said, "Please come with me and heal my son. He is so ill that we are afraid that he will die." Jesus saw how worried the father was and He wanted to help him. But He also wanted the man to realize that God's power was even greater than he had ever imagined it to be. So Jesus was not in a hurry to go with the man.

"Please make haste!" the man pleaded. "Come, before my child dies." Jesus replied, "You may go. Your son will live." The man took Jesus at His word and departed. While he was still on the way, his servants met him with the news that his boy was well. When he asked the time when his son started to get better, they said to him, "The fever left him at one o'clock yesterday afternoon." Then the father realized that that was the exact time at which Jesus had said to him, "Your son will live."

This story is recorded in John 4:46-53 to show us that Jesus can heal a person completely, even if we cannot see Him next to the bed of the patient.

You can pray for somebody who is ill.

13 May

Is Jesus the Savior of the world?

Luke 4 contains a story that is hard to believe. Jesus went to church in His own hometown and was chased away. How was this possible?

On that day Jesus was asked to read to the congregation from Isaiah. It was written on a scroll which was neatly kept in a wooden box, like all the other holy books. The rabbi (the minister of those days) handed Jesus the scroll and He unwound it until He reached Isaiah 6. Then He started reading, *"The Spirit of the Lord is on me, because he has anointed me to preach good news to the poor ... to release the oppressed ... "* Everybody knew that these words were written about the coming Savior that God would send to the world in due time. But then Jesus said something that made everyone sit up straight. He said, *"Today this scripture is fulfilled in your hearing."*

"What! Does He think that He is the Savior?" they asked. "He is only the son of Joseph and Mary. How can He be so arrogant?" They were furious at Him and wanted to throw Him off a high cliff. But Jesus walked right through the crowd and walked away.

Today we still get people who do not believe that Jesus is the Savior. They say that He was an ordinary person like you and me. How can we know for sure that He was actually the Son of God? Only the Holy Spirit can convince us of that. We can ask Him to do it. Just as your mom would never give you a stone when you ask her for a sandwich, so God will also give you nothing less than His Spirit if you ask for it. Jesus, the Savior of the world, made that promise Himself in Matthew 7:9-11.

Read this story in Luke 4:16-28.

14 May

Dirt heap

Stephen's job was to put out the trash every Tuesday morning, because the waste removers came to fetch it on that day. He was not particularly fond of this chore and one morning he was running late. Luckily his dad came to help him with the trash bags.

As his father lifted one of the black bags over the fence, it tore open and a lot of trash fell out. Stephen started picking up the bits and pieces, but his dad told him to go and fetch another bag. He hesitated, but then ran back to the kitchen to do what his dad had said. While he was inside the house, Mr. Giovanni had a look at the things that had fallen from the bag. He was taken aback when amongst the empty tins, cartons and crumpled paper, he saw a few magazines that really didn't belong in a Christian home.

When Stephen came back, his dad asked him, "Have you been reading these?" Stephen blushed. "Yes, but I didn't like them. That's why I threw them away," he added. "At first I thought that it was cool, but later on I found it nauseating. You needn't worry, Dad, I'll never read stuff like that again!"

"I'm glad to hear that," his dad said. "When you read pornography, it pollutes your mind. You keep getting flash-backs of what you have seen and read and later on you have no more room for clean and wholesome thoughts. Not even for God!"

Stephen's dad put the refuge bags on top of the heap that had already been put there by the neighbors. "A real dirt heap!" he said. Stephen wasn't sure whether his dad was referring to the rubbish dump or to his son's thoughts. He made a resolution to get rid of all filthy books and tapes that came into his possession.

Read what 2 Corinthians 7:1 says about unclean thoughts.

15 May

Jonah and the fish

Many people do not believe the Bible story of Jonah and the fish. They say that it is a parable, a story that was written to convey a certain truth. Whatever the case might be, it certainly isn't impossible for God to let something like that happen.

On the Internet you can get a lot of information on whales. They say that a certain type of whale has such a small gullet and such sharp teeth, that no person can go through its mouth without being torn to pieces. But you also get whales with enormous mouths and bony plates instead of teeth. In the Mediterranean Sea a person or an animal might be swallowed by this type of shark-whale. There's even a story about a little dog that was swallowed by such a whale, but was saved again after three days.

But even though there's a lot of information available on whales, nobody can be sure that it was a whale that swallowed Jonah. The Bible only says that God provided a big fish to swallow Jonah, and Jonah was inside the fish for three days and three nights.

What do you think we can learn from this story? Surely it is that we must be obedient to God's calling. If He gives us a job, we had better do it, otherwise we will be very unhappy indeed. Jonah refused to go to Nineveh, as God commanded him to do. And then he landed in big trouble. Only after he had promised to do what God wanted, the Lord spoke to the fish, and it spat Jonah out onto dry land.

If you ever feel unhappy and confused, make sure that there isn't any kind of disobedience that is the cause of your anxiety. Confess your sin and ask God to help you to do His will.

Read in Jonah 2 how dismal Jonah felt in the belly of the fish.

16 May

David and Goliath

This story is probably the best known part of the Old Testament. It tells of a giant, Goliath, who challenged God's people and a young Jewish boy who wasn't scared of him and killed him with a pebble from his catapult. The Philistines (Goliath's army) ran away in fear and David's people chased them and eventually won the war against them. After that the Israelites carried David around on their shoulders and sang songs of praise to him. Not long after that, he was crowned as their new king.

What do you find striking in this story? That a young man can win against big evil forces? That people who dare to defy God will meet catastrophe? Yes, these things are true and are probably two of the reasons why God had this bit of history written in the Bible in 1 Samuel 17. He surely wanted to encourage and warn His children.

David had learned from an early age that he had to trust God. When he was still a young shepherd who had to protect his dad's flock against dangerous animals, he was taught to fully rely on God. During that time he wrote Psalm 23 and it might well be that he was saying these words to himself while he was approaching the giant, *"The Lord is my shepherd, I shall lack nothing."*

Is there somebody in your life who is making things difficult for you? Is there a problem at school or at home that seems too big for you to handle? Then you must remember the outcome of the fight between David and Goliath. Remember, if you are a child of God, you needn't be afraid of anybody!

Do you know a hymn with the words of Psalm 23? (For instance: "The Lord is my shepherd, I shall not want!") Sing it softly to yourself whenever you feel scared.

17 May

Moving away

Wayne and his family were moving because his father had to go and work in another city. This was very hard for Wayne to accept.

He would probably never see his best friend again, he would lose his place in the soccer team and he wouldn't have a chance to be class captain in grade seven at the new school.

His dad could see that he was feeling miserable about everything. "Wayne, let's start thinking about positive things regarding this move," he suggested. Wayne asked reluctantly, "Like what?" "Like all the new things that are awaiting you: new friends, a new neighborhood, new opportunities." "That's exactly what I'm scared of," Wayne admitted. Only after he had said these words, he realized how true it was. It wasn't only the heartache of leaving that upset him. It was also the stress of facing all the new things.

His dad stopped packing his books into a box and came over to Wayne. "You know," he said, "if our ancestors weren't as brave as they were and had not moved from their homes, we would not have been living in this beautiful country today. And we have things that make moving away so much easier." Wayne was frowning. He wasn't sure what his dad was talking about. "The world has virtually shrunk. Long ago it took people months to move from one country to another by ship. Today they can cover thousands of kilometers within a few hours. Even letters took months to reach their destination. Now we have airmail and e-mail and telephones. But one thing remains the same; God's Word. Before we go to bed tonight, I will read you a promise that's in the Bible, especially for folk like us who must move away into unknown territory.

Read Joshua 1:8-9, the Scripture verses that Wayne's father read to him that night.

18 May

The most precious possession

If your home should ever burn down, what would you like to save from the flames? Have you ever thought about it? Your parrot? Your photo album? The trophy you had won? Many people would grab their computer with all its software and some would take their money-boxes. Hopefully we will all first make sure that all the people in the house are brought to safety!

During a war in Europe a group of people literally had to make such a choice. The city in which they lived was surrounded by the enemy. And then came the message: All the women would be allowed to leave the city before the attack and they could take with them one object, their most precious possession. It was promised that nobody would hurt the fugitives.

After a while, to the surprise of the enemy, all the women appeared through the gates of the city, each one carrying a similar bundle on her back. It seemed to be a rather awkward parcel and some of them stumbled under the weight of it. When they got nearer, the soldiers could see what it was: every woman was carrying her husband, her most precious possession! As a result of this action, the city got the name of *Frauentreu* which means "the loyalty of wives".

Not all of us are too happy about our own family. Sometimes they make us furious and sometimes they irritate us. But God put us in a family to teach us how to get along with other people. And always remember, nowhere on earth will you find people who care for you as much as your own family. Therefore we should be loyal to them, appreciate them and thank God for them.

Look up the following verses in your Bible to see what is said about each member of your family: Exodus 20:12; Psalm 133:1 and Proverbs 31:10.

19 May

Eat your veggies!

It's always interesting to hear what parents say to their children on the day they must go out into the world on their own. What did your mom say when you first went camping with friends? Or when you had to go off to boarding school? Some parents say, "Remember to eat your veggies and brush your teeth." Or, "Be brave and remember to phone every weekend."

It is a big step to move out from under the sheltering wings of your parents. You are excited about the new adventure, but also scared of the unknown.

In the Bible there is a description of an eagle that kicks its chicks from the nest, which reminds us of the first separation between parent and child. You find it in Deuteronomy 32:11. There we read, *" … like an eagle who stirs up its nest and hovers over its young; that spreads its wings to catch them and carries them on its pinions. The Lord alone led them."*

One day you will also have to leave your home, maybe to go on a short sports tour or maybe for a long time. Then you must remember the wonderful picture that was drawn here in the song of Moses. The eagle chick is kicked out of its nest so that it can learn to fly. But all the time the mother eagle stays near enough to sweep in and catch the little one if it seems that it won't make it. Then the little eagle can have a free ride on her wings … until the next test! In the same way God is always near enough to help us whenever we need Him.

Read Psalm 31:22-24. Write verse 24 on a card and paste it in your bag to encourage you whenever you must leave home.

20 May

No soap!

A while ago something happened that caused many a business-man to worry a great deal. A group of clever engineers designed a washing machine that can work without washing powder. The machine produces small bubbles that penetrate the washing together with an electrical impulse to take all the dirt out of your laundry.

If your mom should put your muddy soccer jersey and your paint-stained shirt and your grease-smeared trousers into this type of machine, she'll only need to close the door and put on the machine. She needn't use a cup to measure the washing powder and her grocery trolley will be much lighter without any detergents. Of course the housewives who could afford these machines were very excited, but the soap factory owners were most upset.

According to the *Ymium* magazine, that usually reports on new inventions, more than 20 000 of these washing machines had already been sold by September 2001.

There is another type of cleaning device which some people are very glad about, but which causes others to fret. The Bible says that the blood of Jesus can cleanse us from sin. In Zechariah 13:1 we read, *"On that day a fountain will be opened to the house of David ... to cleanse them from sin and impurity."* That day was the day when Jesus died on Calvary and shed His blood to wash away the sins of all people who believe in Him. But can you imagine how unhappy the devil was about this arrangement? He wants us to commit sin and to feel dirty and lost so that we can be separated from God. Don't ever let him have his way!

Write on a card: "The blood of Jesus ... purifies us from all sin" 1 John 1:7. Then fasten it with a ribbon to a piece of soap to remind you of this truth.

21 May

The making of a pearl

Once upon a time there was an oyster that lived in a pool among the rocks. Every day she opened her mouth to take in seawater so that she could be a beautiful part of God's creation. But one day a small grain of sand entered her mouth and it made its bed in the soft tissue of her body. It was uncomfortable and sore to have it there and the oyster tried her very best to get rid of the intruder. But it stayed.

The oyster now had a few options. She could blame her Creator. Why did He allow this to happen? She did not deserve this agony! Or she could decide, "I won't care about being a nice oyster any longer. Obviously I wasn't meant to be a success after all!"

But that wasn't what the oyster did. She realized that the little grain of sand was there to stay and she made a plan. She started to secrete a little bit of milky lime every day to coat the grain of sand. Little by little it became smoother until it did not hurt the oyster any longer. It also became something beautiful to look at: a pearl, for which merchants would be prepared to pay thousands of dollars.

God sometimes allows difficulties to trouble us. Maybe you have trouble at home or at school. Maybe you're not healthy or are handicapped. Maybe you are poor and your dad is unemployed and your prayers seem to be in vain. But don't despair! Do your best with God's help. And one day some rare characteristic might be formed in your personality, something about which people will be amazed!

Jeremiah 31:16 says, "'Restrain your voice from weeping, because your work will be rewarded,' declares the Lord." Remember these words every time you see a beautiful pearl!

22 May

Does God always answer prayer?

James burst into the kitchen and said, "I don't believe the Bible and I'm not going to pray any more." He sat down at the table looking miserable. "The Bible says, *'Ask and it will be given to you.'* Well, I've asked, and I didn't get what I wanted!" His mom was quite calm about this outburst. "What did you ask for?" she inquired. "I asked that I would be chosen as class captain, but everybody voted for Fred."

"Maybe he had the same request," his mom said softly. "Who do you think will gain God's favor in such an event? The one who was most convincing? The one who had the best reputation?"

"Prayer doesn't work that way," his mom said. "When you pray, you can be sure that God will answer your prayer. But you must remember that God knows more than you do. He knows Fred's circumstances and He might think that Fred needs this position more than you do. He also knows you and He knows whether it will be a good thing for you to be class-captain. You never know, maybe He has another job for you."

One thing his mom had said stayed with him. He remembered the day when they had given Fred a lift to his home. James had been shocked to see the poor circumstances in which Fred's family lived. That night he had asked God to bless Fred in a special way. Now James smiled. "At least God heard that prayer," he said to himself.

Read any of the following Scripture verses on prayer: Psalm 91:15; Jeremiah 33:3; John 15:7.

23 May

The broken window

In the suburbs of a big city lived a professor. In front of his house was an open field where children loved playing baseball. One afternoon one of the boys hit a ball right through the window of the professor's front door. Johnny got such a fright that he ran home and hid under the bed. There he stayed, expecting the owner of the house to come and see his parents or to send the police to come and fetch him. But nothing happened.

The next morning on his way to school, he glanced nervously towards the professor's house and then he saw, to his amazement, that the broken window had been repaired! You couldn't even see that it had been in fragments the previous day. That afternoon the children were playing in the park again. But when the professor appeared around the corner, Johnny started running. The man came after him. He got hold of the little boy, who was trembling with fear. "I know that you are the one who broke my window," the man said kindly. "But I forgive you. I have already paid for the damage." Can you guess what Johnny's reaction was to this man's favor? "I hate you!" he shouted at the professor, then he broke loose and ran home.

Why do you think Johnny reacted so strangely? The writer who told this story said that many people react to God's love in a similar way. They cannot accept God's forgiveness for their sins. Maybe they are too proud and want to pay their debts themselves.

Jesus knows about all the things that you have done wrong, and yet He wants to be your Friend. He has already paid for all your sins. Surely you won't run away from Him, will you?

Underline Romans 6:23 in your Bible.

24 May

Empty seats

Mrs. Smith was very tired. "I worked hard for the church fête yesterday," she said as she made herself a cup of tea on Sunday morning. "I won't go to church today. I'll stay at home and read something from the Bible instead."

"I've been trying all week to get rid of this headache," Mr. Hall said. "I'll stay at home today and give it a chance to settle down."

"There's no Sunday school today," said Fred as he turned over in bed to sleep until tea time.

"I've got nothing to wear," Catherine said, going through her wardrobe. "I'll listen to the sermon on the radio today."

In the meantime the church bells were chiming across the city: "It's Sunday! The Lord's day! Come and thank Him! Come and praise Him!" And the pastor knelt at his desk, praying, "Please Lord, let the message from the pulpit stir our hearts today."

Somewhere in the invisible world a few demons were grinning. Today they had done a good job. Many people from that congregation went and bought the Sunday newspaper during church time. Others had decided to watch sport on TV or to write letters. Some families decided to have a picnic.

And the result? When Reverend Scott looked down from the pulpit, he saw only empty seats, with here and there a faithful churchgoer. He was so disappointed. He thought of all the hours that he had spent preparing his sermon. The fire that was burning in his heart when he set out for church that morning slowly cooled down.

Are you one of the people responsible for the empty seats in your church on a Sunday morning?

Read Psalm 84:1-4 and see how keen this poet was to visit the house of the Lord.

25 May

The right friend

It was wartime and all American men had to join the army. One young man wasn't keen to join the army, because both his father and brother had been killed in the war. They were farmers and his mom and sister would not be able to gather the wheat harvest on their own. He decided to go and see the American president about the matter.

But when he arrived at the house of the president, the guards told him, "You can't talk to the president. He is a busy man. Don't you know that we are at war? Go back to the army and do your duty."

The man went to sit on a bench nearby, his head between his hands. A little boy walked up to him and asked, "What's wrong?" The young man told him the whole story. Then the little lad took the soldier by the hand and led him back to the big White House, where the president stayed. They went in through a back door. The guards didn't say a word to stop them.

The boy and the soldier walked through the corridors and hallways of the big building until they came to the room where the president was. He had been busy talking with his secretary, but when he saw the boy, he said, "What can I do for you, Ted?" "You can help this man," the boy replied.

And so it happened that President Lincoln gave permission to a young man to leave the army so that he could look after his family and gather their wheat harvest, just because his son had asked him.

We also have the right to talk to the Almighty God of the universe if we have His Son Jesus with us!

Read in Hebrews 7:25 how Jesus is able to save completely those who come to God through Him.

26 May

Precious to the Lord

All the kids ran out of the classroom when the bell went. Miss Singer stayed behind to tidy up a bit. Then she heard someone crying. A girl was lying with her head on her arms at her desk. It was Margaret, one of the children she had punished because of poor work.

The teacher walked up to her. "What's the matter?" she asked gently. At first Margaret didn't want to say anything. But when she felt her teacher's hand on her hair, she started opening up. "I'm fat and ugly and dumb and nobody likes me!" she sobbed. Miss Singer put one arm around the little girl's shoulders. She lifted her chin with the other hand so that she could look into her eyes. "Do you know that you are precious in God's sight?" she asked. Margaret looked away. It's not easy to believe that. She thought that there's nothing about her that was worth anything.

Miss Singer then said, "You know, I have a little doggie at home. He is my most precious possession. He might never win a prize at a dog show, but I love him! He can comfort me when I'm sad and he brings me joy and laughter. You see, some things we cherish because they are worth a lot, but there are also things that are worth a lot because we cherish them."

Miss Singer walked up to the window and said, "The Lord God made you with a purpose and He loves you very much. Therefore you must never think that you aren't worth anything. Promise me that you will read Psalm 139 before you go to bed tonight. You can start at verse 13 if the whole Psalm seems a bit long. And come and tell me in the morning what you thought of it."

Have you got a photo of yourself? Write on the back of it: Precious to the Lord.

27 May

Do you love yourself?

People who study human behavior, say that it is very important for us to love ourselves. Because if you neglect or hate yourself, you will be a very unhappy person.

But it is also very unhealthy to love *only* yourself. A well-known legend from Greece illustrates this truth.

There once was a young man whose name was Narcissus. He was a very handsome fellow. He was well-built, had sparkling eyes, a healthy skin and long shiny hair. All the girls who saw him were crazy about him. But he wasn't interested in them or in other people. He loved only himself and looked after his own interests. Because of that, he was very lonely. But then one day at the riverside he saw somebody so beautiful that he fell in love immediately. He couldn't take his eyes off this beautiful person and the two of them chatted and laughed the whole day long. Narcissus was so taken up with this new found love, that he could not part with the loved one.

Many people tried to call him away, but he kept staring at the lovely face in front of him. However, there was one draw-back. As soon as he tried to touch this person, the body would vanish. It made him really unhappy. The frustration made him ill and eventually he died there at the water's edge.

Of course this is only a story about a man who saw his own reflection and fell in love with himself. But we can learn an important lesson from it. People who are so in love with themselves that they have no time for others have a tragic life and often a tragic death. God created us to glorify Him and to help one another.

In Acts 20:35 we read, *"It is more blessed to give than to receive."*

Write this verse on a card, decorate it and paste it on your mirror.

28 May

A cheerful giver

One Christmas day a student received a brand new car as a gift from his brother. He was very excited and he went outside several times, just to feast his eyes on his new prized possession. Eventually he took the keys to take the car for a spin. He found a street child walking around the car, admiring it from all angles.

"Sir," he asked, "is this your car?" "Yes," the young man answered. "My brother gave it to me." "You mean to say that you didn't pay for it … that you got it just like that," and he waved his arms as if he was handling a magic wand. "I wish … " The child kept quiet for a while. The young man could guess what his next words would be. He would of course say that he wished that the car had belonged to him. But the student was mistaken. The little boy had a completely different frame of mind. He said, "I wish I could be a brother like that!"

This story illustrates that people can be classified into two main groups, the "givers" and the "takers". Givers are people who love to give of themselves and of their possessions. Takers are for ever looking for ways and means to obtain profits for themselves. The little boy was obviously a giver.

God has something to say about givers. In 2 Corinthians 9:7, He says that He loves a cheerful giver. And in Proverbs 22:9 we read, *"A generous man will himself be blessed."*

By nature we are all takers. You can see this clearly if you watch toddlers at play. "Mine! Mine!" is a favorite expression among them. Have you grown from a taker to a giver?

Make a bookmark and write one of the above Scripture verses on it. You can keep it in your Bible.

29 May

Are you fighting or are you fleeing?

Maybe you have heard the story about the two frogs that fell into the barrel of cream. The one frog soon realized that there was no way to get out of the barrel. So he sighed and said, "Good bye cruel world," as he drowned in the ocean of thick cream that surrounded him.

But the other frog kept on swimming. "Maybe a miracle will happen and someone will take me out of this mess," he thought. "Where there's life, there's hope," he said. And while he was repeating these words over and over again he kept on struggling to keep afloat. Later on it felt as if every movement took more effort than the one before. It seemed as if the cream became thicker. And suddenly he realized that the cream had turned into butter! He scrambled out of the barrel with glee.

Some children can identify with the frogs in the barrel, because they also have difficult situations to cope with. Maybe you are one of them. You might struggle with schoolwork or bad health or poverty. Or maybe someone is giving you a hard time at school or at home. Don't give up! Remember the frog who could keep on swimming until his circumstances changed.

A child of God can always say, "Where Christ is, there is hope." Keep on believing that and make use of God's help. One day you will also feel new ground under your feet and you will walk out onto God's new earth that He has promised to all His children.

Pray Psalm 130:5-6 for yourself and for someone in need.

30 May

Light for the world

The trees in front of her window cast weird shadows against the curtains of Susan's room. She shivered. She thought about the talk that she had heard in church that morning. A missionary told them about his work in India. It was most interesting, because he also showed slides to give them an idea of the lifestyle of the people who live there. He showed pictures of gods and goddesses with many heads and arms and feet. Some had real cruel faces with many protruding eyes. Maybe that's why the shadows against the wall gave Susan goosebumps that night.

"I can't believe that some people worship more than a thousand different gods!" she thought. And apparently they bring presents to their gods hoping for their blessing.

Susan suddenly felt ashamed that she spent so little time with her God. She remembered that she hadn't even said her prayers that night and she had last read from the Bible weeks ago! She put on the light and when she did, the gruesome figures against the curtains vanished. She took her Bible from the shelf and started reading Isaiah 46, which the missionary read in church that morning. She took a sharp pencil and drew a little star next to verse 9. It said, *"I am God, and there is no other; I am God, and there is none like me."* She also read the promise in verse 4, *"I will carry you, I will sustain you and I will rescue you."* How different from the gods that have to be carried around, she thought. Then she prayed, "Please God, put on the light in India, so that strange gods can vanish and people can get to know the one and only true God!"

You can repeat Susan's prayer in your own heart.

31 May

JUNE

Allergic to sin

André seemed to be very uncomfortable indeed. He tried to scratch his arms and legs without his mom noticing. But moms have a way of seeing everything. "André," she asked, "have you been playing in the reeds again?" André dropped his head. "Oh no!" his mom sighed. " You know that you're allergic to those grasses and that your medicine is finished! Why did you do it?" She was really cross.

On their way to the chemist, André said, "I'm sorry, Mom!" He knew that his mom had a lot of things to see to on the farm and now she first had to go to town to get his medicine. "Neville wanted me to play at the river with him and I tried not to touch the reeds that make me itchy." "But you know only too well that that's impossible!" his mom replied. "Haven't we had this conversation before?"

At suppertime his dad read from Psalm 34. He repeated verse 14 and looked over his glasses at André: *"Turn from evil and do good; seek peace and pursue it."*

André expected a sermon from his dad. But instead, his dad was friendly. "To play with your friends in the reeds and then have itchy bumps afterwards is no big deal. Even though it caused your mom a lot of trouble. But there are other things that look innocent and have serious consequences," he warned. "Therefore you must not follow your friends blindly in anything that they do."

"What things do you mean?" asked André. "Innocent-looking things like watching certain videos or reading certain books or visiting places where you will be tempted. We must ask God to help us to steer clear of evil."

Read 1 Thessalonians 5:19-22 and think about the consequences of sin.

1 June

Blind leaders

A friendly man, wearing a neat suit, came to the Barrys' home one day. When Mrs. Barry opened the front door, he immediately started talking about the seriousness of the times in which they were living and how they had to make sure that their relationship with God was right. Then he left two colorful books for them to read and he invited the kids to come to a meeting that was specially planned for children. He mentioned a lot of exciting items on the program, like games and crafts and an interesting video show.

"Can we go, Mom?" asked Judith. "It's going to be fun!" But her mom refused straightaway. Judith couldn't understand why her mom was so firmly opposed to the idea. Usually her parents were keen to cooperate with members of other churches. It seemed as if her mom could read her thoughts and she answered, "These people belong to a sect and they can lead you astray." "What is the difference between a sect and a church?" Judith asked.

Her mom thought for a while and then she said, "I think that sects differ from churches in their beliefs about things that really count. This sect does not believe that Jesus was also God. They say that He was an ordinary man who lived an extraordinary life. We cannot go along with that. We must always be on guard against theories that ignore some parts of the Bible. Jesus warned us against this."

"What did He say about it?" Judith wanted to know. "He said, *'If a blind man leads a blind man, both will fall into a pit.'*" "Where can I find those words?" Judith asked. She was keen to look it up. "You will find it in Matthew 15:14," said her mom, who knew the Bible extremely well.

Also read 1 John 4:1-3 for more light on this subject.

2 June

If it's wrong, it's wrong

Lynn could hear her parents and her brother arguing in the kitchen. He was a college student and usually came home only during the holidays. But that night he arrived unexpectedly because he wanted to discuss something. Lynn and her brother Rudi had to go to their rooms. Lynn could not make out what it was all about. Later she heard the front door slamming and Gerald leaving on his motorbike.

When she joined her parents again, she saw that her mom had been crying and that her dad was very upset. Without her asking, her mom said, "Your brother and his girlfriend want to stay together, because it will be cheaper for them. We are upset about it, because we believe that it is wrong for a man and a woman to live together before marriage."

"Oh Mom! Everybody is doing it!" Lynn said, trying to console her mother. She thought about all the young people that she knew who had the same idea. "Isabel says that it's a good idea. If people do that, they could get to know each other before marriage and then there may be fewer divorces." Her dad spoke up, "God's Word does not agree. Living together means sleeping together and sleeping together before marriage is adultery. God hates that."

"What are you going to do about it?" Lynn asked nervously. Her dad answered, "We will pray for Gerald."

When Rudi came into the kitchen, he found his parents and his sister sitting at the kitchen table, with heads bowed and eyes closed, in serious conversation with God.

Look up a few of the following Scripture verses to see what the Bible teaches on this subject: Genesis 2:24; Exodus 20:14; Matthew 5:27,28; 1 Corinthians 6:9,10; Ephesians 5:3-5.

3 June

The building project

A man once went on a trip to a far-away land. He asked one of his workers to build a house in his absence. The plans and the building material had already been supplied. But as soon as the owner left, the worker decided to use the situation to his advantage. He sold all the good building material and bought inferior wood and bricks with the money. He also sold some of the cement and mixed the rest with sand. He exchanged the good quality paint for a cheaper brand and when the building was completed, he covered the poorly built house with paint. "Now nobody will know that I used bad material!" he said to himself. He smiled as he thought about all the money that he could spend while his boss was away on holiday.

When the man came back, he and the worker went to have a look at the new house. "Thank you," said the older man. He took an envelope from his pocket. "Here are the necessary documents for transferring the house to your name. I want to give it to you as a present and I want to appoint you as the overseer of our team of workers."

The young worker felt terrible. If he had not been so dishonest, he could have had a beautiful, well-built home! Now, however, he had a poorly built house. The walls would soon start cracking and the paint would soon peel off.

In 1 Corinthians 3:8-16 Paul tells us that each one of us is God's building and that we must be careful about how we build.

Let us not be as stupid as the man in the story. Let us not build with sin, bad friends or destructive habits and end up regretting what we have done.

Read the Scripture verses mentioned in today's devotion and ask God to help you to build a beautiful, strong house for Him!

4 June

Freedom!

Today's story goes back to a long time ago, when people used to own slaves. When you had bought a slave, that person had to work for you and you had to care for him until the day of his death. Unless, of course, you as the owner sold him again or set him free. Slaves were sold at an auction and the person who offered the highest bid could buy the slave.

A Christian once visited one of these auctions in America. Among the people who were to be sold, he saw a beautiful girl who was in tears. He felt sorry for her and asked her what the matter was. "Can you see the man over there with the cruel face? He is watching me and I am so scared that he will buy me," she sobbed. The Christian felt deep pity for this woman. When she was put on the table to be examined by the buyers, he made the first bid. The other man offered more. The friendly man smiled at the girl and put his price up again. Now the man with the cruel face was furious. He mentioned an exorbitant price and added, "That's my final offer!" Although it was a very high price to pay for a slave girl, the Christian man took out his wallet and gave all the money that he had in order to buy the girl. Then he loosened the ropes around her wrists and said, "You are free now! You needn't be my slave. I have paid the price to be able to set you free." The girl was so grateful, that she fell on her knees before the kind man and said, "Thank you, Sir! I will work for you out of my own free will for the rest of my life because of your kind deed."

Read in Hebrews 9:12-14 how Jesus paid the price to set you free. Won't you also serve Him out of gratitude?

5 June

Today's portion

"The Israelites had to gather every day's portion of manna early in the morning and they could not save one day's manna for the next day, because then it would turn bad." Anne's father was explaining the story in Exodus 16. "But why did God make that rule?" Anne wanted to know. "If they had worked hard on the one day to gather enough manna for a week, why couldn't they then rest a bit? And if God allowed them to gather Saturday's portion on Friday, why couldn't He allow them to fetch manna every second day?"

"Let me explain it to you by way of a story," her dad said.

There once lived a king who gave his son an allowance every year. On the same date of every year the prince came to fetch the large amount of money. The son began to visit his father less and less and eventually he only turned up when he had to come and fetch the money. Because the king loved his son very much, he made a different arrangement. From then onwards the son had to come and fetch the money bit by bit. He had to come every day to receive just enough money for that particular day! Now the father could see his son more often and could have a little chat with him every day.

Anne's father was silent for a while and then he said, "God did the same with His children in the desert. He wanted them to think of Him every day, because He loved them. That is also why He wants us to have a personal quiet time when we can read His Word and pray to Him. It's not enough if we only think of Him on a Sunday when we go to church."

Read Matthew 6:9-13 as a prayer. Which part of this prayer makes you think of today's story?

6 June

So many problems!

Julia felt like screaming! She felt as if everything was going wrong for her. They were very poor and she had to work hard for everything that she wanted. This included good marks at school. How she wished that she could learn things as fast as some of her more gifted friends!

And now her bicycle had broken and she had to fix it herself, because her brothers had other commitments and her dad came home too late in the evenings. Her mom saw her grumbling and joined her in the backyard. "Mom, I'm sick and tired of struggling," she said and sounded really downhearted.

Her mom gave her a big hug. Then she called Julia to come and see something in the garden. There was a golden cocoon attached to the stem of a rose tree. "Out of that cocoon a butterfly will emerge one day," Mom said. They both watched it for a while. They could see how the little wriggler inside the cocoon was struggling to get out. "Let's help it a bit!" Julia said while going inside to fetch a pair of scissors. "We can make a hole in the cocoon." "Oh no, we must never do that," her mom said. "It will be a serious disadvantage to the butterfly. While it is struggling to get out, its muscles are getting stronger and stronger. By the time it emerges from the cocoon, it will be strong enough to open its wings and fly around. But if we make it too easy for the young butterfly to get out, it will not be strong enough to fly and survive in the outside world."

Julia walked back to her bicycle. "Maybe that's why I must struggle so much," she said. Her mom smiled, "I agree," she said. "I doubt whether you would've been such a capable girl if life had been easy-going for you!"

Read Proverbs 14:23. Do you agree with these words?

7 June

The Lord's money

Psalm 50:15 says, *"Call upon me in the day of trouble; I will deliver you and you will honor me."*

The life of William Colgate is an illustration of this truth.

William's father died when he was 14 years old and his mom was in poor health. He realized that he had to get a job, because they were very poor. One day, after many unsuccessful applications for work, he knelt in the backyard of a soap factory and prayed to God, "Lord, if You give me work in this factory today, I promise that I will give to you a tenth of all the money that I earn."

His prayer was answered when the owner of the factory appointed him to scrub the floors of the whole factory. Because he did his work so diligently, he was soon noticed by the manager, who appointed him as a messenger. This meant that he also got a raise in salary. But William did not forget his promise to God. Each time he got his pay, he put a tenth of the money away for the church.

Later he became a clerk in the office of the firm and still later he was promoted to be one of the directors. Eventually he bought the whole business and at his death he was a millionaire!

When they cleaned out his office after his funeral, his relatives found a drawer in his desk with a neat inscription on it: "The Lord's money". Inside the drawer they found receipts and letters that showed that William had been faithful to his promise to God for all those years.

Being a Christian does not mean that you will be rich. Some of God's children are poor. But we believe that God answers us when we cry out in need and for this He deserves our praise.

Shouldn't you also make an agreement with God regarding your pocket money?

8 June

The visit

It was Sunday afternoon and as usual, the Turner family went to Peace Haven, the local old age home. When they reached the frail care center of the home, they went straight to their grandma's room and gave her a parcel with homemade biscuits as well as a bunch of flowers from their garden.

As always, their granny was glad to see them when they arrived and sad when they had to leave. When she said goodbye, she added, as always, "I'm praying for you!"

On their way home Mr. Turner said, "I wonder if you realize how precious it is that Granny is praying for you. That verse of Scripture that she had framed and put above her bed should be an inspiration to us all." The children knew what he was talking about. "The prayer of the upright pleases Him" (Proverbs 15:8).

Mrs. Turner said, "There's a story in the Bible about two people who prayed for years for the same thing and then their prayers were answered on the very same day. Who were they?"

"Abraham and Sarah!" Dick said immediately. "No, the two people that I have in mind were not married," his mom replied. Now everybody was thinking very hard. "You will have to tell us," they eventually said. Their mom said, "Simeon and Anna. You can read about them in Luke 2. These two elderly people prayed for years and years for the Savior to be born. And then, one day, they discovered that their prayers had been answered!" Dick read Luke 2:38 and said, "Yes, it really seems as if the prayers of grandfathers and grandmothers can bring about miraculous happenings."

Praise God for the prayers of your grandparents.

9 June

Poor me!

"**W**hy am I so thin and sickly?" Martin asked while his mom was giving him his regular medicine. "It's not fair!"

His mom sat down next to him on his bed. She looked sad. "Are you mad at God because of it?" she asked softly. Martin wouldn't admit it, but he knew that that was exactly how he felt. It was God who made him the way he was.

"Ill health isn't God's fault," said his mom. "From the day Adam and Eve chose to disobey God, sickness and suffering have become part of people's lives. It won't help you one bit to feel envious of people who are more fortunate than you. Thousands of others are less fortunate."

Martin was thinking about all the hours that he had already spent in doctors' waiting rooms and hospital wards. He thought of little children in wheelchairs and others who had to be in bed for most of their lives. But he still wished that he could be one of the lucky people who could run around and have fun without getting tired so easily.

"Maybe you're better off than kids who are strong and healthy," his mom said. "What do you mean?" he asked with surprise. "Maybe you are learning from an early age that you have to rely on God because of your own weaknesses. Strong people tend to think that they can handle things without God." Martin gave this a bit of thought. He had to admit that his own weakness had forced him to pray many times a day, because he realized that without God he would not be able to cope. And then he also knew that his relationship with God was very special ... perhaps even more precious that the healthy body that he so badly wanted.

See what Paul had to say about this in 2 Corinthians 12:10.

10 June

The name

One day a married couple came to the parsonage with their three-month-old baby. They wanted the little one to be christened. The minister asked, "What is his name?" "Andrew," they replied in unison. "That's a good name," the minister said. "Who is he named after?" "My dad," the young man said. But his wife called out fiercely, "Never! He will be named after my father." The two people started arguing right there in front of the minister. "My father was Andrew and our first-born should bear his name," the man said firmly. "Your dad was a drunkard who caused trouble wherever he went," the wife exclaimed. "My father was also called Andrew, but he was an honorable, hard-working, good man. How can we give our child the name of your dad?"

The minister spoke kindly to the two people in front of him. "I think you must call your son Andrew. It is a good name and it means 'courage'. One day when he is a grown-up, you will know who he was named after."

Don't you think that the minister gave sound advice to these parents? He knew that a person's name does not determine the outcome of his life. In the Bible, for instance, we read about two people with the name of Judas. The one wrote an epistle in the Bible (Jude) and the other one was the man who betrayed Jesus. What is important, is whether or not you are a Christian who brings glory to the name of Christ. That is why we read in 2 Peter 1:10, *"Therefore, my brothers, be all the more eager to make your calling and election sure."* We should always try to bring honor to the Name that we bear.

Ask Jesus to help you to have a good reputation for the sake of His Name.

11 June

Sheep without a shepherd

Carol's mom came into the living room and turned off the television. "But Mom, everyone in our class follows this serial on TV!" Carol complained. "Everyone except you," her mom said firmly. "Why not?" she asked for the umpteenth time. Her mother explained again, "The people in the story live for money and possessions. They ignore God's laws and their language is shocking."

Carol made a suggestion, "Let's do what Loretta and her mom do. Let's watch the story together and then discuss it afterwards." But Carol's mom was not easily convinced. "Well, I don't want to watch it. Besides, if I have to spend every afternoon of the week watching a story like that, it will be a waste of precious time. It might influence my thoughts negatively, and yours even more! Your worldview and attitudes are not yet formed and your conscience must still be developed. And anyway, we have better things to talk about. Come with me, then I'll tell you a story." Carol followed her mom to the kitchen where they sat down to peel veggies.

Her mom started talking, "When we were still living on the farm, there used to be an old well at the back of the shed. One afternoon there was a commotion. One of the sheep got through a hole in the wall and fell into the well. But the worst part of it was that the other sheep followed him one by one and were overcome by the same fate. When your dad came upon the scene, seven sheep had already drowned and the rest were determined to do the same."

Carol knew why her mom had told her about this incident. She wanted to stress the fact that we should not always follow our friends in what they do, because they can lead us astray. "Silly sheep!" she said with a twinkle in her eyes.

See what Romans 12:2 says about peer pressure.

12 June

Gossip

Nadine couldn't wait to get home. She wanted to tell her sister about the new rumor at school. Darlene, the hockey captain, had not turned up at practice and everyone was talking about it. One of the team members had seen her at the police station talking to an officer. The previous year she had been in trouble for smoking marijuana and everyone was wondering what she had been up to this time.

Nadine's sister listened eagerly to all the gossip. "So that's why she's so fast at hockey, she's taking drugs!" Nadine added. Her mom came into the room and she fell silent. She knew her parents did not like them to spread tales about other people. She acted as if she was fastening her shoelaces and wanted to walk away. But her mom had heard what they were talking about. "Nadine," she said, "what is the first rule about gossiping in our home?" "I shouldn't believe all the bad things that I hear about other people." "And the second?" her mom asked. "I shouldn't repeat negative reports about other people, unless it is absolutely essential." Her mom sounded a bit kinder now and asked, "And the third?" "I must remember that God hears every word that I say."

Nadine's mom was proud that her daughter knew the rules so well. "Well, I think you should try and find out from Darlene what she was doing at the police station. There might be a very simple explanation. And if it is something serious, she needs your love more than ever. Remember that she gave her heart to Jesus after her last offence and we should all support her as much as we can."

Now Nadine felt ashamed about her behavior and she went to her room quietly. "Lord Jesus," she prayed, "Please forgive me for having been so unkind to Darlene."

Read Ephesians 5:1-2 and underline the words "live a life of love".

13 June

God's property!

There once was a little boy who made himself a lovely little boat. He spent much time in the manufacturing of this toy and in the end he was very proud of it. He showed it to his friends and they were most impressed with the fine workmanship. They were keen to try it out on water. So they went to a stream and the boy cautiously launched his vessel. They all held their breaths. The sails bulged in the wind and it glided smoothly along. Cheers went up from the few onlookers and they congratulated their clever friend.

But oh dear! When the boat came to the bend where it had to be taken out of the water, it swayed to the right and the boy who had to take it out could not get hold of it! So the boat drifted away, far out of sight.

The little engineer was very sad indeed. Until one day, when he saw his boat in the window of a pawn shop! "Sir," he said to the owner with great excitement, "that's my boat!" But the man said, "If you want it, you will have to buy it." Yes, the little fellow had to put all his savings together in order to buy his own boat.

When he received it over the counter, he pressed it to his heart. "Now you are twice mine," he said. "First I made you and now I've bought you!"

Have you ever thought that God can make the same claim? First He made us (see Genesis 1:27). Then He lost us when Adam and Eve sinned (according to Genesis 3:9). In the end God had to buy us all back (see Hebrews 10:12). Indeed, God made us and bought us: We are twice owned!

Thank God for creating you and for paying a high price to make you His possession!

14 June

Father's day

It was bedtime before Eric could summon enough courage to talk to his dad. The whole day he had been acting as though he had no idea that it was Father's day. He was embarrassed because his sister had bought an expensive gift which she proudly presented to their dad at the breakfast table. Eric realized that he could have written his dad a nice letter, but it would have seemed so inferior to his sister's beautifully wrapped parcel, that he shunned the idea.

At nine o'clock that evening he knocked on the door of his father's study. "Come in," his father called with a friendly voice. Eric swallowed a lump in his throat. "Dad, I want to thank you for being such a wonderful dad to us!" he blurted out. "I'm sorry that I didn't buy you a gift for Father's day." His dad pulled him closer. "You have given me a wonderful present," his dad said. "What do you mean?" Eric asked with surprise.

Then his dad told him, "Yesterday when we went to the shop together, I knew that you had no money. I saw you taking a slab of chocolate from the shelf at the sweet counter. I got a terrible shock when I saw you putting it into your pocket. I thought that you would leave without paying for it! I realized that you probably wanted to give it to me for Father's day. My heart would have been broken if you had taken it without paying for it." Eric was ashamed at the thought of what he was planning in a moment of weakness. His dad continued, "But then I saw how you put the chocolate back again. I praised the Lord who gave you the courage to correct your sin. It was the best gift that I could have received for Father's day," his dad said. "You showed me that all the things that I have taught you were not in vain."

Read Proverbs 1:8-10.

15 June

A good role-model

If you chose a hero from the Old Testament, who would it be? Maybe Joseph? He's definitely a worthy role-model, especially when it comes to handling temptation. By now you already know what temptation is, don't you? It is a thought that urges you to sin. Satan is the one who sees to it that your path is strewn with temptations.

But Joseph managed to say no to the devil. That was probably one of the reasons why his brothers didn't like him. He was his dad's favorite child and he didn't want to join them in their wicked ways. Maybe he often heard the kind of mocking that God-fearing children still hear today, "Baby! You don't want to play with us? Scared of playing with bad boys? Are we too tough for you?" Yet Joseph stood his ground and he did not join his brothers in sinful practices.

Later on, when he worked for Potiphar, his boss's wife tried to lure him into sin. But again he withstood the temptation. He literally fled away from her. Afterwards she told a pack of lies about him and he was put in jail. There he most likely encountered a different kind of temptation, he would be tempted to become discouraged. You can be sure that the devil often told him, "Trusting the Lord won't help you one bit." Although Joseph had to stay in that dark and filthy prison for many years, he still believed that God would eventually come to his aid. And in the end he was delivered from prison and became the Pharaoh's second-in-command over all of Egypt.

God said in 1 Samuel 2:30, *"Those who honor me, I will honor."* He did that for Joseph and He also wants to do it for you.

Why not read some parts of the history of Joseph in Genesis 37, 39-46? It will be a great encouragement to you!

16 June

Is there a place like hell?

After Peter's mom had said good night, he called her back again. She put on the light and asked, "What do you want, Peter? It's late already and you have to be up early tomorrow morning." Peter sat up straight. He wasn't sure whether this subject could be discussed quickly, but what he wanted to ask his mother was really important to him. "Mom, is there really a place like hell? Children at school say it doesn't really exist."

His mom came to sit at the foot of his bed. "It's definitely not a scare story," she said. "Jesus Himself often spoke about hell. We don't know for sure where it is and what it looks like, but one thing we know, it's a place where God is not present. I think that a place without God will be a frightening place, therefore I want to stay as close to God as possible."

Peter was still not satisfied. "Will I go to hell if I sin?" he asked. "No," she said. "You are a child of God and you will never end up in hell." His mother remembered the night when Peter knelt at his bed and asked God to forgive all his sins in Jesus' name. "Only people who reject God and don't want Him to interfere with their lives, will one day end up in a place where God will really leave them on their own. You're not one of those people, are you?" "Oh no!" Peter said with conviction.

His mom then added, "But we must not keep on sinning just because we know that Christ has already paid for all our sin. All sinful deeds have terrible consequences and we are only safe while we obey God's laws. And that's not a scare story either!"

His mom then carefully tucked him in for the night.

See what Jesus had to say about hell in Matthew 10:28.

17 June

Someone saw

Betty and Harold were always envious of each other. The situation worsened when their grandmother made a lovely rag-doll for Betty on her birthday. She stuffed the doll with beans and dressed it in a frilly dress with ribbons and lace. Betty was thrilled to bits, but Harold sulked. He took the doll and buried it under a mulberry tree in the garden. When Betty found that her doll was gone, she searched everywhere and cried her heart out when she couldn't find it.

Harold was sorry for what he had done, but was relieved that no one had seen him bury the doll. But God saw, and He wanted the little boy to confess his selfishness.

When their mom went to pick mulberries one day, she saw a few bean sprouts emerging from the soil. "Where would these beans come from?" she wondered. She pulled out one of the plants to see what kind of bean it was, and discovered the doll! Now Harold had to come out with the whole story.

"Now you can see, Harold," his mom said, "deceit has a way of showing. But even if the beans did not give you away, you would still have been unhappy because of what you had done. Bad deeds have bad consequences! Tell Betty that you're sorry for what you did. If you mean what you say, you can also ask God for forgiveness."

"What's forgiveness?" Betty asked. "It means that Jesus won't even think about the bad deed again," her mom said. "I'm not sure that I'll forgive him," Betty said. But when she saw how earnestly her brother was talking to the Lord she decided that she would at least try.

Read Galatians 6:7-10.

18 June

The letter

When Humphrey came from school one day, he was delighted to find a letter addressed to him in the mailbox. He quickly put his bike away and was so keen to open the letter, that he even forgot to greet his mom!

The letter read:

Dear Humphrey,

I want to tell you how I miss you. I wait for you at our usual meeting place every day, but you haven't been there lately. I also notice that you are not reading the other letter that I have written to you. It is gathering dust on your bookshelf.

I know that you need a true friend and I want to be there for you. But you must not forget about me. Don't let us become strangers to each other!

I hope to hear from you soon.

From your Best Friend.

Humphrey frowned. He realized that his mom must have written the letter. He knew why she had taken the trouble to send it to him. She had recently talked to him about his relationship with God and how she noticed that he wasn't praying and reading the Bible regularly any more.

He put the letter down and went to the lounge. "Thanks, Mom!" he said. "You have reminded me of the importance of spending time with God." "I think your Friend will be very pleased," his mom said with a smile.

Read what David wrote to his Friend in Psalm 92. Maybe you can write Him a letter too!

19 June

The keeper of the spring

Peter Marshall was a great preacher, and this was one of his favorite stories:

There once was an old man who lived beside a spring in the Alps. From the spring a stream of water flowed down to a village below. The village council paid the old man to keep the spring in good condition. He did his work faithfully. Daily he would take away all the leaves and twigs that landed in the fountain. The people in the valley thus had clean drinking water, enough water for their gardens and a clear pond on which swans and wild geese swam happily.

Then the members of the council decided that the village had to be expanded. Where would they get the money for their new enterprises? They decided to cut down on all unnecessary expenditure. The keeper of the springs was told that his services were no longer needed.

Nothing happened in the first few weeks. However, when autumn came and all the leaves fell into the spring, trouble started. Leaves and twigs blocked the outflow and it wasn't long before the water in the village had a peculiar yellowish color. A slimy layer covered the pond and the water birds flew away. An emergency meeting was held by the councilors and they asked the old man at the spring to resume his duties again.

The story has a message for all of us. What that old man meant to the villagers, we as Christians should mean to the societies in which we live. Maybe your life seems insignificant to you and maybe you think that it makes no difference in a big chaotic world. But remember that as long as you care for the people around you, serve the Lord and pray … your work is indispensable!

See what Jesus said about faithfulness in Luke 16:10.

20 June

The starry sky above

The Rhodes family was camping in the Cederberg Valley for the weekend. After they had pitched their tent, they decided to sleep outside in their sleeping bags around a fire under the open skies.

Because there were no city lights nearby, the stars were much clearer than they had ever seen them before. They were fascinated. Claudia, who was only four years old, remarked, "I'm not scared at all! I know God watches over us. He can see us through all the peepholes in the sky!" They all laughed at her quaint way of observing the skies.

"Can you see the Milky Way?" their dad asked. "It's the street of lights right above us. Do you know that there are more than five hundred billion stars in the Milky Way?" "Wow! I can't even count that high," Chris confessed. His mom said, "Yes, and even if you could count till there, it would take you months to do it!"

"Let me tell you something even more mind-boggling," Mr. Rhodes said. "Beyond what we see, there are a hundred billion other galaxies like the Milky Way."

They all lay quietly, thinking about the immensity of the universe. Then Chris said, "It sure makes me feel very small!" His mom added, "It is very important to think that God, who made the starry skies, is interested in each one of us."

The next evening, in the light of a lantern, Mr. Rhodes read from the book of Job. In chapter 38 God asked Job a few questions: "Where were you when I laid the earth's foundation?" "Can you bring forth the constellations?" "Do you know the laws of heaven?" The whole family now had an idea of how Job felt when God had reminded him of the awesomeness of His creation.

Read how Job answered God in Job 42:1.

21 June

All things bright and beautiful

"All things bright and beautiful, all creatures great and small. All things wise and wonderful, the Lord God made them all!" Helen's mom was singing while she watered the garden. "You like that hymn, don't you?" Helen said. "Oh yes, it helps me to keep the right perspective on life," she said. "Why?" Helen asked. "Well, it helps me to remember how precious God's creation is. To some people money is the most important thing in life. I want to remind myself of the beauty of nature."

"Ah, but money can come in very handy," Helen argued. She was thinking of all the stuff she still wanted to buy. "Of course," her mom said. "We can hardly survive without money. What is crucial though, is what is most important to you. Some people are so busy making money that they don't even notice the nature around them. I read something interesting the other day.

"I heard of a journalist who took a game warden into the inner-city to have dinner with him in a restaurant. On their way the warden suddenly stopped. 'I hear a frog!' he said. Next to the sidewalk he pointed at a little toad. Amidst the noise of the city the man had heard that little croaking sound. Nobody else heard it. If a coin had been dropped nearby, many folks would probably have started looking for it."

Her mom concluded, "People who ignore the beauty of nature miss the best things in life."

After her mom's message, Helen now watched the birds in the bird bath with new interest, while joining her mom in her singing.

David gives the Lord thanks for His many blessings in Psalm 65. Read it and count the things David is grateful for.

22 June

How great Thou art!

There are numerous things in nature that leave us amazed at the ingenuity of our Creator God. Let us think about a few:

Did you know that geese, ducks and swans fly thousands of kilometers just to be able to stay in a different part of the world in winter? When wild geese fly south to get back to their summer homes in spring, they fly at 50 kilometers per hour and they can fly up to a thousand kilometers before they even need a rest! It must be very interesting to know how their built-in compasses function.

Polar bears are just as clever. Some bears can be left three hundred miles away from their homes, and still be able to find their way back. What makes it even more amazing, is the fact that they can do it in spite of the snow-covered environment that leaves no trace of plant life or odors to guide them.

But the most astonishing phenomenon in the animal world is probably the behavior of salmon. They can swim around in the ocean for years and years and then come back to the same river mouth where they were born. Nobody knows how they do it.

Don't you feel like singing a song of praise to our Creator who designed all these extraordinary features? Hymns like "How great Thou art!" must have been born in the heart of someone who stood in awe over similar marvels in nature.

Next time you notice with what craftmanship a little bird builds its nest or when you watch dolphins playing in the sea or if you observe how gracefully eagles fly high up in the sky, stretch out your arms and say with David, *"O Lord, our Lord, how majestic is your name in all the earth!"* (Psalm 8:1).

Why not learn the whole of Psalm 8 by heart?

23 June

Power from above

George quickly finished his test. He was so relieved – and glad that the exams were over! As he put his exam paper on Miss Smith's desk, he crunched up a piece of paper and threw it in the bin. Miss Smith saw what he did and when all the children were out of the classroom, she took the piece of paper from the bin. She was very shocked to discover that George had made crib notes on the paper and that he had used them in his test.

After school, she called him aside. They talked in the entrance hall of the school building. "Did you copy answers during the exam?" George turned red and let his head hang. "I am sorry," he said. Miss Smith was glad that he didn't say "everybody does it", like some other kids did. She looked at him seriously, waiting for an explanation. "My father said I could get a bike if I do well in the exams," he said. "It's the first time I've done something like this," he added. "And I hope it's the last!" his teacher said. "Why didn't you rather work harder and ask God to help you? Marks that you get in a dishonest way, never make you feel good, even if you get presents and prizes for them. I am going to give you a chance to write the exam again," she said. "But if you ever … "

"I won't do it again," George interrupted. "Thanks a lot, Miss!" he said sincerely.

The next day George rewrote the history test. Miss Smith saw how he closed his eyes and softly muttered something before he started writing. "Thank You, Lord!" she whispered softly.

Read Proverbs 2:1-9 and pay special attention to verse 7.

24 June

The blind mountaineer

Mr. Kaneyama once made front page news in Japan's major news-papers. He was a blind man who had climbed to the top of Mount Fuji. This is a mountain that has always been a big challenge to the world's best mountaineers. There are dangerous crevices and diffi-cult rocks to climb before you can reach the top. And of course, you have to be physically fit and spiritually determined if you ever want to reach the summit. And this courageous man did it! He was 44 years old and he had become blind at the age of 20. When he had first become blind, he was too scared to go anywhere, but later on he tried to live a normal life. And then he chose a hobby that wasn't meant for the faint-hearted: mountaineering!

Luckily he was able to buy an audio-identification instrument that used sound waves to tell him when something was in his way.

Everybody who read about this blind man's courage and per-severance admired him. He did not allow his blindness to be a stumbling block. He could still hear and feel and he made full use of these senses.

Have you lost anything in your life? Does it bother you so much that you cannot fully enjoy life? Do not sulk about it. Be grateful for the things that you still have and see how much you can make use of them.

In Philippians 4:13 Paul said, *"I can do all things through him who gives me strength."* You can also ask God to help you to realize your dreams.

Close your eyes and move about in your room for 5 minutes, just to feel how a blind person experiences his surroundings. Thank God for your eyesight.

25 June

Victory

Amy sat with her friend in hospital. She couldn't believe that Glen looked so cheerful. If she had lost her leg, she would have cried herself to death. Glen had been their school's best swimmer, but he was involved in a big car accident and they had to amputate his leg two weeks ago. "They probably gave him pills to feel happy," she thought. "After such a huge disappointment, no one can smile without being heavily doped."

"What does the **PMAD** on that poster on the wall stand for?" Amy asked, just to make conversation. She wasn't really interested in all the medical terms on the hospital's bill boards. But Glen surprised her by saying, "It stands for *PRAYER MAKES A DIFFERENCE.*" Amy frowned. Prayer certainly didn't make a difference in what happened to Glen. Their whole class had got together one afternoon and pleaded with God to save Glen's leg. But the very next day they had heard the terrible news. He would get an artificial leg and would probably never be able to swim again.

"Do you believe it?" she asked, pointing to the letters in big, black print. "Oh yes!" Glen said. "I have seen how it works. I would never have been able to accept that I will be disabled forever, but people prayed for me and I have made complete peace with the thought. Many people don't have arms or legs and still lead happy lives. If you, my friends, will stand by me, I will also be able to make the best of this bad situation."

Amy had to admit that what she was seeing here, was nothing less than a miracle. "Someone who has lost almost everything, was acting as though he had won something! How could one make sense of that? Perhaps **PMAD**?"

Write James 5:16 and PMAD on your pencil case.

26 June

Use your talents!

"Take my life, and let it be, consecrated Lord, to thee!"

The congregation was singing the well-known hymn. Sam cheerfully sang along. His mother glanced at him quickly. "Why did you look at me so strangely in church?" he later asked her at home. "I saw you singing to the Lord that you commit your life to Him. But when they asked for children to sing in the children's choir, you didn't volunteer." "I don't feel like it!" Sam said. "Did you see what the third verse of the song said?" Sam went to fetch the hymnal. He read: "Take my voice and let me sing ... " He didn't read any further.

"The Lord gave you a beautiful voice, Sam. And you also have a very good ear for music. That is a talent. If you don't use it, you'll lose it!" "Where did you get that one from?" he asked. But then he remembered that his music teacher had also said something to that effect. Even so, he was still not convinced that he would lose anything.

His mother fetched a book from the shelf. "Just read this," she said.

It is said that Paganini, the famous violinist, stipulated in his will that nobody should ever play his violin again after his death. When he died, the instrument was put in a show case in a museum. A few years later, people saw that beetles were eating away at his precious violin. If only the instrument had been used, it would not have been ruined by beetles. Then the author added: *If you do not use your talents, you lose them.*

Sam pondered on this for a moment. "I'll go and think about it," he promised.

Read the parable of the talents in Matthew 25:14-30.

27 June

The best

The story I want to tell you today comes from a book about the first missionaries that worked in India.

One day a missionary went for a walk along the banks of the river Ganges. The Hindus believe that the crocodiles in it are holy animals and that feeding them makes the gods happy. The bigger the sacrifice, the more favor one wins with the gods. Some people even throw their children into the river as a sacrifice.

As he was walking, the missionary saw a woman on her way to the Ganges. She had two little children with her. The one was a healthy baby and the other one very sickly. The sickly baby couldn't walk properly so the mother had to drag her along. The missionary then turned away from the river path, but soon met up with the woman again. This time she had only the gaunt little girl with her. She was crying. "Where is your baby?" the missionary asked sympathetically. "I sacrificed him to the gods!" she said. "But why didn't you rather feed this child to the crocodiles?" he asked, surprised. She looked at him, shocked. "My gods only deserve the best," she answered. "And yours?"

Of course all children are equally important, but this story makes one think, doesn't it? How often do we give God our second best? We only pray and read at night when we are tired and sleepy and our offerings consist of our small change.

Our God does not expect us to throw children into the river for Him, but He surely deserves nothing less than our best. Didn't He give us His best on the cross?

Exodus 20:1-17 explains what God expects of us, His children. Pay special attention to verse 5: "I, the Lord your God am a jealous God".

28 June

Found again!

The people at the Bible Society print and distribute the Bible all over the world. They get many letters from people with wonderful stories about what the Bible means to them.

One such story is about a man who traveled all around his country, selling Bibles. One night after a church service, he was selling Bibles again. When he got back to his hotel room, he discovered that his own little pocket Bible had been stolen. He was very sad, because he had always carried it with him. That way he could read his Bible at any time, at a bus stop, in a waiting room or on a train.

Years later he returned to the same town and went to church on the Sunday evening. That night the pastor gave the people in the church the opportunity to talk about their walk with God. A man got up and told the congregation that he had been a pickpocket once. He could steal people's wallets from their pockets without their even noticing it. One evening, so he told them, he stole something from somebody's pocket that looked like a wallet stuffed with bank notes. Back home he saw that it was a small Bible. At first he wanted to throw it into the fire, but then he started reading it. He could not put the book down! After he had read through nearly the whole of the New Testament, he was so gripped by it that he went to a minister to talk to him about it. Eventually he became a child of God. "But," he said, "I wish I could give the stolen Bible back to its owner!"

Then the salesman rose. "Isn't there a name written on the inside cover of that Bible?" he asked. Of course there was, and that is how the owner got his Bible back. But not before he had given the new Christian a beautiful new pocket Bible in return.

Read Hebrews 4:12-13.

29 June

Caught inside

The kitchen door had been slightly ajar and a robin had flown in. Now it was trying to escape. Bernie and his mother heard how it knocked itself against the big kitchen window while trying to get out. Bernie pushed the back door wide open. "Come here, little bird. Here," he called as soothingly as he possibly could. But the robin did not understand human language. It could see the white clouds through the window and knocked itself against the pane again with a thump.

This time Bernie's mother tried to show the robin the way to freedom with a broom. But all in vain! It bumped against the window above the stove in an attempt to escape. It chirped anxiously.

Suddenly Bernie and his mom heard another robin chirping outside. The one in the kitchen turned its head, spread its wings and jumped down from the cupboard onto the kitchen table and from there to the ground. Only a few more hops in the direction of the other bird's call, and it was right on the back porch! Now it flew freely and cheerfully into the sky with its mate.

While Bernie and his mother looked at the two birds, his mother said, "I have learnt something today." "And what is that?" he asked curiously. "That one's friends are the best people to help you on the right way. We might not understand the minister's sermons or listen to the advice of older people. But when a friend shows us the way, we are more likely to pay attention."

Bernie immediately thought of a friend of his who had become indifferent and no longer wanted to attend Sunday school. Maybe he, Bernie, was the best person to suggest that they go together.

Read Hebrews 3:12-13 to find out how we can support each other along the way.

30 June

JULY

Are you a parrot?

At many of the railway stations in Holland and Belgium posters of a multi-colored parrot are displayed. Below the parrot the words, DO YOU SWEAR? THEN YOU'RE A PARROT! are written. The people who printed these posters obviously knew how much damage swear words can do. And they knew that nobody wants to be compared to a parrot.

Yes, all over the world there are people who swear; even one of Jesus' disciples did! You can read about it in Mark 14:71. Here we meet Peter, one of Jesus' best friends. For three years he traveled along with the Master and never heard one curse from His mouth. But from his past as a fisherman he did know quite a few swear words. The evening that he betrayed Jesus, he heard how the people around the fire were using foul language. Then he thought, "If I talk like them, they won't recognize me as one of Jesus' friends." Remember, he was afraid that they would drag him along with Jesus to court!

Later, after the rooster had crowed, he deeply regretted what he had done. *"Then Peter remembered the word that Jesus had spoken to him: 'Before the rooster crows twice, you will disown me three times.' And he broke down and wept"* (Mark 14:72).

After His resurrection, Jesus gave Peter, the curser, the opportunity to repeat three times that he loved Jesus: once for each time that he had denied Him. And Jesus forgave him.

Don't copy your friends when they use foul language. And if by chance you use a swear word, ask God to cleanse the fountain in your heart, so that dirty water doesn't spring forth from it.

Read what James 3:9-14 says about this.

1 July

Little foxes

Sammy was sitting in front of the computer when his dad entered the room. "I don't know that game," he said as he glanced over Sammy's shoulder. "I copied it from Johnny," he said while playing on. His dad put his hand on his shoulder and turned him around so that he had to look him straight in the eye. "Isn't there copyright on this game?" he asked. "Yes, Dad," he replied, "but surely we don't harm anybody if we swap computer games!"

"Not? What about the guy who designed the game? Now he won't get reimbursed for his work," his dad said.

Sammy was still not convinced. His father continued to explain. "The Bible teaches us that we shouldn't steal. When one copies a game without paying for it, it is sin."

"Maybe," Sammy said, "but it's just a little sin!"

"Do you remember the day when we found the snake in the garage?" his dad asked. "Do you remember that Martha said it's only a tiny little snake, so we don't need to be afraid of it? And then you were the one who told her that a snake's size doesn't indicate how poisonous it is." Sammy remembered it clearly. He was terrified when he saw how his sister played with the snake. "Well, sin is just like that. It may look like a small offense, but it is just as bad as a big one, because it poisons your relationship with God. Disobedience is disobedience. The Bible says *'Catch for us the little foxes that ruin the vineyards.'* We have to learn to be honest in small things, otherwise we might later become deaf to the voice of our conscience." Sammy nodded in agreement. Now he understood more clearly what his dad meant.

You'll find the words about the little foxes in Song of Songs 2:15. Look it up in your Bible.

2 July

The Lord's share

Ever since he was very young, Albert had always given a tenth of his money to the Lord. Usually, when he got money from his family at Christmas, he would put aside one tenth of it. Then he would take it to church as an offering.

But then Albert's grandfather died and he left him a large amount of money. It was enough to buy a bicycle. He made a few calculations and paged through the advertisements. He felt very pleased. "And what about God's share?" his mother asked. This startled Albert. He had completely forgotten about that! "A tenth would be a lot of money to give away," he said. His mother sat next to him on the couch. "Come, let me tell you a story," she said.

"There once was a farmer who gave his friend permission to hunt and shoot a deer on his farm every year. All that his friend had to do in return, was to leave the back quarters for the farmer. For years it went on like this. The friend shot a deer, skinned it and gave some venison to the farmer. But one year he hit the jackpot! He shot a huge deer. When they skinned it, the piece that had to be given to the farmer was enormous. 'I can't give up that much meat,' said the man and left the farm."

Albert listened attentively. "Hey, that's not right!" he exclaimed. "Well," his mother said, "don't you think there is a similarity between this story and what you said earlier?" Albert felt ashamed of himself when he thought of his stinginess and he started making new calculations. This time he put the Lord's share aside first.

Read Malachi 3:8.

3 July

Once upon a time ...

Do you like stories that begin, "Once upon a time ... "? Such stories usually have two parts. The first part makes you feel sad and the second makes you feel happy.

In real life, however, things do not always work out this way, because not all stories have happy endings. Children of God nevertheless know that the story of their lives will eventually have a happy ending. God promised that, one day, we will live with Him for ever and that we will be wonderfully happy. If you wonder where in the Bible you can read this, look up John 14:1-2.

Today I want to tell you a true story with a sad beginning and a happy ending. Once upon a time there was a doctor in England who lived near the Tower of London. His name was Dr. Thomas Bernardo. One day, while he was on his way home from the hospital, he saw something odd. A little girl, who looked cold and hungry, scrutinized everybody who came past. She would walk up to somebody, look him in the eyes, and then move on to the next person. "Who are you looking for, little girl?" the doctor asked kindly. Then she told him her story. She was an orphan who stayed with relatives. But she remembered that her mother had said, just before she died, 'Jesus will take care of you, my child.' "And now I am looking for Jesus," came the sad words.

Dr. Bernardo was so touched by what the little girl had told him that he made his own home into a foster home where children who did not have parents could stay. He tried to be like Jesus to those children.

Think of a way in which you can be like Jesus to someone in need. You can be His hands and feet and do His work in your neigborhood.

4 July

Sharp ears

Whales are very interesting animals. They have strange habits that we humans don't yet understand. Clever people who want to know more about the lives of whales, have done all they can to try and find out more about them. But ships following them and satellites monitoring them do not help much because many things that whales do happen under water.

Now a university in Tokyo has made a robot that can swim under water and can react to the signals that whales send out. Isn't that clever? They put the robot in the sea close to a school of whales and then the robot follows them wherever they go. This robot can then send signals to a ship nearby so that humans can follow the whales' every movement.

The robot listens to the call of the whales and then relays these messages to people on the ship. No human being can hear or see those signals, but the robot picks them up!

In the spiritual world we have a similar pattern. God has also made a plan to get His invisible signals to us. He has given us the Holy Spirit who helps us to hear God and believe in Him, even though we cannot see Him.

In Revelation 2:17 and in six other places in Revelation, God says, *"He who has an ear, let him hear what the Spirit says to the churches ... "* We should listen carefully to what God says and then we should do what He says. Where can we hear what He is saying? He speaks to us from the Bible, in church, at youth group and through people and nature. All our antennae should be ready to receive His voice. His Spirit makes it possible and He also makes us eager to hear His signals.

Ask the Holy Spirit to open your ears to God's messages.

5 July

Closed doors

Every Sunday night the Kilians have a family meeting. There, around the kitchen table, they talk about stuff that bothered them or made them happy during the week.

One Sunday night Richard told his family about a big disappointment. He had hoped that he would make the soccer team, but that week he had heard that he hadn't been one of the eleven chosen. "It feels as though a door has been slammed in my face," he said. Everybody felt sorry for Richard, because they knew how long he had been practicing to make this dream come true.

"Did you know that the apostle Paul also had a big disappointment one day?" his dad said. He read from Acts 16:6-10. "Paul was on fire to go and tell the whole world about Jesus and he planned to go to Asia first. But the Lord had other plans and closed two doors for Paul."

"'Not Asia, not Bythynia,' God said. 'Then where to?' Paul probably wondered. And then God sent him the dream we read of in verse 9. Paul had to go to Macedonia. This way the Gospel of Jesus was taken to Europe, where our ancestors heard it."

Richard's mother then told them something she had read, "The famous missionary David Livingstone really wanted to go and do missionary work in China. But all his plans went wrong, so he eventually landed up in Africa, where God used him in a mighty way."

Little Catherine now also joined in. "One day I really wanted to go to Celia's party, but Mom could not take me and that afternoon I found Socks." She stroked her little cat with its white feet.

"Well, even though your stories don't really help me, at least I feel better!" Richard said.

Look up the passage that Richard's father read to them.

6 July

When in trouble: sing!

In Acts 16:16-25 you can read a most unusual story. In Philippi there was a slave girl who had an evil spirit. Paul helped her by casting out the demon with the power of the Holy Spirit. But her owners were furious! She used to bring in a lot of money through magic tricks. Now that the spirit had left her, she was no longer able to do these tricks.

The owners got hold of Paul and Silas, beat them with sticks and put them in jail without a trial. And what did these two missionaries do? Did they moan and groan about their sore and beaten bodies? Did they sulk because they were treated so unfairly? No! They prayed and sang songs of praise to God.

You can imagine how surprised the jailer and the other prisoners were. And think about the disappointment for Satan and his helpers. But, of course, the angels in heaven rejoiced over the victory.

Jesus had once said, *"Blessed are those who are persecuted because of righteousness, for theirs is the kingdom of heaven"* (Matthew 5:10). "Blessed" means something like "three times happy". There are many stories about people who were full of joy even when they had a hard time because of their faith. John Bunyan, a well-known English writer, was put into prison because of his love for the Lord. In his prison cell there was a chair with wooden struts. He took out one of these and made a flute out of it. Thus he could make the most beautiful music to the glory of God in his dark prison cell. The prison warders could never find out where the music came from, because by the time they reached him, the strut was back in its place again!

You can also sing a song of praise to God, even when things are not going well for you. Why not try it now?

7 July

Are you scared?

Carl's heart was pounding in his chest. In the pitch darkness he could not find the light switch. It was the first night in his own room, and he had no idea that he could become so scared. With his hands straight out in front of him, he shuffled forward step by step. Suddenly he tripped over something and fell flat on his face in the dark. At that moment the light went on and his mother was there!

"What happened?" she asked. She helped him get up from the floor. "Are you hurt?" "No," said Carl embarrassed, kicking the sports bag which he had fallen over out of the way. "I couldn't find the light switch." His mother gave him a hug. "Never mind, I will ask Dad to install a bed light next to your bed." "Thanks Mom," he said. His mother waited until he was in bed. "Are you scared to sleep alone?" she asked. "Not really," he lied. "We are all a little bit nervous in the dark sometimes," his mother said. "But remember, when you are a child of God, you need never be afraid. God protects you."

Going to his bedside cabinet, she picked up his Bible. She turned to Psalm 27 and read, *"The Lord is my light and my salvation. Whom shall I fear? The Lord is the stronghold of my life – of whom shall I be afraid?"* "Do you know, Carl," she said, "someone once counted how many times it says in the Bible that we should not fear. He counted 365 such texts. Exactly one for every day of the year! Now go to sleep in peace and thank the Lord that He never leaves us alone." As she left, she put her torch down next to Carl's Bible.

See if you can find another "do not fear" text in the Bible.

8 July

When last comes first

Mrs. Smith was making pancakes for Louis and his friends, seated at the kitchen table. While there were five of them altogether, she could only make four pancakes at a time. "Who is willing to wait for the next batch?" she asked. Dead silence. The pancakes smelled delicious. "I'll wait, Mrs. Smith," Danny said. Then the others tucked in with relish while Danny looked on patiently.

When Louis's mother gave Danny his pancake, she put an extra one on his plate. "That's not fair," came a choir from his friends. "Oh yes, it is!" said Mrs. Smith. "The Bible says he who is first, shall be last. That means that people who think only of themselves, should not be expected to be rewarded for it. I gave Danny an extra pancake because of his unselfishness in letting you eat first."

When the next batch was ready, none of them wanted a pancake. "I'm waiting for the next lot," each one asserted. "Ma'am, then you can start with me, otherwise they'll all be cold," said Danny. So she dished all four pancakes onto Danny's plate. A chorus of protest! Louis protested loudly, "This time he was first and on top of that he gets four pancakes!" "Well," his mother replied, "Danny was willing to eat first when all of you wanted the last ones. Again he was the unselfish one!" Danny grinned broadly and gave each of them half a piece while they were waiting.

After that the children really had something to think about. Perhaps it was sometimes worth the trouble to be satisfied with second best, and then be unexpectedly rewarded for your unselfishness. They would try and remember that.

Read Mark 9:14-37 attentively, and see if you can find the verse Mrs. Smith was thinking about as she dished out the pancakes.

9 July

God's surprises

Pippa's mother was working on her photo album. She pasted the loose photographs into their proper places and gave each a date. Pippa joined her mother. She loved looking at all the photographs and asking her mother about the time when she was a little baby.

Long ago her mother had told her that she was an adopted daughter, but she never tired of hearing how she came to be their very own child. "Daddy and I prayed a lot, asking the Lord for a child. But it seemed as if He was not listening to us. Later we lost all hope and decided that perhaps we should be satisfied to remain childless. But then we heard about a place where you could hand in your name if you wanted a child for adoption. We applied. Exactly a year later they let us know that a little red-head baby daughter had arrived and had been allocated to us. We were so excited! Before the time we had bought pretty outfits for the baby, and on the way to the hospital we praised the Lord for the big surprise. When they put our lovely baby into my arms, I cried with joy."

As Pippa's mother told the story again, she could not help wiping away a tear. She showed Pippa the photograph taken in front of the hospital where she stood holding the little bundle, wrapped in a blanket, with a small tuft of hair sticking out on one side.

Now Pippa moved up close against her mother. "The Lord did not give you a baby because He wanted *me* to come and live with you!" she said with a satisfied smile. "Yes," her mother replied. "And since then I've known that God always hears and answers our prayers. Only, sometimes He does it in a completely different way from what we expected." "I shall try to remember that," said Pippa.

Read Isaiah 55:9.

10 July

The fortune fairy

When Jenny was looking for a pencil sharpener in her brother's book bag, she found two scratch cards. She knew that her parents thought gambling was wrong, so she showed them to her mother.

"Telltale," Gerry said to Jenny on his way to his mother, who had called him to talk to him about the scratch cards. Jenny was sorry about splitting on her brother, but her Sunday school teacher had told them shocking stories about people who had become addicted to gambling. Some people go deeper and deeper into debt, buying lottery tickets while neglecting their families completely. She did not want her brother to turn out like that one day.

From her bedroom, she could hear what her mother was saying to Gerry. "Of course you know that a child of God puts his trust in the Lord and not in the fortune fairy." She sounded troubled. "We believe that we should work for our money, and that everything we have, comes from the Lord. Therefore we must not use our money as we choose. If you use the money the Lord has given you to buy a scratch card, it is money wasted. Your chance of loosing that money is greater than winning anything."

"Yes, Mom. But a lot of the money spent on lottery tickets is given to good causes," Gerry replied. "Well, then why not give your money directly to a good cause?" his mother retorted. "Then you will know that it will be spent in the right way."

Gerry went back to his room still grumbling under his breath. But then he remembered how much money he had already lost through gambling. There and then he decided to use his money more wisely in future.

Look up Proverbs 10:4 and see what the Bible says about the secret to wealth.

11 July

The lesson

A rabbi is a teacher who teaches Jewish children about Judaism and the place where Jewish children learn these things is called a synagogue. Jesus was also taught by rabbis at a synagogue. These rabbis often tell stories to the children in order to explain difficult things to them. Some of these stories have been preserved through the ages and we call them rabbinical legends.

Here is one of them. Once there were three men who were sick and tired of other people always telling them what to do. They wanted to do their own thing. They wanted to be free. So they decided to buy a boat and sail across the sea of Galilee. They would live on the other side of the lake and there they would do just as they pleased.

But when they were almost half-way across, the trouble began! The man who had to bring the food, had brought pickled beef. It was too salty for the taste of the other two and they threw it overboard. After a while the wind died down and then they discovered that the fellow who had to bring the oars, had brought only one. The other two were furious. Rowing a boat with one oar, made it go in circles. But the worst shock came when the third chap took a drill and started drilling a small hole in the hull of the boat. He was just curious to see what would happen. When they eventually reached land again, they were half starved and dead tired from bailing out water. And then they realized why rules are necessary and why people living together could not make their own laws and do whatever they wanted. They had to be considerate towards others.

God has given us a rule book: the Bible. This helps us to know how to live together in unity, peace and happiness.

Read Psalm 119:6.

12 July

Love for love

Adolph's mother couldn't believe her eyes. When she opened the garage door at half past seven, as usual, her car stood there, sparkling clean! She was so used to seeing the car all dirty and dusty, that she hardly recognized it. Since Adolph's dad moved out of their house, she hadn't wanted to ask Adolph to wash the car. There were so many other things that he had to see to.

She wondered why he had done it. Maybe he wanted to ask her a favor. Or maybe he had done something wrong and wanted to prepare her for the news about it. She puzzled over this the whole day while she was at work. When she got home, Adolph was waiting for her outside. "Now he'll spill the beans," she thought. But he casually told her about the things that had happened at school that day. Finally she could not wait any longer. "Why did you wash the car?" she asked. He put his arms around her and said, "Because I love you." "Not because you've done something wrong?" "No," he said. "Not because you want something from me?" "No," he said again. His mom swallowed a big lump in her throat. "Come, let's see if there's anything left in the cake tin."

While they were enjoying a mug of coffee together, his mom said, "God is just as glad when we do something for Him without any ulterior motives," she said. "What does that mean?" Adolph asked. "It's when we do something for Him out of sheer love and not because we are scared of punishment or are looking for favors. He loves us and He is glad when we simply love Him back."

Read in Mark 14:3-8 about a woman who showed Jesus that she loved Him. Why not do something unexpected for one of your parents this week?

13 July

Mister Holy

The leader at the Good News Club had given the children an excellent idea. He gave each one of them a notebook and told them to write down everything that they asked the Lord for in prayer and the date on which the prayer was answered. In this way they could keep a record of which prayers were answered.

One day, when Hopper's mom was cleaning up his room, she found the notebook on his desk. She paged through it and was thrilled to see how many of his prayers had already been answered.

That afternoon his mom asked, "Hopper, I see in your prayer journal that you prayed for a long time about your classmates. You prayed that they would not make fun of you. Why did they do that?" At first Hopper did not want to talk about it. Then he said, "The kids at school call me 'Mister Holy'." "Why?" Mom asked. "Because I walk away when they tell dirty jokes and because I left Archie's party when they started watching dirty videos."

"So what made them decide not to mock you any longer?" his mom asked. "Oh, they still scoff at me," he said. "Then why did you record your prayer as being answered?" his mom wanted to know. "Well, last Wednesday the Lord gave me a Bible verse that helped me accept the situation. Luke 6:22-23 says, *"Blessed are you when men hate you, when they exclude you and insult you and reject your name as evil, because of the Son of Man. Rejoice in that day and and leap for joy, because great is your reward in heaven."* Hopper quoted the verse by heart.

"I am so proud of you!" his mom said, giving him a warm hug.

You can also start a prayer journal and see how God often answers prayer in a most surprising way!

14 July

A new disease

In some countries in the world a new disease is spreading. It is mainly children and young people who fall prey to it. It is not spread through bacteria or a virus, and yet we must be on guard against it, because it can infiltrate our country very easily. The disease is called "cellphone addiction" and people who have this ailment can't be cured with pills or medicine. Not even an operation will be of any use.

Children with this sickness are constantly sending or receiving messages on their cellphones. They see their cellphones as part of their bodies and they get frustrated and panicky if they have to part with them, even for a short while.

These children develop the idea that nobody cares for them if they do not get regular messages on their cellphones. There are kids who send more than eighty SMS-messages a day. And they get irritated if their friends do not respond immediately. Some students even use their cellphones secretly in class. Others send "good night" messages to all their classmates at bedtime. If they don't do it, they believe that they will lose the friendship of these children.

Neil Verwey, a missionary in Japan, says that he has a special message for kids like these. He tries to convince them that there are more important things in life than cellphone connections. To be in contact with God is so much better!

In Job 23:12 we read, *"I have treasured the words of his mouth more than my daily bread."* Let's rather become addicted to the precious messages that come to us from God through the Bible. He will never fail us.

Read Isaiah 54:10 for God's message to you. Say thank You to God.

15 July

A day of rest

He jumped from the stairs of the caravan, grabbed his surfboard and disappeared. Still half-asleep, his mom looked at her watch. "Why has Felix gone off so early?" she asked. "Probably because it's Sunday," his dad answered. "He might be afraid that we will only allow him to go surfing this afternoon."

At lunchtime Felix got back to the campsite. "You must be hungry," his dad said. "You bet I am," he agreed. "Why did you leave so early without having breakfast?" his dad asked. "I could hear the call of the sea," he said. "And not the call of the church-bells," his dad added. Felix tried to defend himself, "But Dad, we're on holiday, remember?"

"A great group of young people conducted a service for all the holidaymakers. You really missed something," his mom said as she put some sandwiches on the table.

"The Lord only asked us to put aside one day a week for church," his dad said. "If you're not even prepared to give an hour of your Sunday to Him, then you are definitely ignoring the fifth commandment."

Felix had more arguments ready. "Mr. Stanley says that the Sabbath was meant for the Jews, not for us." "Hmm," his dad said. "Ask your teacher if he understands Mark 2:27 where Jesus Himself said: *'The Sabbath was made for man.'* He knew that we can't go without spiritual refreshment, just as our bodies cannot survive without food." His dad passed him a piece of sausage.

While enjoying lunch, Felix gave his dad's words some thought. Maybe it wasn't such a good idea to skip a meal or a church service.

Praise God for setting apart one day a week for us to rest and get spiritually refreshed again.

16 July

The quiet corner

Dylan's dad was a mechanical engineer who worked at a big truck-building factory. Dylan had always wanted to see how the big trucks were put together. So one day during the winter holidays his dad took him along to work.

The noise in the factory was deafening. Engines roared, machines clamored, hammers fired away and a radio blared loudly above the other sounds. All speech was drowned by the noise. Dylan's father had to yell to make himself heard. In the one corner of the big manufacturing plant was a room made of glass. It was quiet inside. A man was sitting there working on an engine. "What is he doing?" Dylan asked his father. "He is testing the machine," his dad said. "Just before the truck is finally handed over, a specialist has to listen to the motor. He must make sure that everything is in order. That corner is specially built to keep out all other noise so that he can listen attentively."

On their way home, Dylan's dad asked him, "What was the most interesting thing that you saw today?" Dylan answered straight-away, while rubbing his ears, "The quiet room!" His dad laughed. "Yes, it is a most essential part of our factory. Now you can understand why I want peace and quiet when I get home in the evenings."

Dylan's father drew his attention to something else that was very important. "In Matthew 6, just before Jesus taught His disciples to pray, He also mentioned a quiet corner." "Didn't He talk about a secret place?" Dylan asked. "Yes, Jesus knows that amid the hub-bub of our daily lives, we need a quiet place where we can listen to our own engines and ask the Big Engineer for advice."

If you haven't got a quiet corner where you regularly go to meet with God, create one today.

17 July

Caring for one another

It was three months since Jane heard that her mom had cancer. Jane thought that she was getting used to the idea. That morning however, while she was combing her mom's hair, clumps fell out and left bald patches on her mom's head. Jane went to her room and cried her heart out. Although they had been warned that her mom would lose her hair as a result of medical treatment, it came as a shock when it actually happened.

After a while Jane wiped away the tears and decided to go to her friend Beth. She was so glad that her best friend lived nearby and that she was a committed Christian. Beth had already meant so much to her. People at church or at school often asked her, "How's your mom?" But Beth asked, "How are *you* coping?" Beth realized that her friend was going through a difficult time because of her mom's illness.

When Jane rang the doorbell, Beth opened immediately. She offered Jane some fruit juice and let her talk. Then she said sympathetically, "You look stressed out. I'm sure you're worrying about what will happen to you if your mom should die." To Jane it was a great relief to be able to talk to somebody about it. Sometimes she was scared and sometimes she was angry and at other times she was just plain sad. It was wonderful to have someone with whom she could share her feelings. All her other friends looked uncomfortable when she started talking about her mom's illness.

When she left, Beth gave her a hug. "I am praying for you," she said. "I thank God for a friend like you!" Jane said with a smile.

Beth took the words of Galatians 6:2 to heart. Read it and think how you can apply it to your friends.

18 July

Living bricks

"**W**hy are we having so many Sundays this week?" asked Andy when his mom told him to get ready for church. "Don't complain," said his mom. "It's only once a year that we have this special series for kids at the church. It's a great privilege. Only a few churches can afford regular youth rallies."

Later that evening Andy and his sister came home after the meeting. Courtney was very excited. "Mom," she said, "it was fabulous! The music was so good and the message was awesome."

"What was the topic?" their mom wanted to know. Andy answered, "The preacher mixed things up a bit. Last night he said that we were sheep and tonight we were bricks." "Oh, for goodness' sake," Courtney interrupted. "If you don't understand what the preacher had to say, your brain-cells must be frozen! Let me tell you, Mom." Courtney was very enthusiastic. "He built a wall on the stage and said that we were living stones in the church of God. Then he pulled out one of the bricks to show us what will happen if any one of us did not do his share." Now Andy joined in, "Yes, the wall tumbled down and one of the bricks fell on Jimmy's foot and everybody roared with laughter."

"It sounds as if you enjoyed the meeting," their mom said. "I take it we will have to let you go again tomorrow night." "For sure!" said Andy. "Otherwise the church wall might tumble down. By the way, the preacher said that our parents were appointed by God to shape us, the bricks."

"Well, if that's the case, come closer for a really impressionable hug," his mom said, laughing.

Read 1 Peter 2:5. The preacher explained this verse to the youth at the meeting that night.

19 July

Guard your mind

Matt hummed while he washed the car. He was enjoying himself. "Do what you want, want what you do!" he sang rhythmically.

His mom came out to see his progress, and asked, "What are you singing?" "Oh, it's a song from my new CD," he answered. "I think we will have to scan that CD together," his mom replied.

"Don't worry, Mom," he said. "It's just a nice song with a nice beat. I hardly notice what they're singing." "That's what you think," his mom said. "The truth is that your brain gathers those words and stores them in your subconscious mind, like a computer."

Matt's mom took a cloth and helped him to dry the roof of the car. "Why do you think people spend so much money on advertising?" she asked. "It's because they know that it is worth their while to send 'Fizzy Delite makes life bright' over the airwaves. It conditions people to ask for a Fizzy Delite when they're thirsty."

"Maybe you think that it doesn't matter what you are listening to, but the truth is that everything that enters your ears, settles somewhere in your mind. Music can sell cooldrink and it can also sell ideas. That's why choosing songs is so important. Today you might sing 'Do what you want!' and tomorrow you might do exactly that, instead of doing what is right. God's Word teaches us that we must not do what we want, but what God wants."

Matt ducked into the car and put on the car radio. An instrumental band was playing a lively tune. He started polishing the car to the beat of the drums. "Are you satisfied now?" he asked his mom. She smiled and went to fetch them each a glass of Fizzy Delite.

Read Matthew 12:33-37 and write these words on your CD-shelf: What the heart thinks, the mouth speaks!

20 July

A man's best friend

There was an interesting bit of news in a newspaper the other day. A girl who was paralyzed in her arms got permission to study at a famous university. A person with her disabilities could not attend classes on her own, carry books around or take care of herself. How did she convince the authorities that she would be able to cope?

Tatebaya got injured in a car accident when she was in high school. She was so severely maimed that she completely withdrew from society. She stayed in her room during the day and spent a lot of time on her computer. Then she learnt about a place where dogs were trained to help handicapped people. Her parents took her there and bought her a beautiful Labrador! At the school for dogs Tatebaya and her dog Atom got to know each other very well. He followed her wherever she went and he was trained to do all sorts of things for her.

Tatebaya and Atom applied to be accepted at a university, and to her great delight, she was successful.

Are you grateful that you are not seriously handicapped? And if you are handicapped in one way or another, do you realize that God wants to be your special Helper? In Hebrews 13:5-6 we read, *"'Never will I leave you; never will I forsake you.' So we say with confidence, 'The Lord is my helper; I will not be afraid.'"*

Do you know a handicapped person? Think of something you can do for that person this week to make things a little easier.

21 July

The Matrushca dolls

Have you ever seen a set of Matrushca dolls? They are made in Russia out of soft wood and the faces and clothing are painted on them in bright colors. You get between three and ten dolls in a set. What makes them so special, is the fact that they all fit into each other. When you turn the upper part of the doll, it comes off and another one is found inside. You can go on like that and in the end you find a tiny doll in the middle. Then you have a whole set of similar dolls ranging from big to small.

Susan had a set like this. She had four dolls that were beautifully painted with a bright hat and apron on each of them. She never got tired of them. All her other toys had been given away as she grew older, but the Russian dolls remained on her dresser. She loved stacking them into one another as if in a little nest.

On her eleventh birthday her grandma sent her a card with a picture of Matrushca dolls on it. In the card she wrote: John 14:20: *"On that day you will realize that I am in the Father, and you are in me and I am in you."* Her granny also included a letter with money in it. She wrote, *"You are now eleven years old and almost a young lady. Buy yourself a nice gift and remember that you are safe between God the Father, Jesus the Son and the Holy Spirit, just as the dolls on your dresser snugly fit into each other."*

Suddenly the dolls became more meaningful to Susan. She realized that the Holy Spirit was inside her, Jesus was around her and they were all enclosed by God Himself. There was no need for her to be afraid of the strange world of grown-ups that awaited her!

Choose today to be safely enveloped by the layers of God's love and protection.

22 July

A difficult decision

A tricky situation cropped up in the Smith household. John was keen to participate in a cycle race, but it was on a Sunday, which meant that he would have to skip church and Sunday school. His parents were very concerned. To them it was important that John should love and revere the Lord above all else.

A week before the event, John's father called him to his office. "Mom and I decided to help you prioritize things you want to do on a Sunday. We took three envelopes and labeled them Never, Sometimes and Maybe. We also took a number of cards on which we wrote possible situations that can arise on a Sunday. You can help us to put the cards into the right envelopes."

John loved games, even though this one seemed to involve serious matters. He chose a card. You went to bed late on Saturday night and don't feel like church the next morning. "No doubt where this one belongs!" he said as he put it into the "Never"-envelope. The next card stated, A friend is in hospital and visiting time is Sunday mornings. John put this one in the "Sometimes"-envelope. He drew a third card, A cycle tour sponsored by a leading newspaper takes place once a year, but on a Sunday. You want to take part. John stuffed this card into the "Maybe"-envelope and then looked pleadingly from one parent to the other.

"OK," his father said smilingly. "You may go, but then you'll have to write a letter to your Sunday school teacher and you'll have to catch up on next Sunday's lesson." His mom added, "I hope you'll be singing God's praises as you peddle along." "For sure!" John said. He was also keen to tell his friends how his parents had helped him to make the right choice.

Read about keeping the Sabbath in Exodus 20:8-10.

23 July

A sad story

"**M**-m-must we finish all the work by to-m-m-morrow?" Frank asked his teacher. He was stammering as usual and his classmates snorted with laughter. Paul, the biggest boy in the class, was mocking him, "Y-y-yes D-d-dummy!" he said. Frank should have been immune to all this teasing by now, but it still hurt when the kids in class made fun of him.

When Frank was a baby, he had contracted a rare kind of illness and he had to stay in hospital for months on end. Now he was much smaller than his classmates and he had a speech impediment. The children at school were cruel. They loved chasing him around with wet towels in the locker room and sometimes they threw pieces of bread at him during lunch time. They would shriek with laughter when they saw how embarrassed he became.

Frank never complained about it, because he realized that he would then be mocked even more. He could hear the boys saying, "Sissy!" "Mommy's baby!" if he dared to tell anybody. Many of the boys at school felt that it was "cool" to bully others.

Frank became a real loner. Only one guy was friendly towards him. It was Selby, who was fat and ugly and also received his share of scoffing from the boys at school. Sometimes Frank wondered why the teachers didn't do anything to protect those who were being teased. Maybe they thought that it was good to leave them to fight their own battles.

When Frank got home that afternoon, he opened his Bible at his favorite text: *"The Lord is my helper; I will not be afraid. What can man do to me?"* (Hebrews 13:6). Then …

Finish this story for yourself. Ask God to show you how you can act towards children who are victimized at school.

24 July

A bright idea

Once there was an old man without a job who walked from house to house begging for food. But nobody could give him anything, because in that neighborhood the people themselves were very poor. Eventually an old lady had compassion on him and said, "I have no food to give you, but you can have this pot. It's the only thing that I have to spare." The old man looked at the pot and got a bright idea.

"Thanks ma'am," he said. At the next house he asked for a meat bone. The lady who opened the door gladly brought him a few leftover meat bones. He put them in the pot and went further. At the next house he asked for a few veggies. He received a potato, an onion and a carrot. Then he saw a man working in his herb garden across the street. "Please may I have some parsley?" he asked. "Certainly," the man said and gave him a piece of celery as well. At the last house he asked for salt and pepper and gratefully received it. "Now I am going to cook myself some tasty soup," he said. He walked to a park and on his way he picked up twigs for a fire. At a tap he got water and after a while he had a fire going with a steaming pot of soup on it!

We can learn something from this story. Today there are thousands of people in the world who have no work and are very hungry. They say that there is one person who dies of hunger every half a minute. Maybe you feel that you cannot help these millions of people. But if each one of us contributes our share, we can help hungry people to help themselves.

Read how Jesus could feed a crowd of people with the contribution that one child made (Mark 6:30-44).

25 July

Animal rights

It was March in Alaska. The fields of snow were glistening in the morning sun. There was movement across the snowy landscape. Hundreds of baby seals wallowed in the distance. One could hardly distinguish them from the white snow in the background, because they were a light creamy color. Coming closer, you could see their big brown eyes.

Suddenly something else could be seen on the horizon. A ship was coming towards the land. As it touched the shore between the snow-clad rocks, a group of people disembarked. They went straight to the colony of baby seals. They had batons with them and one by one the little animals were beaten to death. Then the dead seals were skinned on the spot. All the furry skins were taken to the ship. Those skins would be processed in huge factories to make glamorous fur coats for which rich women would pay an exorbitant price.

Does it make you furious to hear stories like this? Rightly so, because animals also have rights. They have the right to be protected by us. God appointed us to look after His creation.

From the beginning of time animals have been slaughtered to be eaten. Some animals were also slaughtered as an offering to God. But later people started killing animals for other reasons. Elephants were killed for their ivory tusks. Rhinos were killed so that all kinds of ornaments could be made from their horns. How selfish and cruel mankind can be!

God is very angry with senseless killing. He created man to look after all the other creatures on planet earth. We should do all we can to protect our plant and animal species and we should fight pollution whenever and wherever we can.

Read about the animals God created in Job 40:15-28

26 July

Fire!

It was a beautiful autumn day in the Western Cape. Nicolene was doing homework at her desk in front of the window. She could see her father raking together the fallen leaves in the garden. When he had made a big heap, he went to fetch a can of petrol and sprinkled it over the leaves. Then he put a match to it. The next minute he was aflame!

Nicolene got a terrible fright. She cried, "God, please help me," and ran to where they kept their coats. She tried to remember all the things they had learnt in school about handling a crisis.

When she reached her dad, she threw the coats over him. He sank to the ground and he rolled over to put out the flames. She realized with a shock that underneath the heap of clothing her dad lay and he needed help urgently!

Again she cried to God for help as she ran to the telephone. There was nobody else at home. Quickly she scanned the list of emergency numbers. She phoned the ambulance and gave them their address in a shaky voice. Within a few minutes they were there to take her dad to hospital. Only then could Nicolene phone her mom at work.

"Thank You, Lord," she said as she sank down on the couch. But there was still a lot of crying and praying in store for her family, because her dad had been seriously burned. He had to stay in hospital for months. All their friends and relatives said, "If it wasn't for Nicolene who reacted so bravely, then the story would have had a very different ending." Then Nicolene would say, "If it hadn't been for the Lord … !"

Be sure to display all emergency numbers near your telephone and write the words of Psalm 50:15 next to the list.

27 July

Never give up

Mary Verghese was a missionary in India. She was an excellent surgeon who could perform the most intricate operations. She especially tried to help the leprosy patients at the Vellore Christian Hospital so that they could get the use of their hands and feet back.

She was one of many doctors who left their home country to go to places where people did not know Jesus, so that they could provide medical assistance and spread the gospel. But something about her was even more extraordinary – she was in a wheelchair! Shortly after she started working in India, she was in a bad car accident in which her back was broken. She was paralyzed from her waist down.

Everybody thought that she would go home to England after this major setback. But Mary Verghese was determined to finish the task that she believed God had given her. She underwent a few operations to strengthen her back so that she could sit up straight in a wheelchair. Then she started to practice using surgical instruments in the operating theater from her wheelchair. It proved to be extremely difficult, but she persevered. People who watched her performing operations afterwards were amazed. They were also impressed that she did not pity herself at all.

In 2 Samuel 22:29-30 David said, *"You are my lamp, O Lord; the Lord turns my darkness into light. With your help I can advance against a troop; with my God I can scale a wall."* Dr. Mary, as she was called by everybody at the hospital, showed that God can help a person to do things that others regard as impossible.

You can pray for doctors and nurses who must sometimes do their work in very difficult circumstances. Pray especially for those who do their work as witnesses for Jesus.

28 July

Who was to blame?

Three old men sat at the roadside, begging for food. The one was blind, the other was crippled and the third one was lazy. One day the lazy one came up with a clever plan. He asked the blind man to carry the crippled one to the nearest vineyard, where they could steal a basketful of grapes. "If you bring it here, I will sell it and we can divide the money amongst us," he said. If the farmer should inquire about the lost grapes, the lame man could say, "I am lame. How could I get to your vineyard?" The blind one could say, "I am blind. How could I pick your grapes?" And lazybones could say, without even telling a lie, "I wasn't near the vineyard!"

Yes, people are forever denying the fact that they are sinners. It started right in the beginning, when Adam blamed Eve for the sin that he himself had committed. When God asked him why he had been disobedient by eating of the fruit that was in the middle of the garden, he immediately blamed Eve. "The wife that You have given me, she gave me some of the fruit," he said. Eve did not admit her sin either. She said, "It was the snake that told me to eat of the forbidden fruit." In the meantime both of them were to blame, just like the three old men in the story.

If we sin, we should not blame other people for our wrong deeds. We must confess them and ask God to forgive us. He knows about your share in treating a classmate badly. He saw the time you copied homework from your friend. The Bible says, *"Anyone who knows the good he ought to do and doesn't do it, sins"* (James 4:17).

Read Numbers 5:5-7.

29 July

Golden years

"**M**ust Mrs. White come with us on the picnic?" Elizabeth wanted to know. "She is always so slow!" "Yes," Penny complained, "and she repeats a story over and over again." "We invited her and she is coming," their mom said. "We will all be old one day and we won't want people to forget about us in the old-age home, will we?"

Mrs. White was waiting for them on the porch of the home where she stayed. She got into the car with difficulty. The twins watched their mom as she patiently attended to the old lady. While they drove to the park, they didn't talk much, because Mrs. White could not hear their voices above the sound of the engine.

They parked their car in the shade near the dam and the two girls fed the swans. Mrs. White was watching them, her eyes laughing. She remembered her childhood on a farm.

They all enjoyed a picnic lunch consisting of chicken sandwiches and fruit juice. Elizabeth had to help Mrs. White open the tight fruit juice cap, while Penny helped her down the steep hill to the car.

On their way back, Mrs. White sang softly. The two girls couldn't help laughing. "She's going dotty," Elizabeth said. Her mom looked sternly over her shoulder at them.

After Mrs. White had been taken to her little room again, their mom had a serious talk with the girls. "I don't ever want to hear you make fun of Mrs. White or any other older person," she said. "She looked after me when my mom died and other senior citizens have done their share for society when they were younger. The least we can do, is to have respect for them in their old age."

Write Leviticus 19:32 on the back of a photograph of your grandparents.

30 July

A smell that sticks

"**P**hew!" Anne said as she got out of her uncle's car. "That car smells awful. Next time Uncle Gerald gives us a lift, I'll take along a few pegs." She pressed her fingers to her nose. Her mom smiled. "Yes, I don't think that people who smoke realize how smelly they are. Every time Mrs. Gregory comes to visit, I have to take special trouble to get our furniture and carpets clean and fresh again. That's why I have bought this air freshener," she said, while unpacking their groceries.

"Can't Mrs. Gregory smell the tobacco herself? She seems to be so neat and tidy." "I think that people who smoke hardly notice the smell on themselves."

While her mom was putting the groceries away, she said thoughtfully, "You know, that is exactly how it is with sin." "Why do you say that?" Anne asked. Her mom explained, "When you mix with a crowd who does things against God's laws, you are upset about it at first. But if you spend a lot of time in their company, you begin to scarcely notice their foul language and bad habits."

Her mom took off her jacket and hung it in the doorway. "The smell in the car has worked its way into my clothes and is even in my hair. Just like sin! Before you know it, you have joined the gang in doing wrong. That's why you should be careful about whom you spend most of your time with."

The next Sunday Anne's Sunday school teacher asked, "Who knows what 2 Corinthians 6:14 means? It says: *'Do not be yoked together with unbelievers.'*" Without hesitation Anne answered, "Because their smell can get stuck on you."

Read Psalm 1 and see which type of friends David warns us against.

31 July

AUGUST

Someone is following in your footsteps!

"Mom, today I saw the funniest procession! Uncle Steve has a duck that follows him wherever he goes. And behind the duck comes a goose. Wherever Uncle Steve goes, the two birds follow him, waddling and quacking away." Quentin imitated the duck and his mom couldn't help laughing.

"Aunt Sara said that the duck thinks that Uncle Steve is his mother. He helped the little duck to hatch out of the egg, and that's where it all started. Apparently the first thing a duck sees after his birth, is 'mother' to him. If it was Rex, the duck would have had a dog for a mom."

"And the goose?" his mother asked. "Well, this poor thing first laid eyes on the duck when he came out of his shell. Now he thinks that he is a duck and he follows his duck-mother wherever she goes. What a picture! Luckily it doesn't work the same way with human beings," Quentin said. "Otherwise I would probably be trotting behind a nurse for the rest of my life."

His mom had a good laugh and then she said, "In a way this is true about humans too, you know. They say that children copy the habits of the people they live with. That's why your father and I try our best to live the way the Bible teaches us. We hope that you will follow us and that you will also learn to love and serve the Lord." Quentin sat down. "Do you mean to say that Wendy will copy me?" "Oh yes!" his mom said. "Just listen to her as she talks to her friends on the phone. Where do you think she gets 'Cool man, cool' from?"

Quentin decided there and then to be more careful about what he did when his little sister was around.

Think about the words of Titus 2:7.

1 August

The false label

Ricky was at a youth camp and their group was planning a midnight feast. When it became quiet in the camp on the Friday night, they crept out of their sleeping bags. All their food was packed out on the floor by the light of a candle. Ricky had brought a can of peaches. He opened it with a can opener and said, "Come on, folks. Give me your mugs for some peach delight." But oh dear! What did they find? The tin contained green beans instead of peaches. Ricky looked at the label. It said *Peach Halves* and it also pictured some mouthwatering yellow cling peaches. At first his friends were annoyed. But later they laughed. "What a blessing that we didn't put Derrick's custard on the beans!" they said.

The story about the sixth graders' nocturnal disappointment spread like wildfire through the camp. On the Sunday morning the youthworker even made a sermon out of it. "Boys and girls," he said, "today you get a lot of people who call themselves Christians, but who do not really belong to Christ. Some even attend Sunday school or church. They show one label, but in their hearts they are something quite different. They are living a lie. You should only call yourself a Christian if you know the Lord Jesus as your personal Savior. To me you all look great, but only God knows what is going on in your hearts. If you invite Him into your life, He will see to it that you are just as attractive on the inside as on the outside."

Then he asked one of the older children to read Hebrews 4:13: *"Nothing in all creation is hidden from God's sight. Everything is uncovered and laid bare before the eyes of him to whom we must give account."*

Ask God to cleanse you from sin so that you can live an honest life before God and men.

2 August

Humphrey and Theresa

"Humphrey Dumphrey sat on the wall, Humphrey Dumphrey had a great fall!" Three boys were making fun of Humphrey who was sitting on the merry-go-round in the park. One of them suddenly stopped the wheel and Humphrey fell in the dust. He had trouble getting up again. The others roared with laughter.

Humphrey walked timidly to a bench nearby and sat there. The others laughed at the funny faces that he was making in an attempt not to cry. They all knew that Humphrey attended a special school. They thought it was very funny that a child of twelve still acted like a toddler.

Theresa was watching everything from where she was playing. She remembered what the lady at the children's club had told them. They should be kind to other people and especially to those in need. She went up to Humphrey and wiped the sand from his knees with her hanky. She smiled and talked kindly to him. Humphrey soon forgot the nasty encounter with the other kids and he laughed happily to show Theresa that he appreciated her friendliness.

Then Humphrey's mom turned up. "Thanks for being kind to Humphrey," she said. "He hasn't got many friends. He got injured at birth and now he is way behind other children of his own age. But he is learning a lot at his school. We believe that he will be able to look after himself one day."

"I will come and play with him sometimes," Theresa offered. "I'll bring my ball, then we can roll it to each other." "Thank you my dear!" Humphrey's mother said with tears in her eyes." I can see that you are a true child of God." She gave Theresa a warm hug.

Read John 15:9-14. The lady at the children's club explained these verses to Theresa.

3 August

The missionary

"There was a missionary at youth club today," Pauline said enthusiastically at suppertime. "What is a missionary?" asked her four-year-old brother Eddie. "It's a fanatic!" retorted Jonathan, their elder brother. "You don't need to trek across the world to serve the Lord. There's enough work around here."

"If that is what a fanatic is, then I also want to be one!" said Pauline. "Mr. Thomas said that he came across hundreds of people in the country where he works who begged him to stay with them and to teach them about God. We can't act as if we don't know about them. And anyway, Jesus instructed all His followers to go to the ends of the earth to tell people about Him. If we can't go ourselves we should give money so that others can go. And of course, we must pray for the fanatics who are prepared to go."

"And who will do the work amongst us?" Jonathan asked. "You and I," said Pauline. "We witness to people around us and missionaries tell people in faraway places. In that way all people will know about Jesus."

"Bring my Bible," Dad said. "I'll read you a very interesting passage." Eddie fetched the Bible and their dad opened it at Matthew 24:14. He read, *"'And this gospel of the kingdom will be preached in the whole world as a testimony to all nations, and then the end will come.'* God wants people of all countries to hear about His love and mercy. After that He will come to fetch His children."

Jonathan said, "Well, then I guess it's a good thing to be a fanatic!"

Keep a photograph of a missionary in your Bible to remind you to pray for him. And remember that you are also a missionary to the people around you.

4 August

Remote control

The owner of a shop that sold televisions, video-players and other electronic appliances, was taking stock, when he discovered something odd. He was suddenly selling five times more remote control devices than before. "Why would so many people suddenly buy remote controls?" he wondered.

He asked the cashier which customers were buying all these devices. "They're criminals," she said. "Those remote controls can open the doors of certain types of cars." The shop owner reported this to the police and they discovered some interesting facts. Thieves were buying the controls and trying them on cars with remote-controlled locks. If they succeeded, they could open the car without breaking a door or a window. Then they could steal anything that was in the car. Some thieves even knew how to start a car without a key and then they could simply drive away.

The Bible teaches us that Satan is just as cunning as these thieves. He wants to enter our lives and influence our thoughts. He knows which things we like and he is always trying to get to us through them. If you like reading, he will see to it that you read books that are full of ideas that contradict the truths of the Bible. Or you might be very fond of music. Then Satan can use the words of some popular songs to infiltrate your thoughts. The singer might encourage you to do things that a Christian shouldn't do. Later on you might find it difficult to know right from wrong.

Beware of the devil's remote control!

2 Corinthians 11:14 says that Satan masquerades as an angel of light. Next time he wants to control your actions, do what James 4:7 recommends.

5 August

God is holy

"**T**rrrrrring!" the telephone rang in the Nigels' home. Mrs. Nigel picked up the phone and her husband could hear her saying, "All right dear, we'll be there right away." He looked up from his newspaper in surprise. Melany had been dropped off at a friend's birthday party only an hour ago. Why would she want to come back already?

"She says that her friends are watching a video where the characters are swearing all the time and she'd rather come home." "I'll go and fetch her," said Mr. Nigel.

When he arrived at the party, Melany was already waiting at the garden gate. "Did you say 'good bye' and 'thank you' to the hostess?" asked her dad. She nodded. "And do your friends know why you are leaving so early?" "Yes," replied Melany. "Actually Danny left first. He was upset by all the blaspheming. When he left, I decided to phone you to come and fetch me."

"I'm proud of you," her dad said. "Maybe we should think of an alternative if something like this crops up again." "Like what?" Melany asked. "Well, perhaps we can plan a good game that you can all play together. Maybe it will take some effort to prepare for it, but it might be worthwhile."

When they got home, her mom said, "You did the right thing today. God is holy and we should have the highest respect for Him. That's why the Ten Commandments prohibit us from taking His name in vain. You have definitely given your friends something to think about!"

Pray the prayer found in Revelation 15:4: "Who will not fear you, O Lord, and bring glory to your name? For you alone are holy. All nations will come and worship before you!"

6 August

God is faithful

In the Bible we read about many people whom God helped in their trouble. You probably remember the stories of Daniel in the lions' den and Peter in jail. God still answers the prayers of His people.

The following true story was recorded in *Lights from Many Lamps* by Watson. During the Second World War a plane was shot down and crashed into the sea. Luckily the pilot and seven other men could get into rubber boats after the plane had sunk. They fastened the boats together and hoped that somebody would find them in the middle of the ocean. But nobody spotted them and they drifted aimlessly while the sun burned down on them relentlessly. They had no food, except for four oranges, and no water either.

What they did have with them, was a captain who was a true Christian and who had a pocket Bible with him. Captain Eddie Rickenbacker read parts of Scripture to the men and encouraged them to pray and to trust God.

Soon three of the men fell ill from thirst and exhaustion. Captain Eddie read to them from Matthew 6:31-34. The next minute a seagull landed on his head. He caught the bird and it became a source of food. And then, after a while it started raining! This supplied them with water which they could catch in containers. They realized that these coincidences were nothing less than miracles. After a fortnight they were seen and rescued by a helicopter. When curious journalists asked the crew how they could survive in such dire circumstances, they just said, "We prayed!"

Whenever you are in trouble, don't give up. Pray and believe that God will never forsake His children.

Read the passage the captain read to his crew.

7 August

Too good to be true

One day a minister visited a man who told him, "I have sinned too much in my life. I have wasted my parents' money, I have been a thief, I have ill-treated my wife. I have also been a bad parent and have been divorced. Then I started drinking. How can God pardon me? I deserve to go to hell."

Then the pastor said, "Let me read you something from the Bible. Isaiah 1:18 says, *"'Come now, let us reason together,' says the Lord. 'Though your sins are like scarlet, they shall be as white as snow, though they are red as crimson, they shall be like wool.'"*

The man answered, "That is too good to be true."

The minister did not give up, however. He said, "My friend, what would you do if you tried on a jacket in a department store and it fitted perfectly, but was too expensive. Then just as you are leaving the shop, the owner calls you back and says, 'Sir, that jacket fits you beautifully! I want to give it to you as a gift. It will give me great joy if you take it and tell your friends about my shop.' Will you say, 'It is too good to be true!' and walk away?"

The pastor continued, "God wants to forgive all your sins. He wants you to become His child and He doesn't want any payment for it. Jesus has already paid the account for your redemption. It will really be foolish of you not to accept this offer."

These words made the man think. A week later he came to the minister again. "I decided to accept the gift of salvation," he said. They prayed together and the man who had previously been so desperate now started a new life with the Lord.

Thank God that He is prepared to forgive all your sins.

8 August

Plugged in

Henry was waiting for his best friend outside his house. They always cycled to school together. When Conrad came around the corner from the garage, his mom called, "Have you got your lunch?" "Yes, Mom!" he answered. "And are you plugged in?" "Yes, Mom! Good bye Mom," he called over his shoulder.

"What did your mom mean when she asked if you are plugged in?" Henry wanted to know. Conrad laughed. "My mom has the most curious way of explaining spiritual things to us. She says that if we don't pray in the morning, we won't be plugged in. You know, like an electric plug in the wall. She believes that we get power from above when we pray. And if we don't make contact with the Lord through prayer, then our power supply is cut off. Like an electric wire that's been disconnected."

"Do you believe that?" Henry asked, very interested. "I don't know," his friend confessed. "All I can say is that I do not want to go anywhere without the Lord, not even for a single day. I tell Him that every morning and then I feel plugged in."

"Maybe that's how you keep your calm when Andrew bullies you." "Yes, it also helps me when I have trouble with Science. I'm really not good at it and I would have given up long ago if it wasn't for the constant power supply."

That afternoon when Henry opened his sports bag, he found a letter in it. *The God of Israel gives power and strength to his people (Psalm 68:35).* He recognized Conrad's handwriting. He smiled and closed his eyes before he ran onto the soccer field. He was planning to stay plugged in himself!

Write Psalm 68:35 on a card and give it to somebody in need!

9 August

Patience

Today we are going to talk about patience. Having patience means that you are able to wait. But waiting isn't easy!

You want to go for a swim, but your mom says, "I'm not ready yet. Bring in the washing so long." You are hungry, but the food is not ready yet. Your mom says, "Lay the table so long."

You want to play with your ball, but it is raining outside. Your dad says, "Do your homework so long, and when the rain stops, you can go and play outside."

You want a bicycle, but your parents say that you must wait until you are twelve. They say, "Save your money so long, then you can help to pay for the bike."

Yes, waiting can be very, very difficult indeed.

It is also not easy to wait for the Lord. Maybe you have been praying about something for a very long time, but God does not seem to answer your prayer. Maybe you need a friend, but He says, "Be kind to everyone. At the right time I will answer your prayer."

The Bible says that we must have patience. In 1 Thessalonians 5:14 we read, *"Be patient with everyone,"* and according to Galatians 5:22 patience is one of the fruits of the Holy Spirit. Therefore we must ask God to make us patient.

An impatient person says, "I want it now!" A patient person says, "I can wait. I can do something else so long."

In the Bible we read about many people who had to wait. Joseph had to wait until somebody came to release him from prison. The Israelites had to wait before God led them out of Egypt.

We must also be able to wait. We must be patient and trust God.

Is there something you really want? Say to yourself: I am God's child. I can wait if I must!

10 August

God always has a plan

God's children must be able to wait. In the Bible we find many stories of people who had to learn how to wait. One of these stories is the history of how the Israelites had to travel through the desert for forty years before they reached the land of milk and honey that God had promised them. When they came to Canaan at last, they saw that there was a broad river that first had to be crossed. How would they do it?

God had a plan. He made a road through the river so that they could all reach the other side. Now they wanted to take the land and settle in it. But God said, "Wait! First build me an altar as a reminder to you of what I have done for you." So the Israelites first built an altar and praised the Lord for bringing them safely to Canaan.

"Now we can settle at last," they thought. "We have waited long enough." But oh dear! The walls of the city of Jericho where they wanted to stay, were strong and high. They certainly hoped that God would have a quick solution for the problem. God had a plan, but again they had to be patient. Their leader said, "God knows the right time. We must be patient and do as He tells us."

Then God told them to walk around the city once a day, for six days in a row. After that they were really tired of waiting. But Joshua said, "You are God's children. You must be patient. You must trust God."

And on the seventh day God said, "Today you must walk around the city seven times and the walls will come tumbling down."

Everything happened just as God said.

We must also learn to wait and to trust God. He always has a plan.

Read this story in Joshua 6.

11 August

A miracle!

Joy and her husband Colin were missionaries in the Congo. When their third little boy was three years old, Joy discovered that she was pregnant again. She was unhappy because she didn't want more children and she didn't know where she would get clothing and other things for the new baby. She had already given away all her baby things and she couldn't afford to buy any more.

But Joy realized that she ought to be grateful for the little one who was on its way because every child is very special to Jesus. So the mother went to a quiet spot under the trees to pray. She asked the Lord to forgive all the angry thoughts that she had and to help her be glad about the new baby. While she was praying, all the bitter thoughts vanished. "Lord," she then asked, "will You please supply all the things that we will need for this baby?"

A fortnight later her prayers were answered in a miraculous way. A huge container arrived at the missionary station. What was inside and for whom was it intended? A letter came with it. It said, "Please give this to somebody who is expecting a baby." The container had been sent away months before and inside was everything that a baby could possibly need: clothing, bedding, baby furniture and everything else that a pregnant mother could dream of. A church in South Africa decided to send this gift of love to the Congo. God must have given them this idea, because He knew about a mother who would need it for a little baby boy that was about to be born.

This is a true story and it teaches us that God knows beforehand what little children will need and that He wants to take care of each one of them.

Read Mark 10:13-16 to see how much Jesus cares for little children.

12 August

Have you ever heard of an MK?

Do you know what an MK is? It stands for Missionary Kid and it is a name that has been given to the children of missionaries who work in faraway countries.

Many of them live in countries where there are no other people from their own culture nearby. The children with whom they attend school are usually not Christian and often speak a different language.

Nico de Wet is an MK from South Africa who lives in Japan. He was twelve years old when his parents decided to pack up and go to Japan to tell the people of Fukuaka about Jesus. Here is an extract from one of his letters:

Schools here are completely different from the ones in South Africa. Our school starts at 8:30 and only closes at 16:00 in the afternoon. After school we have sport activities which last till at least 19:00. Then many Japanese children still attend "juku" three or four times per week, which ends at 22:00 at night. "Juku" is special classes in different subjects. Unfortunately we have no real school holidays. Each day of the holidays is filled with sport activities or matches and we get tons of homework and research projects to finish during the holidays. Please pray that I will get to know the Japanese language better. Pray that I will be able to make friends with these kids. I really miss a good friend. Pray that I will be a witness for the Lord to the children at our school. 'Pray that I will declare it fearlessly, as I should,' according to the second part of Ephesians 6:20.

Pray for MKs like Nico, especially for the three things that he mentioned.

13 August

The little blind girl (a true story)

Nomhase was a little Xhosa girl who grew up in the Transkei. She was very unhappy, because she could not play with other children or go to school like them. She was blind.

When she was six years old, her mom took her to a witchdoctor to see whether he could help her. He ceremoniously threw a few dry bones on the ground and told her that the trouble with her eyes was because of an ailment of her eyelids. He treated the eyelids with all sorts of herbs, but she could still not see and the lids became infected.

Out of desperation her mom decided to take her to a hospital in Zitholele. The doctors and nurses who work there are Christians and they treated her very well, so that her eyelids healed. Then they told her about the Efata school in Umtata. It was founded by the reverend André Scheffler and it was built specially for blind and deaf children. There Nomhase could learn how to read with her fingers. Yes, the books at that school were written in braille, which meant that the letters were composed of little knobs that you can feel with your fingers. At the school Nomhase also heard about Jesus and she learned to love Him. She worked hard and in 1973 she became one of the first four students at the school who passed grade 8. The next year she went to Efata aftercare center where she was taught how to look after herself. Eventually she found work in a post office and she lived a happy, normal life.

In Mark 8:22-26 we see how much Jesus cared for a blind man. We can also help blind people by praying for schools like Efata. Can you think of something else that we can do?

Thank God for your eyesight and pray for institutions for the blind.

14 August

Being a billionaire

ohn D. Rockefeller was a billionaire. Do you know how much money you must have before you can be called a billionaire? In America you must have more than a thousand times a million dollars in the bank! Yes, he was one of the richest people who ever lived. But people who wrote books on his life, say that up to the age of 53 he was a very unhappy person. He earned more than a million dollars a week, but he wasn't healthy at all. He could only eat dry toast and drink milk and he was a lonely man, because he never had time to build any friendships.

He did not sleep well at night. One night as he was tossing and turning on his bed, a terrible thought struck him. If he should die, he would not be able to take even a single cent of all his money with him. He remembered how he had made sand castles when he was a small boy. Then the tide would come in and the water would destroy his carefully built castles. "That is exactly what will happen when I die," he realized with a shock.

The next day he went to the bank to organize a few things. He had decided to start the Rockefeller Foundation. With his money he helped poor people, schools, churches, universities and hospitals. Many books have been published about the numerous institutions that benefited from his generosity. He donated huge amounts of money to research on malaria, tuberculosis and other diseases.

And do you know what? The minute he started to distribute his money and to make friends, his health started to improve. He could sleep again, he could eat normal food and he lived to be 98 years old! He discovered the truth of the words in 2 Corinthians 9:6, *"Whoever sows generously, will reap generously."*

Read the rest of that verse in the Bible.

15 August

Beware of witchcraft

We read about Satanists in newspapers and magazines and we wonder, "Why would anybody want to pray to Satan?" Maybe his followers think that he will give them everything they ask, while God only gives us the things that He knows are good for us. These unfortunate people do not realize that nothing that they receive from Satan is free of charge and that they will have to pay a dreadful price in eternity.

People who are involved in Satanism usually became hooked gradually. They might have been curious to know more about the rituals at a Satanic meeting or about witchcraft in general and before they knew it, they were heavily involved in Satanic practices.

Some children say that they got interested while they were still quite young. The heard about "wicca" or white magic and they wanted to try it out. Some say that they had heard about magic potions with which they could put a spell on someone and harm them. Others had been to parties where they played with a Ouija board or called up spirits to answer certain questions. Yet others went to fortune tellers.

However, the Bible teaches us that we should not have anything to do with sorcery. In Leviticus 19:26 we read, *"Do not practice divination or sorcery."* God knew that if we were involved in these practices, Satan could easily get a hold over our lives.

Halloween parties might be quite innocent sometimes, but it was originally a night when people tried to make contact with the spirits of the dead, so God's children should rather do something else on that night.

Read what the Bible has to say on these matters in Deuteronomy 18:10-19.

16 August

The cheap gift

It was Sunday morning and Kylie asked her mom for money to put in the church collection plate. Her mom said, "From now on I'm not going to supply your church offering. You will have to give some of your own money." Kylie wasn't very happy about this. She didn't get that much pocket money.

The sermon of the day didn't make her feel better either. The pastor spoke about the widow who put two coins, the only ones she had, into the temple treasury. He said that it takes a real miracle to get a rich man into heaven. Did he mean that a rich man would be too fat to get through the gates of heaven?

But at home she had nicer things to think about. "Dad," she asked, "can I give you my wish list for my birthday so long?" In their home it was customary for birthday-persons to provide the rest of the family with wish lists before their birthdays. That helped them a lot when it came to choosing birthday gifts.

"Don't worry," her mom said. "You can choose something from our jumble sale box this year." Kylie could not believe her ears! "But that won't be a gift," she complained. "Then you would've given me something that didn't cost you a thing." "Well, isn't that what you give to the Lord every Sunday?" her mom asked. "You give Him collection that doesn't cost you a thing." Suddenly Kylie understood the whole business about being rich and giving offerings. The poor widow gave something that really cost her something, while rich people often give without even feeling it. She decided there and then that she wanted to give part of her own pocket money to the church.

Read about the widow's contribution in Mark 12:41-44.

17 August

What about Harry Potter?

"The kids at school are arguing about Harry Potter," Todd told his mother. "What do they say?" his mom asked. "Brenda says it comes from the devil himself. Her dad said that kids who read those books will all end up being Satanists, because they learn all about sorcery and witchcraft from Harry Potter. But Stella said that her parents have given her the whole series. They are so glad that she is at last reading something."

"What do your friends say?" Todd's mom asked. "Tim thinks we should go to the Harry Potter movie. It shows the war between good and evil and the power of good deeds. It also teaches friends to stand together. But Dan said that there is no such thing as good sorcery and bad sorcery. Witchcraft is witchcraft and the Bible says it's sin."

"Who did you agree with?" his mom wanted to know. "Well, Bill said that he can't see why there is such a to-do about Harry Potter. After all, it's just a story. In real life there isn't anything like magic potions, magic wands and spells. I agree with him. Things like that are only make-believe and anything that stimulates our imagination is good for the development of our brains, not so?"

Todd's mom smiled. "Yes, a good imagination is worth a lot. That's why I have been telling you stories ever since you could understand them. But the problem is that there really are witches, sorcery and evil spirits around. Maybe that's why Brenda's father is concerned about it. He's probably worried that kids might be caught off guard when it comes to the real stuff. If you get a chance, you should warn your friends about the reality and dangers of real witchcraft."

Read the warning about sorcery in Isaiah 47:10-15.

18 August

Holding a record

What makes someone dance 371 hours non-stop and another one tell jokes for 52 hours on end? People do these crazy things because they want to be record-holders. The craving to do something special made one man stand on his one leg for 34 hours. It inspired a youngster to blow a bubble 42 centimeters in diameter and it challenged a caddy to balance seven golf balls on top of each other! People practice for years to achieve something extraordinary so that their names can be published in *The Guiness Book of World Records.* Borrow this book from your library. You will be astonished to see what people have actually done just so that they could become famous.

The man who holds the record for talking incessantly gave a lecture on Buddhism for 159 hours without stopping. Another man was able to lick and stick 72 stamps within four minutes. And then there was a fellow who could eat 17 bananas in two minutes. Some of these achievements really seem senseless. But certain records are really worthwhile. One life guard saved 907 people from drowning! Another chap had been searching for his sister for 79 years and eventually found her. And a teacher stayed on the job and taught for 76 years. Wow!

For what would you like to be remembered? Do you want it said at your funeral that you could sit in a tree for 71 hours? Or that you could eat 21 hamburgers within 10 minutes? Or would you rather want people to say that you had meant something to them during your lifetime? Won't it be more meaningful if people could say that you helped them to come to know Jesus as their Savior?

The moral of the story? Choose goals that are worthwhile!

Read Philippians 3:10-12 to see what Paul's goals were.

19 August

Spiritual fitness

One weekend Mark attended an adventure camp that was organized by their church. When he got home, he was tired and looked scruffy, but he couldn't stop talking about all the fun they'd had. "Dad, we had a swim early in the morning and right after that an obstacle race. After lunch we did absailing and in the late afternoon a canoe race!"

"Your muscles will be sore by tomorrow," his dad warned. "Maybe," he said, "but from now on I'm going to try to stay fit. Next camp I'm not going to be one of the drop-outs again."

"And how did you like the Bible sessions?" his mom asked. "It was cool. We learned about keeping spiritually fit as well. The theme was MORE AND MORE LIKE JESUS. Our leader said that we have to practice every day to become more like Jesus." He took a notebook out of his bag. Mark looked in his notebook and told everything with great enthusiasm. "First you have to do eye exercises. You must turn your eyes away from filthy stuff. Then there's ear exercises. You should listen to the voice of God. Mouth exercises mean that you must control your tongue and hand exercises that you must do things for God. Brain exercises mean thinking wholesome thoughts and knee exercises means praying regularly."

"I'd love to have the scriptures that accompanied those lessons," his mom said. We can all do with a fitness program for our spiritual lives. Dad can put it up somewhere where we can all see it."

"All right," his dad replied, "I'll do that, provided that you see to it that our son gets himself respectable for school tomorrow."

These verses tell you how to become spiritually fit: Matthew 6:22-23; Revelation 2:7; Psalm 34:13-14; Hebrews 12:12; Philippians 4:8 and 1 Thessalonians 5:17.

20 August

Honesty

When his granddad raised his eyebrows three times in a row, Justin knew that a lecture was on its way. "Yes, Granddad?" he asked. "Do you think that stealing is wrong?" Granddad started. "Of course," he answered. "And to copy answers during tests?" "Yes!" he said emphatically. "And what about taking steroids for sport?" "Never!" Justin said. He wondered where this conversation was leading.

"Then why were you dishonest when you played soccer?" Justin turned red in the face. He didn't realize that his grandfather had been watching while they were playing on the front lawn. "But it was only a game," he protested.

"You insisted that you definitely didn't move the ball. Come here." His grandfather made him sit next to him. "Do you know how many people are in jail today just because they started being dishonest during childhood? They cheated in games and then in schoolwork and eventually in business. But eventually they were caught and brought to justice."

"Would you like us to pray about it?" his granddad asked. Justin knew that his grandpa prayed about everything. "All right," he agreed, still a bit embarrassed. His grandfather said, "Dear Lord, there are so many people in this world who are dishonest. Don't let Justin or I walk into this trap of Satan. Let us be honest in small things and in big ones."

The next day when Justin came home from school, he found a parcel on his bed. Inside was a leather belt with a card fastened to it. It said, *Remember to wear the belt of truth every day. From Grandpa.*

See where Justin's granddad got this idea from (Ephesians 6:14).

21 August

Colorblind

Cedric was colorblind. His friends often made fun of him because of this. "Hey, Cedric," they would say, "The tree that you've drawn has a green stem and red leaves and brown apples!" And when Cedric had carefully marked his pencils according to their advice, he found out that they had given him false information.

Because of his own disability, Cedric had a heart for other children who were different. That's how he and Desmond became friends. Desmond had a different skin color and the other kids avoided him. "Cedric," his classmates would then say, "just as well you're colorblind. Otherwise Desmond wouldn't have a friend!"

One day their science teacher wanted to teach them about helium. He brought a few colored balloons along. He filled them with helium and the children took bets about which balloon would reach the ceiling first. "One, two, three!" Mr. Walters counted. All the balloons rose together and bumped into the ceiling at the same time.

"What do we learn from this experiment?" their teacher asked. "That color doesn't matter!" Cedric answered immediately. "And also that the helium makes it possible for all the balloons to move at the same pace," Mr. Walters added. "What is important is not the color of the balloon, but what's inside," he said. He waited until all the kids were back at their desks and then he said seriously, "It is the same with people. The color of one's skin is not important. What is important, however, is the character inside. I have received complaints about some racism in your class. I want to remind you of what the Bible teaches us in James 2:9, *'If you show favoritism, you sin and are convicted by the law.'* We should all be colorblind when it comes to judging people."

Read Acts 17:26.

22 August

Are you a snob?

Have you ever said, "I'm glad I'm not as ugly as that guy," or, "I'd rather die than drive around in a ramshackle car like that." Or, "He can't join our club because his dad is a drunkard!" Then you are probably a snob and you should know that God is not happy with your thoughts and deeds. Read Romans 12:3, Galatians 6:3 and Psalm 138:6. What do these Scripture verses teach us?

The Bible says that we should not be proud. God wants us to be humble. Jesus was the most humble person who ever lived. He, who was the most important among men, was prepared to wash the dirty feet of His disciples.

God does not want His children to belong to a clique of people who exclude the disadvantaged or anybody who is "different". He doesn't want us to brag about the things that we have received or achieved. Of course there's nothing wrong with being glad when your team has won a match or two. And it is also right to be grateful for the talents that God has given you. But to insist on V.I.P treatment and to look down on others because you think that you are better than them, only shows that you lack the love of Jesus in your heart.

A matron once wrote an article on her experiences in a boarding school. She recorded an incident about a little boy who said to her at the beginning of the year, "Miss, if there's a room in the hostel that nobody wants, you can put me there." He was the son of a rich and well-known statesman who could have insisted on having the best sleeping quarters available. She said that the memory of that incident helped her stay humble for the rest of her life.

Pray that God will show you when you are snobbish and ask Him to teach you humility.

23 August

Enough faith

Aunt Ethel came to visit her sister and the Ryan children were very excited. Their aunt had a book of missionary stories from which she could tell the most interesting tales. Especially when their dad made a fire in the fireplace and they sat on the carpet at their aunt's feet … then a story went down very well indeed!

The Saturday night of her visit was exactly such a night, with the wind howling outside and the whole family snugly in the lounge.

Aunt Ethel started, "Tonight I want to tell you about Hudson Taylor." The children already knew that he was one of the first missionaries to China. They had often heard stories about him, how he fearlessly went into the foreign country, trusting God. He believed that God had called him for this mission, and that, as long as God wanted to use him, he would be safe.

"Well, tonight's story is about the time he was on his way to China in a sailboat. They were in the doldrums because there was no wind to carry their ship forward. The ship floated about aimlessly. Not far away was an island that was inhabited by cannibals. If the ship should be stranded on that shore, they would certainly be caught and eaten! The captain of the ship said, 'Mr. Taylor, you will have to pray for us.' 'I will do that,' said Hudson. 'But you will have to set the sails!' The captain set the sails as if a mighty wind was on its way. When the sails were set, Hudson prayed and God sent a fresh wind to take them away from the dangerous island."

"Wow! That man must've had a mighty faith," said Iris. "Oh no," her aunt corrected her. "What he had was a normal portion of faith in an almighty God!"

Look up Luke 17:6 to see how big your faith needs to be.

24 August

On safari

Eric and his family were visiting an uncle who had a farm in Mpumalanga. During the day they went out on safari to look for wild animals and at night they sat around a fire near their *rondavel*. Then they could hear the sounds of the bush, even lions roaring. In the mornings they woke up to bird song.

Sometimes baboons would come right up to the fence, but Eric's uncle said that they shouldn't feed them. Wild animals get lazy and spoiled when they got fed and they soon forgot the secrets of fending for themselves.

Eric hated to see the small baboons with pleading eyes. He wished that he could give them something to eat. But his dad said, "Rather sit tight and ignore the little beasts. If you really care for them, you will not feed them now."

One thing that spoiled the holidays, was a science project that Eric had to bring along to finish before the new school term started. One afternoon when he was really fed-up with it, Eric said, "Dad, please help me with this stuff." His dad looked up from the book that he was reading. He winked at Eric. "I'll also have to sit tight," he said. "If I help you now, you will never learn to complete a task like that on your own."

After a while his dad said, "You know, I think that sometimes the Lord also allows us to struggle before He helps us! That way we learn a lot." Eric remembered the time when he had to help his dad in his office to earn enough money to buy a mountain bike. He sure learned a lot during that time. If the bike had fallen out of the sky after he had prayed for it, he would not have learned how to use a computer.

See why Eric's dad read Colossians 1:9-11 to him that night.

25 August

Banned from the garden

Gillian was playing with Bert, her little brother. She liked to tell him Bible stories. She wanted to be a Sunday school teacher one day. "Adam and Eve lived in a beautiful garden," she started. "They were very happy there. They had lots of fruit, vegetables and nuts to eat. But God said, 'You may not eat of the fruit in the middle of the garden!' But the snake came along and said to Eve, 'I hear that you are not allowed to eat the fruit from the tree in the middle of the garden.' 'Yes,' Eve answered. 'God said that we will die if we eat it.' 'That's not true,' said the snake. 'God doesn't want you to eat that fruit, because then you will be too clever!'

"So Eve tasted the fruit and she also gave some to Adam. When they had eaten it, they immediately knew that they had done something wrong and they were ashamed. When God came to visit them, they hid behind some trees. God called, 'Where are you?' When they came out of the bush, He banned them from the beautiful garden. From that day on they had to work very hard. The sweat ran from their bodies and they were very unhappy."

Bert started to cry. Gillian didn't know how to console him. Luckily her mom had heard everything and came to pick the little boy up. "Don't cry, dear," she said. "On the same day when God banned Adam and Eve from the garden, He promised to send Someone who would make everything right again. That's why Jesus came. He paid for the sin of Adam and Eve and also for our sins on the cross. So one day it will again be possible for us to live with God in the beautiful garden." Bert's little face lit up and he wiped the tears from his face with both hands.

Read Revelation 2:7.

26 August

Cruel people

Are you scared of anybody? Not a burglar or a criminal, but somebody you often have to spend time with? It could be a teacher who is unreasonable or an uncle who humiliates you. It could also be someone who bullies you at school or who spreads lies about you …

Two passages in the Bible might help you in this regard. First read Luke 12:4-7. Do you realize that God knows everything about you and that He wants to protect you?

Then read Psalm 56:11. There David says, *"In God I trust; I will not be afraid. What can man do to me?"* Remember, David had many enemies and he even had to defend himself against bears and other wild animals when he was a shepherd. Yet he could say, "I will fear no evil, for you are with me."

You should talk about your fears to someone you trust. If somebody is molesting you or misusing you in any other way, you should seek help from your parents or any other grown-up person whom you trust. God can use one of them to help you.

Sometimes one has reason to be scared. Did you know that even Jesus was scared about what people would do to Him? In Gethsemane His sweat fell like drops of blood to the ground out of sheer agony over the prospect of what men would do to Him. He knew that they would scorn Him and hit Him and nail Him to a cross. Therefore, if you talk to Jesus about your fears, He will fully understand. And what's more, He'll send His angels, saying, "Go quickly! Go and help My child."

Talk to Jesus about people who scare you and do as Matthew 5:44 says. Pray for those who want to harm you.

27 August

The six pear trees

A man once went to his orchard to see how his six new pear trees were doing. To his disappointment they looked rather withered and wilted. So he asked the first tree, "What's wrong?" "I've been planted in the wrong place," said the tree. "I get too much sunshine here." "And what's wrong with you?" he asked the second tree. "I grew from the seed of a no-good pear tree," he said. "I will never be successful." "And what is your complaint?" he asked the third tree. "There are too many trees in this orchard," he said. "There's not enough water and food for all of us." When he asked the fourth tree the same question, there was no reply. The tree had already died. The farmer dug it out and threw it away.

Before the farmer could say anything to the fifth tree, it started talking, "If I keep on pushing my roots deeper into the soil for water and if I keep on sending my branches up into the air, I will become a big, strong tree." "Good luck to you," said the farmer as he moved on towards the sixth tree. "What's your problem?" he asked. "I need water," said the tree. "There's not a drop nearby. Will you please water me regularly so that I can grow and bear fruit?"

The farmer listened to the plight of the last tree and brought him some water every day. It became a huge pear tree from which his owner could pick lovely juicy pears.

People are often like these pear trees. Some people who suffer, blame others for their misfortune. Some lose heart. Others try to manage on their own. However, it is only the ones who realize that they need God who are truly successful. Jesus said in John 15:5, *"Apart from me you can do nothing."*

Think about this story. Which tree do you resemble?

28 August

Being scared of the future

During their English oral class the sixth graders were asked to talk about the future. Each of them had a turn to say what he or she thought the world would be like in twenty years' time. A few interesting views were expressed. Peter said that there would be no telephones. "People will be virtually connected to each other," he said. "What does that mean?" asked Steve. "It means that when I talk to you, even though we are far apart, I will appear right before your eyes." The girls shuddered at the thought. When it was Don's turn, he predicted that people will be living on Mars and that it will be possible to go for a holiday on one of the planets. Two other boys believed that bicycles would be completely out of fashion. Instead a conveyer belt would be set up in all major cities to transport people from one place to another.

Some children painted grim pictures of the future. Valerie said that there might not be enough food and water for everybody. Gertrude envisioned a world that had gone back to the ice-age and that many people would freeze to death.

Here and there someone came up with a more promising idea. Yasmin said, "People will have learned to live together peacefully. There won't be any more wars!"

Iris was the one who made everybody sit up straight. "In twenty years' time there won't be an earth any more! The world will have gone up in smoke and we will all be dead," she said.

Their teacher said that her thoughts were way too grim. He encouraged them to read Psalm 46. "Whatever the future holds," he said, "God's children need never be afraid."

Tell Jesus if you are scared about the future and ask Him to help you trust God.

29 August

Try a chain of hugs

Nicola came home in a terrible frame of mind. She kicked the cat out of the way and answered gruffly when her younger brother wanted to play. Her mom did not allow such rudeness. She ordered her to go to her room until she felt better. Later on her mom went to her. "Who made you angry?" she asked. "How did you know?" Nicola asked with surprise. Her mom smiled. "Let me tell you a story," she said. "There once was a man who got bitten by a mad dog. You probably know that a dog gets this disease from another mad dog that has bitten him. A whole chain of the sickness is then spread from one victim to another.

"When the man realized that he had contracted this deadly disease, he grabbed a pen and paper and started to write. His wife thought that he was writing his last message. 'Darling,' she said. 'let's rather go to a doctor. He might still heal you.' 'I'm not writing my will,' he said. 'I'm making a list of people whom I'm going to bite!'"

Nicola couldn't help smiling at this story. Her mother continued, "I gather that somebody at school hurt your feelings and now you are taking it out on the cat and on all of us. That's not how Jesus taught us. He said in John 15:12: *'Love each other as I have loved you.'* Jesus has the right medicine for your ill feelings. He loves you very much and He wants His chain of love to be stronger than Satan's chain of hatred. So, don't bite when somebody rubs you up the wrong way. Do something quite different. Sit down and make a list of people whom you want to hug!"

"It won't be easy, but I'll try," Nicola said, hugging her mom.

Remember this advice next time someone makes you cross.

30 August

Don't be a vidiot!

Do you know what an idiot is? It is somebody who does something without thinking about it. Well, to be a vidiot is almost the same. It is someone who watches videos without thinking what he is doing. Remember, children of the living God do not simply do the things that they feel like doing. They do what the Bible prescribes for them to do. Of course there weren't cameras or television sets or video machines in the days when the Bible was written. But Jesus said that if our eye causes us to sin, we should gouge it out and throw it away. This means that if a certain video or film could pollute our minds, we should leave it.

A lot can be said in favor of videos and films. One can learn a lot by watching some of them and it is a relatively cheap type of entertainment. However, if the film is interspersed with bad language, intimate sex scenes and violent crimes, we should have the guts to turn it off or leave. If you've hired the video, you should take it back. The money that you might lose, costs far less than the damage that could be done to your thought life.

There will always be children who don't care about the age restriction on certain films and the video shop owner often doesn't care. But you should be prepared to explain your point of view to friends who insist that you join them in doing something that makes you feel uncomfortable. Practice to say NO. You can even do it in front of a mirror. Say, "I don't like that type of film." Or, "I don't feel like watching this."

We should love the Lord enough to say under the heaviest social pressure, "No! I won't do it because I'm a Christian!"

Read in 1 Thessalonians 4:7-8 how God wants us to live.

31 August

SEPTEMBER

Remember Daniel

Some people think that everything will be smooth and easy once they're Christians. But the truth is that when you're a Christian, you will still have trouble like everyone else. You might even have more than the normal load of problems, precisely because you're a child of God.

Read the sixth chapter of Daniel if you want to see how bad things can get for somebody who wants to obey God. Since childhood Daniel had been taught that he should not pray to any other God. It was the first commandment that Jewish boys had to learn. So, when King Darius made a law that forced everybody to pray to him, Daniel refused to do so. Although he knew full well that he could be fed to hungry lions for disobeying the king's order, he still knelt in front of his window three times a day to pray to the living God. For that he was thrown into the lions' den.

However, the next morning, when the king went to the lions' den, a real surprise awaited him. "Has your God, whom you serve continually, been able to rescue you from the lions?" he asked. And he received an answer. "My God sent His angel, and he shut the mouths of the lions. They have not hurt me, for I was innocent in His sight." After that the king issued a decree that in his kingdom all people had to fear and revere the God of Daniel.

Remember Daniel when people who do not fear God scorn you for being obedient to Him. You might influence others by your commitment. God is with His children in a very special way when they have to suffer for His sake.

Ask God to make you His faithful follower, even in the face of hostility.

1 September

Healthy habits

Gail's parents were very strict about what she ate and drank. She was not allowed to eat any sweets, because they were bad for her teeth. She had to eat lots of fresh fruit and vegetables and she never had white bread in her lunch box. She had to drink lots of water. The result was that Gail was healthy and always full of energy.

Frank's parents didn't worry about his eating habits. Sometimes he even had chocolates for breakfast! They enjoyed fast foods and Frank's favorite food was French fries with soda. But Frank was lazy and inattentive in class. He lacked energy and wasn't interested in sporting activities. It took too much effort, he said.

What do you think, whose parents did the right thing? Surely it was the parents who cared for their child's health, not so?

Maybe that's also the reason why your parents are strict about the kind of spiritual food that you consume. If you never read a good book, but spend all your time watching shallow television shows, or hang around with friends who do not love the Lord, then you will not become spiritually strong and healthy.

You have a responsibility towards your body, because it is God's temple. But you also have a responsibility towards your spirit. Therefore you must guard your eyes and ears so that nothing can enter that will be harmful. You must also keep your mind clean and healthy by reading good books and choosing friends who will help you to stay in God's will.

Proverbs 4:23 gives this good advice: *"Above all else, guard your heart, for it is the wellspring of life."* This means that you must love the things that are wholesome and good for your body and soul.

Make a poster for your room with photographs of sports heroes on it. Write Proverbs 4:23 underneath.

2 September

The newcomer

In the Calder home things would never be the same again because a new baby had been born! Mealtimes, which always used to be strictly on time, now shifted to irregular time-slots in order to accommodate the baby's many needs. Some mornings Fred, the eldest son, had to iron his own shirt for college and all the children had to prepare their own sandwiches for school. Not to mention the nights! The baby girl could cry for hours on end. So much so, that their dad often practiced his golf putting on the lounge carpet, when sleeping was impossible.

One afternoon Katy couldn't keep quiet any longer. "You love the baby more than us!" she cried. "She can just whimper and she will have your full attention. And what about us? We must fend for ourselves." Her mom tried to put her arms around Katy, but she wriggled herself loose. She was fed-up with the whole new set-up and she wasn't in the mood for hugging.

"Let's talk about this," her mom said. "You know, there was a time when you were the baby in the house and we all had to adjust to your whims. I can still remember how depressed even our puppy was because we often neglected him for your sake. It was during that time Tony had to start making his own bed, because he wasn't the baby of the family any more and Ellen started making the breakfast porridge every morning."

Suddenly Katy's face lit up. "It's like climbing a ladder!" she exclaimed. "When a new member arrives, the rest must all move up one step." "Yes," her mom said with a smile. "And at each new level the Lord is there to help us with our new responsibilities."

Read 1 Corinthians 13:4-7 to see what our attitude towards other family members should be.

3 September

A winning team

Brett had been to a leadership seminar and when he came back, he put up some colored strips in his bedroom. On them he wrote in big bold letters:

> I AM A WINNER!   I CAN DO ANYTHING!
>
> I'M IN CHARGE OF MY OWN LIFE!
>
> I'M ON MY WAY TO A BIG FUTURE!

Proudly he went to fetch his father to come and have a look. His dad said with a shiver, "Wow! All these positive vibes tickle me." "That's exactly what the seminar speaker said," Brett said with enthusiasm. "We should do and say things that send out positive energy. Mr. Goodman said that we should stand in front of our mirrors every morning and say all these things to ourselves." Brett pointed to the various slogans on the wall. "Within a month these attitudes will be part of our thinking and we will never again have negative feelings towards ourselves. In this way we can become real leaders, because people admire people who admire themselves."

Brett's dad went to sit on the window-seat. "Where does God come into the picture?" he asked seriously. "Oh, He will help us if we ask Him," Brett said. His dad answered, "The speaker at the seminar was right. Anybody can be a leader in the eyes of men. He only needs to do the things that others are too lazy or too timid to do. But if you want to be a leader in God's sight, you should remember that you can't do anything without Him. If I were you, I would write next to every 'I' on these placards, 'Jesus and I.'" "Not a bad idea!" Brett said and picked up his marker for a few alterations.

Learn Philippians 4:13 by heart.

4 September

The lady in the caravan

There were lots of fun activities and numerous stalls at the annual community fair. The Grant family drove in from the farm to enjoy the festivities. The children each received some spending money from their dad. While their dad visited the gymkhana, mom took Billy to the merry-go-round. Derrick tried his skill at target shooting and Fiona had her face painted like a clown. Popcorn and candy-floss were the favorite snacks.

"What did you do?" Fiona asked her younger sister on the way home. Debbie was lying on the back seat of the car, staring with dreamy eyes at the stars. "I visited Madame Kay," she said. "What!" her mom exclaimed. "You visited a fortune-teller?" "Yes," Debbie answered. "And she said that I will marry a handsome guy who will be rich and famous." "How can she tell?" Derrick wanted to know. "She looked at my hands, and then she predicted my future."

When they got home, Mr. Grant called the whole family together. "I realize tonight that there is something that we as parents have forgotten to teach you. That's why I can't punish Debbie for visiting the fortune-teller. However, I am going to explain something to you now and afterwards I hope that none of you will ever waste your money on something like that again. People who want to tell you what the future has in store for you, are only interested in your money. Leaves in tea-cups, crystal balls and playing cards can't determine the future. The fact that some predictions work out, is nothing more than coincidence. And furthermore, God forbids us to have anything to do with things like that. He wants us to trust in Him alone."

See what happened to people who were superstitious and believed in divination in Isaiah 2:6-9.

5 September

Lonely?

Mary and her family had moved to a new city and during the first school holidays after the move, her grandmother came to visit them. Mary was very fond of her granny. Grandma never bought them expensive gifts like scooters or roller blades, but she could make the most scrumptious oatmeal cookies. She helped her brother when he built model planes and she had also taught them to play chess. Her granny always had time to listen to her stories and she often read to them from the Children's Bible.

"How do you like the kids at your new school?" her grandma asked one morning while they were busy cleaning up the kitchen. Mary did not answer immediately. She was busy with the garbage bag. Then she said, "I have no friends here, Grandma." "Why not?" her grandmother asked. "I don't know. Nobody wants to talk to me." "And do you talk to them?" "Not really. What if they think I'm a nuisance. What if they don't like me. What if they make fun of me." "Oh no!" Grandma said. "Take all those 'what-ifs' and put them in the trash can together with the garbage. Now listen to me. If you want friends, you must be friendly. Maybe you are too stingy with that lovely smile of yours! When school starts again next term, you must try to have a friendly talk with at least three people a day. Then tell me what happened."

A month later Mary's grandmother received a telephone call at Green Pastures, where she lived. "Gran, it's Mary! I just phoned to tell you that it worked. I have two friends here with me and I am teaching them how to make oatmeal cookies. Thanks for the good advice!" she said. "Thank You, Jesus," Gran said softly.

Choose seven words from Ephesians 4:32 that match Grandma's advice.

6 September

Jesus is with you

Ryan had leukemia. This is a disease from which one can die. He had been in hospital for a few weeks already, but his condition was getting worse. His classmates had made him a card on which they had all written their names. On the card was also a picture of a shepherd who was carrying a little lamb. A verse from Psalm 23 was printed on it. The nursing sister had put the card up against the wall of his ward and told him to look at the card each day.

His parents took turns to come to him every night and on weekends his younger brother also came to visit him. One evening, when it was his father's turn to come, his little dog Scamp came along. Of course he wasn't allowed to come into Ryan's room, but Ryan could hear him sniffing and whining at the door. Ryan wished that he could feel his doggy's warm body against him once more and feel him licking his ears like he always did.

"Dad," he asked unexpectedly, "what will heaven be like?" His father wasn't sure how to answer that question. "We don't know much about heaven," he said. After thinking for a while, he got a bright idea. He said, "Scamp has never been to see you in hospital, but he is very keen to come in. It is because I'm here and he knows me and trusts me. We don't know what will be waiting for us in heaven, but we do know that Jesus is there. He loves us and we can fully rely on Him!"

"Even though I walk through the valley of the shadow of death, I will fear no evil, for you are with me," Ryan was reading these words from the card on the wall. A big tear ran down his father's cheek.

Sing any hymn that you know that is based on the words of Psalm 23.

7 September

Stepfamily

Do you belong to a 'try-again family'? In other words, did one of your parents marry for the second time? Then you have a stepfather or a stepmother. Today there are many families that have been reconstructed as a result of remarriage and it would be silly to assume that step-parents are vicious and unreasonable like the ones in *Hansel and Gretel* or *Cinderella*.

Some people talk about an instant family, because the members of this type of family didn't have a chance to get to know each other like in a normal family. Suddenly you must obey someone whom you've never even known before and you might have acquired a new brother and sister as well. Things can become really tricky if both your parents married again after their divorce. To have four parents and eight grandparents must be pretty complicated. And you are expected to live in harmony with all these people. Talk about being thrown in the deep end!

Maybe you feel unhappy about the fact that your mom or dad has fallen in love with someone new. Maybe you miss your mom or dad. It would help if you could bear in mind that the new situation is also difficult for your new parent.

Try never to say, "My mom (or dad) wouldn't do that!" Try to notice the things that your new parent is doing for you and show him or her that you appreciate it. You will be surprised to see what a magic phrase "thank you" can be.

Paul once said, *"I have learned to be content whatever the circumstances"* (Philippians 4:11). He could make the best of any situation: good or bad. Of course he could never manage that on his own. He had God as his helper. He can be your helper too.

Read Psalm 55:16-18.

8 September

How to become part of God's family

A neighbor had sent lovely flowers to Nan's grandmother. "Aren't they beautiful!" Nan exclaimed. "Mrs. Norman is the sweetest person I know. I'm sure she's going straight to heaven one day." Her grandmother was arranging the flowers in a glass bowl. "Why do you say that?" she asked. "Because she is so good to us. She gives us lots of presents and she works hard for the Red Cross."

"Yes," Grandma replied, "I also think that she is a very kind person. But I am praying for her. She once told me that she does not believe in Jesus Christ. Good works can never get us to heaven. Only Jesus can."

"But Granny, she lives a better life than a lot of Christians I know." "I know," her grandmother admitted. "What a pity that is. We Christians should be the most generous and lovely people imaginable. However, even if we were wonderful people, we could never earn a ticket to heaven. Only if we know Jesus as our Savior, can we hope to be with God in heaven one day. Mrs. Norman, you and I and all the people in our church are still far from being holy enough to be admitted to heaven. Jesus even told Nicodemus, who was a faithful member of the church of those days, that he would have to be born again if he wanted to have everlasting life."

"Tell me about being born again," Nan asked. "Well," Grandma said, "it happens when you ask God to adopt you as one of His children. If you say that you are sorry about your sin and that you are glad that He bore the punishment for it, then you become His child." "Wow, Grandma, that means that you and I are doubly related. We are both Smiths and we both belong to God's family."

Read how Jesus and Nicodemus talked about this same subject in John 3:1-16.

9 September

God knows best

It was Sunday night and various people were busy praying. Percy was lying on his bed, his eyes closed tightly, saying, "Please, Lord, don't let it rain tomorrow. You know that we have a class outing to Walker Bay. If it rains, it will be a total disaster."

A farmer stood in front of his house and scanned the sky where there wasn't a cloud in sight. "God Almighty," he prayed with his eyes wide open, "if it doesn't rain by tomorrow, there will be no harvest this year. The seedlings that sprouted so beautifully, are now withering without water."

Mrs. Davids knelt at her bedside and prayed vigorously, "God, have mercy on us. Let there be sunshine tomorrow. Everything has been arranged for the garden party. We won't know what to do if it should rain. You know how much we need the money from the function for the orphanage. We can only trust in You!"

A few miles from the shore a boat was drifting aimlessly with two men on board. They had lost their oars in a storm during the previous night. "Dear heavenly Father, won't you send rain, please. The drops will supply us with enough water to keep us alive until the tide can take us back to shore."

What do you think, whose prayer should be answered? Can you see why some of your fervent prayers cannot be answered? God knows about all our needs and He knows what is best for each one of us. We must trust Him to do what is best. That doesn't mean that we shouldn't ask Him for things like good weather conditions. We can take all our requests to Him. He will take everything into account. However, if for some reason or other, He cannot give you what you ask, He will come to your aid in some other way.

Read Philippians 4:19.

10 September

A bad decision

Danny didn't feel like going to school. He wanted to go fishing. "Why not? What does one day matter? It's such a beautiful day," he said to himself. He put on his school uniform, but stuck a T-shirt and a pair of jeans in his satchel. In the kitchen he grabbed a piece of bread for bait.

At the turn-off opposite the park he took the road to the dam. He forgot all about his dad's warning not to go there on his own. Donald and he often went fishing there and they had a special hiding place for their rods. He took out his fishing gear and settled on the rocks amongst the reeds.

Time flew. Every now and then he smiled when he thought of the rest of the children in school. He didn't catch any fish, but he loved watching the wild birds on the dam.

Suddenly he heard a movement in the bushes behind him. When he turned around, he saw an ugly, dirty face peering through the leaves. He grabbed his stuff and ran away as fast as he could. He was completely out of breath when he reached the park. There he saw Donald on his bicycle. "Where were you today?" Donald asked. "You really missed something! Your hero Michael Jordan was visiting the school today and he talked to the whole school. We all got his autograph!"

At home Danny sneaked to his room. He sat on his bed, feeling miserable. He should rather have gone to school that morning. Now he had lost a fishing rod and he had missed the chance of a life-time. He went up to his calender and drew a red circle around that day's date. "That will remind me never to do such a stupid thing again," he said to himself.

Read Solomon's advice in Proverbs 2:1-15.

11 September

Rules! Rules! Rules!

Mabel was busy with a pair of scissors and glue. Their youth-group were going on a camp and she was making a poster to put up in the foyer at the church, so that more kids would want to attend. Her baby sister came toddling along. "Mine!" she said, as she always did when she wanted to help, and with that she grabbed the pair of scissors. "No!" Mabel said, and took it from her. "You will get hurt." The little one cried bitterly and went over to her brother Chris, who was sitting in a corner, reading.

Mabel felt like complaining. "You know what?" she said. "Gerald had a whole sheet of rules printed out for the camp. Imagine! 'Nobody will be allowed to leave the camp site without permission!' 'No talking after lights-out!' 'No radios or CD-players!' Who wants to go on a camp with so many restrictions?"

Chris had been to lots of camps. He smiled. "I know how you feel, Sis!" he said. "But a camp without rules is much worse than the strictest army camp. With such a big group of people, things would be chaotic without rules. If all thirty campers were allowed to come and go as they wished, do what they wanted to, and went to bed when they felt like it, nothing would come of all the good plans that you have for the weekend."

Mabel thought about this for a while. "Maybe that's why God made rules for His children as well," she realized. If we could do as we pleased, nothing would come of the good plans that He has for our lives. We often say "Mine!" as her little sister did, but then the Lord takes the scissors from our hands because He has seen the danger signs.

Read Romans 13:1.

12 September

Are you a rocket-Christian?

The preacher had a target next to him on the stage while he was addressing the children of the congregation. He gave a piece of paper to ten of the kids and told them to fold a paper jet with it. Then each one of them had a chance to try and hit the target. Some of them made really cute aero-jets, but none of them could hit the target. A jet would float neatly in the right direction, but just before it came to the target, it would swerve away. The preacher reminded all the children that a paper jet was really no match for a rocket! He said that Jesus' followers should all be rocket-Christians instead of paper jet-Christians.

Do you know what the difference is? Yes, a paper jet has no power from within, while a rocket has built-in power! (Maybe you can think of some more differences.) If you want to be a Christian who is right on target, you should allow the Holy Spirit to fill you with His power. As long as you try to be good in your own strength, you will go off track. All your beautiful intentions will not work out. You will aim at being faithful with schoolwork, but you will find that you don't succeed. You will try not to lose your temper, but will fail dismally when somebody provokes you. Maybe you have sworn an oath on the Bible that you will never swear again. But before long, you find that you have used bad language.

Don't despair! The Holy Spirit will help you and give you the power and strength you need to live a Christian life.

Read Romans 5:3-5. Thank God for the Holy Spirit.

13 September

Be a magnet for the Lord!

Have you ever seen how a magnet can attract a metal object? When a magnet gets near a nail, it grabs hold of the nail and the nail clings to it. One then really has to use force to get it loose again. If the nail has been clinging to the magnet long enough, the nail itself becomes a magnet. It is then able to pick up other nails. However, if it loses contact with the magnet for a while, it loses its ability to attract other pieces of metal.

When Jesus was on earth, He once said to His disciples, *"But I, when I am lifted up from the earth, will draw all men to myself"* (John 12:32). Since then Jesus has attracted people from all over the world to Himself. On the cross He demonstrated how much He loved them. People who were tired of their sinful lives found Him irresistable. They were drawn by His love and mercy and they took hold of Him for relief from guilt and sin. That is why many people today are clinging to Him like metal objects to a magnet.

But Jesus wants to use these people to draw others to Him. He wants His followers to radiate love and joy so that more unbelievers can be attracted to Him. Therefore, like nails that have been saturated with magnetic power, we should live in unity with Christ so that we will have enough power to draw people to Him. We should stay close to Him through regular prayer and Bible study and we should never allow wrong habits or indifferent people to come between us and our Magnet.

Try to get hold of a magnet and a few nails. See how long it takes for a nail to lose its magnetic power after it has been separated from the magnet.

14 September

Your name on a planet

How would you like to have your name written on a planet? The American spaceship, *The Cassini*, took a DVD-disc with 600 000 names of people from 80 different countries to Saturn. And people in Japan are spending thousands of yen to have their names engraved on a metal plate that will be taken to Mars when the first Japanese satellite is launched.

Maybe you don't want to spend your money on something like that. But wouldn't you like to have your name written in a book that is kept in heaven? In Revelation 21 you can read about a new heaven and a new earth where all of God's children will one day live forever. But, according to verse 27, only those people whose names are written in the Book of Life will go and live there.

Is your name in that book? If you believe that Jesus Christ paid for all your sins on the cross and if you are one of His followers, then your name is already written in that book! Then you will one day live in the New Jerusalem. We don't know much about that heavenly city, but here is a description that is given in Revelation 21:3: *"Now the dwelling of God is with men, and he will live with them. They will be his people, and God himself will be with them and be their God. He will wipe every tear from their eyes. There will be no more death or mourning or crying or pain, for the old order of things has passed away."* That sure sounds like a wonderful place, doesn't it?

Make a list of the things that you would like to have in heaven and then look at 1 Corinthians 2:9. It seems as if all our best wishes will one day be granted to us if our names are in God's book!

15 September

Bible stories

"Holidays, here we come!" Paul shouted as they left home on their way to their grandparents' farm. The road was long and tiresome, so their mom came up with an idea. She asked, "Which Bible story do you like best?" Paul replied immediately, "Daniel in the lions' den." "Why?" his dad asked. "It teaches us that God always takes care of us." "The story of David and Goliath is my favorite." Johnny said. "The giant could do nothing against David, since the Lord was on his side." Beth said, "I like Esther. She was lovely and she did lovely things."

Then Paul spoke again, "We know which is your favorite story, Mom. You like Ruth's story because your name is Ruth!" He turned to his dad. "And you, Dad?" His dad thought for a while. "I think Job is the most inspiring character. He stayed true to God, even when things went horribly wrong."

Their mother gave each one an apple and then tried something else that could shorten the trip. "Who can remember anything from the days before they went to school?" she asked. The children could think of very few incidents. Their parents of even fewer.

"That's funny," Paul commented. "Things that happened to us are soon forgotten, but the things that happened in Bible times are remembered for ages." "Yes," replied his dad. "That's because God saw to it that the history of His dealings with people were properly written down in the Bible and then He preserved it through the ages. He wanted us to know Him better through those stories."

Paul, Beth and Johnny looked forward to the holidays even more. They knew that Grandpa would read stories to them from the Children's Bible every night before they went to bed.

Read Isaiah 46:9.

16 September

Have you ever eaten tears?

In his book *Church, Why Bother?* Philip Yancey tells how he regularly visited children's wards in hospital. There were children who had cancer, others who were badly burned and some who had been in serious car accidents. In the beginning he dreaded going there, because it was awful to see little children suffering. However, certain verses from the Bible, like 1 John 3:18, encouraged him to go every week. He realized that it wasn't worth anything just to feel sorry for those kids. He had to go and visit them and try to cheer them up. So he asked his wife to make him a colorful clown's outfit out of red and green material. He also bought a red plastic nose and enormous shoes with turned-up toes to wear when he went to the hospital.

During his visits he played with the kids and made them laugh. He talked about Jesus to the ones who were hurting and he demonstrated Jesus' love to all of them by being loving and kind.

Later on he developed the habit of buying popcorn on his way there. The children loved it when he shared it out among them. Sometimes he would come across a little fellow who was crying because he was homesick, or scared before an operation. Then Mr. Yancey would take a piece of popcorn and mop up the tears with it. After that he would put the popcorn, salted with tears, in his mouth and chew it. It made the little ones smile. "He's eating tears!" they would say.

God expects us to eat people's tears. This means that we should not only feel sorry for suffering people, but we should also help them feel better.

Read 1 John 3:18 and think of what you could do to make things easier for someone who is having a difficult time.

17 September

Who says?

Peter couldn't wait for his dad to come home. At school a man had given a lecture on world religions. He stated that all religions were equal. "Practicing religion is like climbing a mountain," he said. "Everybody wants to get to the top, but there are many paths that will lead you there. Whether you are Christian, Buddhist, Hindu or Muslim, it's all the same. Your religion will help you to live a good life. Therefore none of you should think that your religion is better than that of another." Peter was curious to know what his dad would say about that.

When his dad had settled down with a cup of coffee and the newspaper, Peter told him everything. His dad stayed calm. "Well," he said, "that's not what Jesus taught us. Jesus said that there is only one way to get to God the Father, and that is through Him. You can read that in John 14:6."

"But how do we know that Jesus was right?" Peter asked with concern. His dad sounded reassuring, "It's clear from Scripture that He certainly wasn't a liar. And He definitely never acted like someone who was insane. So what He said must be the truth."

"But are you sure that He really existed?" Peter asked. "There are children at school who say that Jesus is a made-up story." "That's not true!" his dad said with certainty. "The Bible isn't the only book that tells about Jesus. Other history books have similar accounts of His life to those in the Bible. However, I do agree with one thing that the lecturer said. We should never look down on people of different faith. We should show them the truth of our beliefs by our lives."

Read John 18:37.

18 September

You can make a difference!

An athlete went for an early morning sprint along the beach. He noticed that the tide had brought thousands of fish ashore. Some were still struggling, while others had already died. An old man was moving amongst them, bending down every now and then to pick up one of the fish. Then he would throw it back into the sea.

The athlete stood still for a while to catch his breath. "Old man," he said, "do you really think that your method of saving one fish at a time will make any difference to the thousands of fish that are lying here?" The old man looked the younger one straight in the eye and then picked up yet another fish. "No," he said, "but it will make a difference to this one!" With those words he threw the fish into the ocean.

Some people think that there are too many poor and struggling people on earth to try to do something about it. "What difference would my small contribution make?" they say. You could give a blanket to the supervisor at the night shelter so that he can give a homeless person a bed to sleep in. You could give a sandwich to a child at school who is hungry. You could start a friendly conversation with a lonely person in your neighborhood. And you could pray for a lost person in your family.

Proverbs 3:27 says, *"Do not withhold good from those who deserve it, when it is in your power to act. Do not say to your neighbor, 'Come back later; I'll give it tomorrow' – when you now have it with you."* Surely that also means that you should not think that you are too young to make a difference in the lives of other people.

Underline Proverbs 3:27 in your Bible.

19 September

Guess what!

There were still fifteen minutes left before the bell and Miss Smith said that the children could ask one another riddles. A lot of hands went up. Each child had a riddle to puzzle his friends with. "What did the one curtain say to the other?" Peter asked. Nobody knew. "We didn't commit murder so what are we hanging for?" The kids laughed.

"What is the greatest sign of stupidity?" Betty asked. There were many guesses. But Betty said, "To plant macaroni and wait for the holes to come up!"

Then Miss Smith asked, "What has four legs first, then two legs and finally three legs?" The kids were puzzled. "A baby, a young man and an old man using a stick," chuckled Miss Smith.

Now Bert stood up. He was the son of the local pastor. "Guess what?" he said. "There is something that God can't do. What is it?" The children frowned over this catchy question. "There's nothing that He can't do," Gillian said after a while, "because He is almighty." Brainy Steve jumped up. "I know!" he said. "He can't make a stone that's too heavy for Him to pick up." Everybody applauded Steve for that clever answer. "He can't sin either," said Anna. However, Bert wasn't satisfied with their answers. He was thinking of something that his dad had said in church on the previous Sunday. He was glad that he could share it with his friends. "God can't pardon sin unless it has been paid for," he said seriously. "It is against His nature. That's why Jesus had to pay for our sins on the cross."

It became very quiet in the classroom. Miss Smith added, "He can also not break any of His promises. He said that those who believe in Him, will not perish, but have everlasting life."

Praise God for His promise in 1 John 1:9.

20 September

What a carpet!

You must have heard about magic carpets – the ones princes ride on in Arabian stories! It is fun to imagine to be on such a carpet, floating in the air high above the world.

But do you know that one can buy another type of magic carpet, one that can save lives? Yes, in some countries they have carpets that are laid between the railway lines to warn the train driver if anybody is lying there.

This invention was necessary because there have been so many people lately who wanted to take their own lives at railway stations. Some people jump from the platform and others go and lie down in front of an oncoming train.

What a sad state of affairs! However, it can also happen that people land in front of a train by accident. The engine of a car crossing the railway line could seize and the train could arrive before the people in the car had a chance to get out!

There have also been occasional reports about elderly people who lost their balance and fell from the platform. The magic sensor carpet has been invented for all these different emergencies. Railway companies can buy these carpets and use them so that a train driver can be warned if there is anything unusual on the railway line. He can then put on the emergency brakes of the train and precious lives can be saved.

If you know Jesus, you needn't ever feel that you have nothing to live for. And if you are in trouble, you can pray to Him at any time. He is always available to come to your aid. He is even better than a sensor carpet!

Try to draw something you are scared of. Write Psalm 46:1 underneath the drawing.

21 September

It's cool to say no

Marge and Keith were upset and disappointed. They were at a holiday resort for the holidays and they went to the beach on New Year's Eve to watch the fireworks. Although the display was beautiful, they were upset about the behavior of the college students on the beach. Many of them were drunk and they were making a nuisance of themselves, swearing and doing all sorts of vulgar things that they would never have done if they hadn't been drinking.

"What do you think about all the things that you've seen tonight?" asked their dad as they were walking home. "It was nauseating," said Marge. Her brother Keith kept quiet. His mom prompted him, "What do you say?" "I was wondering what I would do if I landed in a group that wanted me to drink with them," he said. "Oh, that'll be easy," Marge said. "I'll change the subject or I'll just walk away." Keith didn't think that he would do that. Maybe he could try to ignore them or make some kind of joke about it. He solemnly decided to think of a variety of responses that he could have ready if the crowd he was with started drinking.

"Maybe you could come up with a plan for some other kind of activity when your friends want to drink alcohol," their mom said. "And I also think that you should show your disgust when people suggest it's fun to get drunk. Who wants to drink himself into a state where he loses control over himself, anyway?"

Now their father had something to say, "The quickest way to get out of a situation like that, is just to say 'No thank you' immediately. You will find that most of your friends and other people will admire you for it. And the Lord will support you in a very special way."

Read Romans 13:12-14.

22 September

A miracle in Korea

Korea is a country in the Far East, yet almost a quarter of the people in South Korea are Christians. Although they are surrounded by people who follow other religions, they are serving the true God. How did this come about?

A hundred and forty years ago a Welshman, Robert Thomas, went there to preach the gospel. Amongst his belongings there was a trunk full of Bibles which he wanted to distribute amongst the Korean people, so that they could learn about God.

When the captain of the *General Sherman* saw a suitable landing spot, he sailed closer to the shore. But the Korean people thought that they were enemies and started shooting at them. The ship caught fire and all the passengers had to get into lifeboats. The young missionary with his load of Bibles was also picked up. He and his precious cargo landed safely on the shore. However, a Korean officer was waiting for him. Robert opened the trunk and offered the man a Bible. But what did the officer do? He took out his sword and chopped off the young man's head.

Was this the end of the story? Oh no! The man who killed the missionary took his Bible and read it. When two other missionaries went to Korea 22 years later, they discovered a group of Christian believers in that faraway place! Today more that 500 missionaries work in Korea and 3 000 Koreans are doing missionary work in other parts of the world.

In Romans 10:15 we read, *"How beautiful are the feet of those who bring good news!"* Robert Thomas was obedient to God, although it cost him his life. However, thousands of people were eventually saved as a result of his courage.

Pray for the Christians in Korea.

23 September

Who wants to be salt?

At his funeral, a lot of people said that Graham's grandpa was like the salt of the earth. "What does that mean?" he wondered and asked his mom about it. "It is a big compliment to Grandpa, because it means that his life had great value. Do you remember how tasteless your porridge was last week when I forgot to add salt to it? Salt gives a special taste to the food we eat. It brings out the flavor. Jesus said that His followers should be the salt of the earth. We should improve life in the same way that salt improves food. We should be the most joyful, kind and enthusiastic people around." Graham thought about his grandfather. It was true, when he was around, life always looked more promising!

Later that afternoon his mother called Graham to the kitchen. "Want some peanuts?" she asked. She had no need to ask him twice. "Thanks, Mom! You know how I love salty snacks," he said and was reminded about their conversation that morning. He had already decided that he also wanted to be a salt-of-the-earth type of person.

Now his mom said something very interesting. "Do you know why we season food with salt?" she asked. "It's because it will go off if it isn't rubbed with salt. The salt acts as a preservative. That's another reason why Jesus wants us to be like salt. He wants us to act like an antiseptic in the world around us. We should fight evil and preserve what is good. That's why we should always try to discourage people who are planning to do wrong things. Otherwise we will be like salt that has lost its value."

See what Jesus said in Matthew 5:13 about salt that loses its flavor.

24 September

Checkmate!

If you play chess you will know what "checkmate" means and you will also know that it is a word that a chess player would rather not hear while he is playing an important match! When your opponent says that word it means that your most important piece, the king, has been placed in danger.

Another fact that you will also know about if you are on your school's chess team, is that many chess games are played nowadays between people and computers. The most famous competition between a man and an electronic brain took place in America in 1997 between the world's chess champion Gary Kasparov and the computer *Deep Blue*.

Actually, the tournament was a bit unfair, because the computer had the ability to consider 50 million moves within three minutes. After six games Kasparov lost the prize-money of 3 million dollars. And yet everybody who watched the game felt that the human player actually surpassed the computer by far. The electronic device had no expectations of the match and it wasn't even glad when it was announced the winner.

The computer was, after all, designed and built by human beings. When you think about it, you realize once again what a marvelous organ a human brain is, much better than the *Deep Blue* computer that weighed more than a ton and was connected to 256 other processors. This man-made brain may "think" at a breathtaking speed, but it was compiled by a God-made brain whose Inventor had given him more than the ability to plan a chess game. God made man so special that he can also laugh and cry and love.

Read the words in Isaiah 40:12-14 and think about the fact that nothing can be compared to our God!

25 September

A light in the dark

A group of tourists visited the Cango caves. Among them was a twelve-year-old girl and her brother, who was seven years old. They were amazed at the stalactites and stalagmites, the tunnels and rooms that had been formed underground. At one stage, while they were in the big hall, the tour guide put off all the lights. The visitors could then get an idea of how dark it must have been in the grottos long ago before mankind ever entered it. It was pitch dark ...

Everybody fell silent, but the little boy got scared and started to cry. And then the voice of his sister could be heard, whispering clearly, "Don't be afraid. Somebody knows where the light is and he is going to put it on just now."

Are you scared of the dark? Or do you feel as if the world is a dark place because of all the bad things that are happening around you? Maybe you are treated badly at home or at school. Maybe you feel that nobody really has time for you or really cares for you. It might be that you are scared of things that might happen to you. Your dad could lose his job or your parents might get a divorce or somebody whom you love dearly may be taken away from you. Worries like these can make the future look very dark indeed.

However, God knows about all our fears. The prophet Micah once said, "Though I sit in darkness, the Lord will be my light." We can also be calm like the young girl in the caves, because we know about Someone who can turn the lights on again. As the hymn says, "Though the night be dark and dreary ... child look up: the dawn is near!"

Underline the words of the prophet in Micah 7:8 and draw a candle next to them to remind you not to be afraid in the dark.

26 September

Not good enough

A pastor once asked his barber whether he knew Christ as his Savior. "Don't bother me with questions like that," the man said. "I do my best, and that's good enough!" The pastor said no more. He wondered how he could convince the man that he needed Christ in his life.

When the barber had finished cutting the pastor's hair and was busy cleaning up, the next customer arrived. Suddenly the pastor thought of a good idea.

"I'll cut his hair," he said. "You can't do that," the barber objected. "Why not? I'll do my best, and that will be good enough." Then he smiled, paid his bill and left the barber with something to think about. The barber started to realize that doing one's best isn't always good enough. Sometimes an expert is needed to do the job. When the pastor came for a hair-cut again, the barber asked him a few questions.

"Jesus is the only one who is good enough to please God," the pastor explained. "That's why we must know Him as our Savior. Even our best efforts are not good enough. God looks at them and says, 'That's not what I'm looking for.' Only if we accept Jesus into our lives, will God be pleased with us."

We should all realize that it's not good enough to go to church and Sunday school and to try not to swear or lie or steal. It doesn't even help if we try to be loving and kind towards other people. We will never be able to live the holy lives that God expects from us, even if we do our best. Pray to Jesus and ask Him to take over your life. Then when God looks at you, He will see Jesus, the Perfect One. That pleases Him.

See what Hebrews 7:25-26 says about Jesus.

27 September

Foot washing

Casper came home later than usual. "Where have you been?" his mom asked. "I helped Mr. Williams in the library," he said. His mother was surprised. She knew that this teacher had often been unfair to Casper. Once he had accused him of writing obscene words in one of the library books. Although his mom knew that Casper would never do something like that, the teacher insisted that it was Casper's handwriting. "That was kind of you," his mom said. "Have you forgiven Mr. Williams?"

"Yes," Casper said. "At the Good News Club we decided to do foot-washing this week. We're all going to do things for other people that nobody else would want to do. Jesus had washed the dirty feet of His disciples and He said that we should do the same. He even washed Judas' feet, although he knew that Judas would betray Him."

Casper's mom was very glad that he belonged to the Good News Club. They definitely made no secret of their commitment to Jesus.

The next morning she found a piece of paper with a list of tasks on Casper's desk. At the top of the list was written: Footwashing to do this week. She read through the list: Empty trash can; pick up litter on the school grounds; help pre-schoolers on the bus; clean fire-place ...

Underneath was written: John 13:15, "I have set you an example that you should do as I have done for you."

She prayed softly, "Lord, please help Casper to stick to these resolutions. Let him discover the joy of being obedient to You!"

Think of a foot washing job that you can do for someone this week.

28 September

The empty chair

A pastor once visited an old man who was seriously ill. Next to his bed was an empty chair and the pastor took a seat there. While he was talking to the old man about the Lord, the sick man said, "Pastor, I know the Lord! He usually sits in that chair when I speak to Him. I never knew how to pray, but an old friend of mine told me that I should imagine Jesus sitting in a chair next to me. Then I can tell Him everything that is on my mind and also listen to what He has to say. The rest of my family will not understand this, but you, being a child of God, will understand. That's why I am telling you this secret!"

The pastor left the house with great joy. The old man knew Jesus as a Friend and he fully understood that prayer is a conversation with God. The pastor hoped that he would get a chance to lead the rest of the family to Christ somehow.

A week later the daughter of the old man called to say that her dad has passed away. "Will you conduct the funeral, Pastor?" she asked tearfully. "I would be honored to do it," the man of God replied. "We can learn a lot from your father's relationship with God," he added. "A strange thing happened," the daughter said. "We found him kneeling next to that old chair in his room, with his head resting on the seat." "I wish we could all die like that," the pastor replied softly.

Do you talk with God as with a friend? And would you like to lay your head on His lap when you are feeling lonely?

Pull up a chair next to you and imagine Jesus sitting in it. Talk to Him about everything that is on your mind. He always has time to listen if you have time to pray!

29 September

Fishing

Michael and Claude smiled when they heard that the theme of the youth service was *fishing*. That was their turf! Every weekend they spent lots of time on the jetty trying to catch the big one. At first they used to bring home only small fry, but since they had learned about different techniques, fishing gear and bait, they had often had good catches. They had also learned a lot from studying the tides and the weather.

The youth pastor read Matthew 4:19. It was Jesus' words to Peter and Andrew: *"Come follow me, and I will make you fishers of men."* "We have to take Jesus' command seriously," said the pastor. "We must look out for opportunities to tell people about Jesus and to 'catch' them for the Kingdom. That means that we will have to know God's Word, so that we can apply it to different situations. The fish will not come crawling in through the front door," he said. Michael and Claude laughed. They knew that for sure! It took skill and hard work to catch a fish. During the sermon they started to realize that their friends and thousands of lost people would not become Christians without someone telling them about Jesus.

"Some people will have to pray, others will have to pay and some will have to go to frontiers where the gospel has never been taken," he said. "And the rest of us will have to be Christian examples to those around us. We must make the bait very attractive, so that people will want to become Christians," concluded the preacher. Then he asked, "Are there any of you who are prepared to commit yourselves to being fishers of men for Christ?" Michael and Claude's hands went up simultaneously.

Ask God to show you what you can do to "catch" people for Him.

5 October

The love of money

A farmer once came to his wife in great excitement. "Darling," he said, "our cow has given birth to two calves, a white one and a black one. I'm going to keep the one and give the other to the Lord out of gratitude." "Which one is ours?" his wife asked. "I don't know yet," he said.

The man took good care of the calves and after a few weeks he planned to sell them. He would keep the money for the one for himself and the money for the other he would give to the church. He still could not decide which calf to keep. Then, one afternoon, he came home very depressed. "What's wrong?" his wife asked. "The Lord's calf has died!" he said.

In Luke 16:13 Jesus said that we could not serve God and Money. Of course nobody will ever pray to his money box or his purse, but there are many ways in which we can make an idol out of money. It must never be more important to us than God. The farmer in the story was more keen to fill his own pocket that to give anything for God's cause. If he really loved the Lord, he would still have given a portion of the money for God's work.

We must not love money more than God. 1 Timothy 6:10 says, *"For the love of money is the root of all kinds of evil. Some pople, eager for money, have wondered from the faith and pierced themselves with many griefs."*

Of course there is nothing wrong with making money. Jesus worked in a carpenter's shop and the things that He and His father made, were sold for money. However, we must make sure that money does not become our master.

Read Luke 16:1-13 to see what Jesus said about money.

6 October

The new home

Diana was crying when she entered the kitchen. "What's wrong?" her mother asked. "It was all a bunch of lies!" she said through her tears. "You said that Lulu was in heaven and now I've seen for myself that she is still lying in her grave in the garden." Her mom was shocked. "Who opened it?" she asked. "The neighbor's dog." She started to cry again.

"Come and sit here with me," her mom said. "Why are you so upset by what you have seen?" "Because now I know that you also lied to me about Granny," Diana said. "Grandma is still in that cold dark hole in the ground and she's not with Jesus, like you told me."

"Wait, wait," her mom said as she put her arm around the little crying girl. "Grandma's body is still in the graveyard where we put it. But her spirit, the true Grandma that we knew and loved, will live for ever and ever. Do you still remember when we moved into this house? We brought along everything that was valuable to us. Only the house in which we lived in Kimberley, stayed put. In the same way Granny's body stayed behind when she moved to heaven, because she will not need it there. She now has a better 'house' to live in."

"And Lulu?" Diana asked. Her mom thought for a while. "I personally think that there will be room for pets in heaven. That's why I comforted you with those words at Lulu's grave. However, nobody knows for sure. Remind me tonight to read something special from the Bible. It is a description of what the new heaven and earth, where we will live one day, will look like. Then you can decide for yourself whether you think that Lulu will be there."

Read the passage Diana's mother was referring to: Isaiah 11:6-9.

7 October

The rich farmer

In Luke 12:13-21 Jesus told a story that makes us think about all the possessions that we gather for ourselves here on earth. It is the story about a rich farmer who eventually decided that he had treasured up enough earthly goods. He thought, "Now I am going to retire and eat, drink and be merry!" In the Bible God called him a fool and shortly afterwards, he died.

In which ways did the rich farmer act like a fool? He was foolish, because he remembered himself, but forgot about others. The word *I* was very important to him. In verses 17 to 19 he used it seven times! But he had no concern for other people. His own barns were filled to capacity, but apparently it didn't occur to him to give some of it to people who were less fortunate. He decided to build bigger barns instead.

He remembered the world, but forgot about God. He had remembered to plow and to sow and to harvest, but he had forgotten about God in heaven to whom he should've been grateful. He never thought about the fact that the rain and the sun and his own health were gifts from God. He also forgot to give a part of his income to God. When he died, he had to stand before God with empty hands.

Jesus said in Luke 9:25, *"What good is it for a man to gain the whole world, and yet lose or forfeit his very self?"* That means that we should not just gather earthly possessions, but we should also think of life after death and spend time nourishing our souls and obeying God.

Read this story in your Bible.

8 October

The two lost sons

In Luke 15 we find the well-known story of the prodigal son. Remember? It's about the son who asked his dad for his inheritance and then went and spent it all. When he had nothing left and was starving, he ended up working in a pigsty. There he came to his senses and decided to go home again. He was now willing to be one of his father's slaves. But his father was so glad to see him, that he ran out to meet him and immediately organized a big welcoming party. We all know this part of the story quite well but we are apt to forget the rest.

The second part tells us about another son who was also lost and about whose eventual salvation we cannot be sure. The elder brother, who stayed at home, was very unhappy when his younger brother returned home. He thought that it was highly unfair that this brat, who had brought so much disgrace to the family, was now honored like a hero. The father was greatly saddened by this attitude.

That is why people say that this is actually a story about two lost sons, because the brother who stayed at home had also gone astray. He was with his father all the time, but he did not share his father's love and concern for the younger brother. He did not care about him and wasn't glad when he came back.

We must be careful not to be like the elder brother. We can spend much time with God's Word and in God's house without having God's love for other people. Then we won't care about the fact that they are lost and then we won't rejoice with the angels when they are redeemed. If this is so we are also lost and our heavenly father is just as concerned about us as He was about the prodigal son.

Read Luke 15:1-32.

9 October

God works behind the scenes

Did you know that there is a book in the Bible that doesn't mention God's name once? It is the book of Esther, where we read the beautiful story about a very special Jewish girl. Even though God's name is nowhere to be seen, He is very much at work in this story. It was God who influenced King Xerxes to fall in love with Esther. It was to God that Esther and all the Jews prayed for deliverance when Haman wanted to murder them. And it was He who arranged all the circumstances so that a whole nation could be saved, even after the king issued a decree to have them killed.

Every year during March the Jews still celebrate the Purim festival, to commemorate the time when God saved the people of Israel through the bravery of Queen Esther. When Jewish children get together on that day, the story of Esther is read to them. When the reader mentions the name of Haman, the perpetrator of the evil plan, all the children boo loudly. Then they say, "That wicked man! His name shouldn't even be mentioned!" But when they praise God afterwards for the deliverance of their people, Esther's name is mentioned with respect and reverence. Through her courage Esther held the name of God high. God used her to protect His children. Even though His name was never mentioned, He could do His work in a heathen palace through a young Jewish woman.

God is still present in all the things that happen on earth, although He is not always acknowledged. And He has a special task for each one of us, as He did for Esther. He wants us to take His presence into places like homes, schools and neighborhoods, where there might be people who don't ever think about Him.

See what Esther's Uncle Mordecai told her in Esther 4:14.

10 October

A new person

Sandra came home from the youth camp with her face aglow. "Mom," she said, "I am now a child of God! On Saturday night at the camp I asked God to forgive my sins and to adopt me as His child." Tears ran down her mother's face. "I am so glad," she said. "I believe that God set you apart when you were still a baby and we made a covenant with God to bring you up as His child. Your dad and I have been praying that the day would come when you would decide for yourself to serve the Lord. Now that day has come and we as your parents can rejoice about it like the angels in heaven do when a new convert comes into the kingdom."

"The leader at the camp said that my life will change now," Sandra said as she pasted a little fish on her school bag. "There you are," she said. "Now everybody will know that I belong to Christ."

"I hope that there will be many more ways in which you will show the world that you are a true Christian," her mom said. "Like what?" Sandra asked. "Well, hopefully they will say, 'My, but Sandra has changed. Look how faithfully she does her homework. What has happened to her? She is so kind to everyone and she's not gossiping like before. See how patient she is with that old lady and watch her as she helps her mom with the dishes.'" "Flattery will get you nowhere, Mom!" she said with a smile. However, she grabbed a dishcloth to help her mom. She really wanted the Holy Spirit to transform her life. She hoped that nobody would ever have to wonder whether she was a true child of God.

Read 1 Timothy 1:12-15. See what Paul said about his old life as opposed to his new life.

11 October

Birds with a message

Birds are often mentioned in the Bible and we can learn valuable lessons from them. In Psalm 84 the writer mentioned sparrows and swallows. He said that they made their nests in the house of the Lord, because it was a place of safety. In verse 4 he says, *"Blessed are those who dwell in your house; they are forever praising you."*

Jesus also talked about sparrows. He wanted to let people know that nothing ever happened without God's knowledge. So He said, *"Are not two sparrows sold for a penny? Yet not one of them will fall to the ground apart from the will of your Father"* (Matthew 10:29).

Eagles are such majestic birds and every now and then you will read something about them in the Old Testament. Moses once wrote a song in which he said that God looked after His children like an eagle that carries its young around on its wings. And Isaiah said, *"Those who hope in the Lord will renew their strength. They will soar on wings like eagles; they will run and not grow weary, they will walk and not be faint"* (Isaiah 40:31).

Another bird that is frequently mentioned in the Bible, is the dove. Jesus said that we should be shrewd as snakes and innocent as doves. A dove is the symbol of purity. Jesus' most famous words about birds are probably those that we find in Matthew 6:26, *"Look at the birds of the air; they do not sow or reap or store away in barns, and yet your heavenly Father feeds them. Are you not much more valuable than they?"*

Collect pictures of birds and make a poster with the following verses: Deuteronomy 32:11; Isaiah 40:31; Matthew 10:29; Psalm 84:3-4. Read the birds' messages to you!

12 October

Danger!

One Friday night Geoffrey and his parents went for dinner at their neighbor's house. Geoffrey's friend wanted to show him something on his dad's computer while the grown-ups were chatting on the patio. They could hear what their parents were talking about. "I'd much sooner give my child the car keys and let him drive without a license than let him surf on the Internet without supervision," Geoffrey's father said.

The two boys looked at each other and raised their eyebrows. "Can I show you something?" Dan asked secretively. Although Geoffrey was very curious, he remembered what his dad once told him, "One day you will be tempted to watch explicit sex scenes. Don't even consider looking at them once. What you will see there can become a nasty flashback that might bother you for the rest of your life. And apart from that, you could get hooked on pornography just as easily as on drugs. It could arouse urges within you that you can't control and your body will for ever be asking for more."

"No thanks!" Geoffrey said. "Rather show me a website about soccer." "As you wish," Dan said. They spent the rest of the evening talking about their favorite soccer players.

When they were home again, Geoffrey said to his dad, "I heard what you told Dan's father. Can I get the car tomorrow?" His dad laughed. "Been eavesdropping!" he said jokingly. "Of course I won't give you the car keys before you have a license. I said that because I take Jesus' words in Luke 12:4 seriously." He paged through his Bible and then read, *"Do not be afraid of those who kill the body and after that can do no more. But I will show you whom you should fear: Fear him who has power to throw you into hell."*

Read Matthew's version of these words in Matthew 10:28.

13 October

How well do you know your Bible?

The reverend Jan Pit often visited Eastern Europe when the Bible was banned there. He said that he once attended a secret gathering of Christians in Romania. Nobody had a Bible with him. But the preacher said, "We will read together from Ephesians 2." Then a man stood up and recited the whole chapter. If the reading had been from another chapter in the New Testament, somebody else would have been able to recite it. Because all their Bibles had been destroyed, each Christian regarded it as his responsibility to memorize at least one chapter from the Bible. In that way the Bible could be preserved for them.

A similar case was reported by a missionary to China. He related that he found two hundred people in one village who knew the whole New Testament by heart. They were also afraid that their most precious possession might be taken from them. So they decided to keep it in the safest place they knew, in their hearts and in their minds.

But this wonderful deed needn't be restricted to faraway places. At one stage of her life a certain teacher had to travel long distances in her car. And what did she do to shorten the road for herself? She learned the whole book of Hebrews by heart.

Would you be able to remember Bible passages if you were thrown into a dark prison for days on end? Or would you be able to encourage people from the Bible if you were stranded on a lonely island?

Choose a book from the Bible that you find inspiring and start to learn it by heart. You will never be sorry that you did. You could even get a grandparent to sponsor your endeavor!

See what God's Word is compared to in Psalm 119:103.

14 October

WWJD

Nowadays many children are wearing a WWJD band around their wrists. The letters stand for WHAT WOULD JESUS DO? You also see this slogan in car windows, on hats, T-shirts and keyrings. People who wear these tokens, know that Jesus always did the things that gladdened His Father's heart and they want to follow His example. In every situation we have a choice – to do things in the world's way or to do things Jesus' way.

God has given us the Holy Spirit to guide and teach us. If we study God's Word, we will know which things make Him smile. And if we are in doubt, the Holy Spirit will tell us what Jesus would have done.

You will soon find out that it is not possible to live like Jesus in your own strength. To be able to live a Christlike life, we need the power of the Holy Spirit. Just as an electrical bulb cannot glow on its own, but needs an electrical current, so we need God's power to be a shining light for Him.

It's a good idea to wear the FROG band as well! The letters stand for FULLY RELY ON GOD. If we want to live like Jesus, we will have to rely on God to supply the power for such a life. The devil does not want us to live like Christ, but God can equip us with special weapons to fight evil. What would Jesus do? He would trust God completely and rely on Him for everything!

Read John 5:30.

15 October

First things first

When Mrs. White left the house she said, "Remember, first things first." "Okay," said Sylvia from where she and Nora were doing homework. "What does that mean?" Nora asked. "Nothing much really," said Sylvia. "It's a well-known phrase in our home. To my parents it is very important that we keep our priorities straight." "Like what?" Nora asked. "Like finishing your homework before you start chatting!"

Nora nodded, "That's true! Important stuff should get the most attention. What is important to you?" Sylvia thought for a while and then said, "God comes first, then my cat and then my friends." She passed Nora a donut. "To me my figure and my clothes are the most important. So I won't have any of that fattening stuff, thank you," she said. "And then, there's my money and my CDs."

That night Nora was thinking about her conversation with Sylvia. Her own parents weren't believers and it was always interesting to hear what went on in Sylvia's home. She always heard something that was worth thinking about from them. "First things first" sounded like good advice. Now she let her imagination run wild. What would happen if their town got flooded? What would come first in a situation like that?

She knew that she would not really worry about her clothes or her money or her CDs. She would much rather save her family and her pets. While dozing off, she thought that it would be handy to know God in a situation like that. I must ask Sylvia after school how I can become God's friend. Or rather, I should ask her that before school starts. "First things first" she said to herself, smiling.

Read what should come first in our lives in Matthew 6:33.

16 October

An eye-opener

Susan was fed-up. Her mom had convinced her that going to a church camp would be the best way to spend the long weekend. Now she was at a horrible camping site that had cold showers and outside toilets! The beds were hard and the food was awful. To make things worse, they were not allowed to bring cellphones, so she could not phone her parents to come and fetch her.

She dragged her feet to the wooden hall where somebody was going to give them a lecture on … she wasn't sure what! She couldn't care less. The young man who stood up to talk seemed very uninteresting … until he opened his mouth! He read Philippians 4:11-13 and then started to talk. He said God called him to work in a squatter's settlement. He was living with the squatters in his own shack. There were no taps where he stayed and nobody came to empty their trash cans or clean their streets. They had to look after themselves. Some days he, like his neighbors, had nothing to eat. Then he would tighten his belt, take out his guitar and start to play. Many squatters started drinking to try to forget about their problems and there were often brawls. However, there were people who loved the Lord and who would come and join him to sing praises to God and to listen to His Word.

Every day they would pray, "Give us this day our daily bread," because many of them were jobless and really didn't know where food for the next day would come from.

When he had finished his talk, he gave each person a sheet of blank paper. "Write a letter to God about what you have heard tonight," he said. Susan took a pen and wrote in big letters: Dear God, thank You!

What would you have written if you were at the camp?

17 October

Miracle in Chicago

Believe it or not, a moth once featured on the front page of a daily newspaper in Chicago! Yes, a group of scientists conducted an experiment and the results were so amazing that they invited local journalists to come and witness the miracle for themselves.

The team of scientists found the male and female of a very rare type of moth. Because they were quite sure that there would be no other moths of the same species in the vicinity, they realized that they could now find out whether the male would find the female if they were separated by a great distance.

They put the female in a room, and they closed the doors and windows. Then they traveled 8 kilometers with the male and let it loose. Would the moth find his mate through the dense smog of the city, the heavy, noisy traffic and all the flashing lights around him?

A few hours later the people in the laboratory where the female moth was kept, heard an unusual sound at the window. It was the male tapping on the window.

How can we ever explain something like this? It is a miracle! This is only one of the many wonderful things that God made and that can be seen in nature every day. No wonder David was so excited about the things that he could learn about God through nature. In Psalm 19:1-4 he said, *"The heavens declare the glory of God; the skies proclaim the work of his hands ... Their voice goes out into all the earth, their words to the ends of the world."*

What message is the universe sending out? God is almighty and awesome and He cares for His creation.

Decide today to spend time in nature to marvel at the wonders that God has created.

18 October

Make Him the guest of honor

In Revelation 3:20 Jesus said, *"I stand at the door and knock. If anyone hears my voice and opens the door, I will come in and eat with him, and he with me."*

According to this image, our life is like a house with a door that can be opened to let Jesus enter. And when He comes in, He stays there, as 1 Corinthians 3:16 says.

However, there are many people who do not allow Jesus to dwell in all the rooms of their lives. Maybe they allow Him into the laundry so that He can wash away their sins, but they prefer not to have Him in the lounge. That's the place where they receive their friends and where they do their gossiping. He must also rather not come to the television room, because then they will have to be careful about what they are viewing.

The study will be out of bounds for Him as well, because who wants somebody to look over your shoulder all the time to see whether you are doing your best with your studies? And your bedroom is utterly private! Nobody, not even Jesus, can come and go in there as He wished!

That is how many Christians treat Jesus. They shut Him up in one area of their lives and they themselves inhabit all the other rooms of their existence.

These folk can usually not understand why some of God's children are glowing with joy and fulfillment, while they are so unhappy. Their lives are not joyful as Jesus planned them to be. The reason is that they are walking around with the keys of all the rooms of their lives, instead of handing them over to Jesus.

Ask Jesus to be the guest of honor in all the rooms of your life.

19 October

Like a mother

"**M**om, if God is the Father and Jesus is the Son then the Holy Spirit must be the Mother," Vera was saying this to her mother after she and Simon had listened to their daily Bible reading. Their mother smiled. "One could say that," she answered. "There are many things about the Holy Spirit that remind me of a mother."

"Tell us about them," Simon said. "Well, a mother usually wants to give her children only the best. I know, because I am one! And the Holy Spirit is the same. He wants to encourage us and comfort us and help us to live beautiful lives. But He can also become heart-broken like an earthly mother. Ephesians 4:30 says that we can grieve the Spirit of God. I can identify with Him, because I know how sad I sometimes feel. Especially when I have taken trouble in preparing your food and you don't even want to eat it. Or when you forget to say good-bye before you leave for school in the morning." Simon blushed. He knew that his mom was talking about him.

Their mom had more to say, "Sometimes I see things that make me sick with grief. I try for years to teach you good habits and then I still don't see any results." Vera thought about the many times that she still kicked her dirty laundry under the bed in spite of all her mom's lectures. "In the same way the Holy Spirit of God can be grieved if we do not listen to His advice," concluded their mom.

Vera and Simon stood up from their chairs and went over to their mom to give her a hug. They decided to take heed not to grieve their mom or the Holy Spirit unnecessarily.

Ask God to make you sensitive to the leading of the Holy Spirit in your life.

20 October

Caring

The managers of a kindergarten announced a competition. It wasn't to find the cleverest or the cutest or the fastest child in the school. It wasn't even to see who could collect the most money. It was to see who cared the most for other people. The competition matched the school's motto: *Learning to care.*

But how would they choose the winner? The principal invited people to let the school know about caring deeds. Beautiful stories came to the ears of the judges. A little girl had taken flowers from her garden to an aunt in the old age home, without her parents even knowing about it. A granny said her grandchild phoned her every evening to say good night. The school caretaker wanted one little boy to win because he always shared his lunch with him. Yes, the judges had a difficult task!

But one story touched everybody's heart. Little Mandy's mom reported that their neighbor was very lonely after his wife had passed away. One day Mrs. Walker saw him sitting on a bench in his garden, staring in front of him. Then she saw how Mandy climbed over the fence and sat down next to the old man.

That night her mom asked, "What did you and Uncle Chris talk about this afternoon?" "Nothing," said Mandy, "I just helped him to cry." Do you think that her deed deserved the prize? The judges thought so. She received a beautiful Children's Bible as a reward.

Romans 12:15 says, *"Rejoice with those who rejoice; mourn with those who mourn."* That means that we must be able to place ourselves in somebody else's shoes and show that we care. That was what little Mandy did.

Think of something that you could do to show someone in need that you care.

21 October

God's property

Maura was trying to guess which subject her Sunday school teacher was going to choose. He read from 2 Corinthians 8. In verse 2 he read about people who were poor, but whom Paul called rich. In verse 9 it said that Jesus was rich, but He became poor for us. And in verse 14 Paul said that those who had plenty, should help those who had little. Then Maura knew that the lesson would be about being rich or poor.

She was right! The teacher showed the class an enormous picture of a man in a smart suit. Behind the man was a grand house with an expensive car. The man was saying, "Mine! Mine!"

"What's wrong with this picture?" asked the teacher. At first there was no response. Then Maura said, "That man is not a child of God." "Why do you say that?" the teacher asked. "If he was a child of God, he would not be selfish," she said.

"Yes," said the teacher. "The Lord gave this man many possessions, but the proud man thinks that it was all meant for his own use. If he were a child of God, he would know that he was only a manager of God's property. He could use some of it for himself, but he should also give some of it to the needy and some for God's kingdom. His car should sometimes transport others and the door of his house should sometimes be open to others."

Maura's teacher concluded by reminding the class that you cannot take any possessions to heaven with you when you die.

Read Luke 14:33.

22 October

To listen with one's fingers

"With eager fingers I listen to the flood of sounds" is the first line of a poem. But why would the poet listen with her fingers? Because she was blind and deaf. Blind people can hear when somebody speaks to them and deaf people can lip-read. But when you are blind and deaf, life becomes very difficult. This is the problem that Helen Keller had to face. When she was only two years old, she became very ill and afterwards she could not see or hear at all.

She grew up to be quite wild, because nobody knew how to teach her anything. However, her parents found a teacher who had enough patience and love to try to help her. Anne Sullivan understood Helen's frustration, because she herself had to cope with blindness for a while during her childhood.

After many attempts, her teacher made Helen realize that everything had a name. One day she held Helen's hand underneath a pump while the water was running. In the meantime she spelled w-a-t-e-r in the palm of her hand. It was as if the little girl broke out of a prison. She became eager to learn the name of everything around her. She soon learned to read braille. She also learned to write. To everybody's surprise she even went to college and finished a course in languages with the help of Miss Sullivan. She wrote a book about her life called *The Story of My Life.* With the proceeds of this book and through lectures, she collected a lot of money which she donated to schools where deaf or blind children could learn to look after themselves.

What a courageous person!

Read Psalm 146:7-8 and thank God for the fact that you can see and hear.

23 October

God

"What is God like?" the teacher of a pre-school asked the toddlers. "He is like a king!" a little one promptly answered. That is probably one of the best ways in which one can describe God. David also thought about God in this way when he wrote Psalm 99. He started this song of praise with the words, *"The Lord reigns, let the nations tremble."*

However, there are good kings and bad kings. Some kings couldn't care less about their people. They love making laws and punishing those who do not abide by them. God is not like that at all. He is personally interested in each one of us. According to the Bible He even knows how many hairs you have on your head.

Another toddler said, "God is a kind old man with a beard." She pictured God as a loving, laughing old man like her grandfather. And yet it can be dangerous to think of God only in this way. Because He is not like some grandfathers who wink their eyes and laugh at the mischief of their grandchildren. Oh no, He hates sin! He knows that sin is like a poisonous spider that you dare not allow your children to play with. He hates sin so much that He sent Jesus to come in between us and sin to save us from it. He is willing to forgive us if we confess our sins, but we should never forget what it cost Him to be able to do that.

He is also not too old and weak to help us. You get kind old gentlemen who cannot work any longer and who sit in the sun on the veranda all day long. But God, our Helper, is strong and mighty! That is what Psalm 24:8-10 says. *"Who is this King of glory? The Lord Almighty – He is the King of glory."*

Aren't you glad?

Read the whole of Psalm 24.

24 October

What about dinosaurs?

Jack's science teacher took them to the museum. There they learned about animals that have become extinct. When he got home, he found his mother in the garden. "Mom, why don't they say anything about dinosaurs and other pre-historic animals in the Bible? Some of my friends say this is proof that the Bible isn't true." Jack's mom was upset to hear that kids could come to such a conclusion so easily. Yet she answered calmly, "Some scientists who are also Christians believe that God created the earth during six very long periods of time and that dinosaurs had already died out by the time man was created. Whether that is true or not, the fact that the Bible doesn't mention these animals isn't so strange. Only animals that had something to do with Bible history are mentioned. You could draw up a long list of other animals that are also not mentioned in the Bible."

Jack decided that he was going to make such a list. He could use his dad's concordance, which is a thick book in which you can find every single word that is written in the Bible, like in a dictionary.

Jack's mom spoke further, "It is an established fact that dinosaurs roamed the earth at one stage in the history of the world. One can learn a lot about them through excavations and fossils. God must be proud of human beings who have been able to discover so much about His creation." Jack could hear that his mom was worried, though. "However, it must make Him very sad to see that this knowledge makes people doubt the truth about the Bible. One day we will see that there is no difference between what the Bible says and what we see in nature."

Read how excited David was about God's creation in Psalm 65:5-13.

25 October

Chopsticks

You probably know that people in the East eat with chopsticks instead of knives and forks. "Easy on the dish washer!" you probably say. But not so easy to eat with. To pick rice and peas up with two sticks and then put them into your mouth is really an art.

Most Japanese have their own set of chopsticks which are washed and put away separately. Each owner has a pair of these sticks carefully designed to suit him. Hand sizes are especially taken into account because the chopsticks for a big, hefty man are quite different from those for a small, dainty lady. Besides that, you can choose from about 200 different styles.

After your set of sticks has been designed to suit you, it is carefully crafted in eleven stages. Yes, the people of the East see their eating utensils as an extension of their bodies and as an important tool.

Have you ever thought about the fact that God created you in a very special way for a very special purpose? You are not the way you are by coincidence. Before you were created, God took everything into account. He knew in which type of home you would grow up and in which neighborhood you would stay. That is why he has given you special looks, a special personality and special talents. Maybe you are living among people who are unhappy and God has given you a sense of humor or a gift for music with which you can cheer up everybody around you. Maybe there are sickly people around you and you have been given a strong and healthy body so that you can help these unfortunate ones. Try to discover which gifts God has given you so that you can serve Him and other people. You can be a most useful tool in the hand of God!

Read Romans 12:6.

26 October

Remember to remember

Have you ever heard the story about Androcles and the lion? Androcles was a slave who fled from his masters because they treated him so badly. He hid himself in a cave. One day he heard a deep roar at the opening of the cave. A young lion stood there looking for shelter, because he had a nasty thorn in his paw. Androcles slowly moved closer to the lion and carefully took out the thorn. The lion licked its wound and walked away.

Soon afterwards Androcles' hiding place was discovered by his owners and he was thrown into prison. Then the Romans decided to use him as a gladiator to fight against the lions in the arena. In those days thousands of people came to watch these fights. Usually the poor gladiator was torn to pieces after a short struggle with a hungry lion. This time however, when Androcles walked into the arena and the lion was released, something extraordinary happened! The lion walked up to the slave and started licking his hand. The crowds had never seen anything like that before. And when the lion rubbed himself against the slave's legs as a cat would do, the people went mad with excitement. The officials had to let Androcles go free. All these things happened because a lion remembered a good deed that was done to him.

In Luke 18:8 Jesus asked His disciples not to forget the miracles that He had done. And in Revelation 2:5 the Lord asked His church not to forget how He had saved them. We must be like that lion and remember all the good things that God has done for us. By remembering His loving-kindness we can live lives that are pleasing in His sight.

Remember to thank God for all the things that He has given you and trust Him for the future.

27 October

The unsinkable ship

Anne wanted to know from her father why her granddad always said "God willing" when he was planning anything and why he always concluded his conversation with "If it is the Lord's will". Her father told her this story. "The *Titanic* was a luxury ship that undertook its first voyage in 1912. It was at that stage the biggest vessel that had ever been built for sea travel. The ship had a double hull and 16 watertight compartments. People said that this ship was unsinkable, because even if four compartments were flooded by water, the rest of the ship would still stay afloat.

"However, just before midnight on 14 April, while the ship was sailing at about 41 kilometers per hour, it crashed into an iceberg. An enormous hole was gouged in the hull and five of the compartments flooded with water. The boat sank and one and a half thousand people drowned! Only after an hour and a half did another ship come to the *Titanic's* rescue, so that the people who were still alive could be taken out of the icy water."

Anne shivered. Her dad took the Bible and read from James 4:13-16: *"Now listen, you who say 'Today or tomorrow we will go to this or that city …' Why, you don't even know what will happen tomorrow … Instead, you should say: If it is the Lord's will, we will live and do this or that. As it is, you boast and brag. All such boasting is evil."*

Anne knew why her dad had told this story. The people who built the *Titanic* had said that it was unsinkable and they boasted about its reliability. They were certain that they would reach America safely. But they forgot to trust God to help them travel safely.

Read James 4:13-17.

28 October

Bending the rules

"Mom, you are too rigid!" Gerald said one day. "William's parents aren't nearly as strict as you are." "In what way?" his mom wanted to know. "In many ways! We are not allowed to pass the traffic lights on yellow, not allowed to watch videos with an age-restriction and not allowed to park in a parking spot for the disabled, even if we are late for an appointment.

"William's dad said that if you don't harm anyone, it's okay to bend the rules," he said. "That's interesting," his mom said. "And who will decide whether you have been doing any harm while you were breaking the rules? Many people have been in accidents because they ignored the traffic lights. They too thought that there was no danger, but they were mistaken because other people who were also bending the rules a little bit, pulled away just too soon."

"And what about films and videos?" Gerald asked. His mom answered, "You know very well why we are strict about that. The people who decide which films are suitable for different age-groups, are highly qualified people who know which material is not suitable for children. Parents can't scan all the films to see which ones are appropriate. That's why the authorities pay specialists to do the selecting."

"The reason for not parking in sites for disabled people is that these people struggle to get to the shops and these parking spaces make it easier for them."

Now Gerald had a lot of ammunition ready if his friends called him a nerd again for sticking to the rules. He also decided to choose this subject for oral discussions in English class!

Read 1 Peter 2:13-17.

29 October

Our Lifesaver

Beth and her friend Cindy went for a swim. The sea was fabulous. There were big swells, so that you could drift on your back and just relax in the water while you floated up and down. The two girls stayed close to each other and chatted happily. They did not notice that a current was taking them far away from the shore.

Suddenly Beth noticed that the other swimmers were far away and looked pathetically small. "Cindy, we'll have to swim back!" she shouted. The two friends swam as best they could, but they had to battle against a very strong current. Cindy got tired first. "I can't go further," she said and put her arm into the air.

Luckily there was a lifesaver on the shore. He was watching the two bathers through his binoculars. When he saw Cindy's arm stretched out in the air, he blew his whistle and he and another young man ran into the water. With a few strong strokes they reached the girls, so that they could bring them back to safety.

A little later Beth and Cindy arrived at the Smith's beach house. They were still out of breath, but they told Beth's mom everything. "Let's praise God that you are still alive!" she said with tears in her eyes. They prayed right there and then. Beth's mom said, "Today could have been an especially tragic day if one of you drowned and we weren't sure whether you knew Jesus as Savior. This is an opportunity for both of you to make sure about your relationship with God."

"Don't worry, Mrs. Smith, I accepted Christ as my Lifesaver long ago, just like Beth!" Beth's mom drew them close to her and gave them each a warm hug.

Read Acts 16:31. Here Paul tells us how we can get to know Jesus as our Lifesaver.

30 October

Fridges that can write letters

Is there a computer in your home and can you receive e-mail? It is a wonderful invention, isn't it? You can get mail from all over the world and answer letters immediately. To think that there was a time when letters were sent with a carrier pigeon or a mail-coach! If you wanted to send a letter overseas long ago, it had to go by ship and it took months for a letter to reach its destination.

But nowadays you even get fridges that can send e-mail messages! These fridges have a screen on their door, which enables a housewife to watch a video or follow a recipe while preparing supper. On that same screen a message can appear that will tell the owner if the food inside the fridge has gone off or if the machine is not functioning properly. Wouldn't your family love such a clever fridge?

But unfortunately all new inventions are not without problems. Receiving e-mail can be a hassle. People with Internet facilities often complain about all the junk mail that they have to sort through every day. Somebody might get hold of your e-mail address and send you hundreds of advertisements and news snippets and letters that you have to attend to. You can't just throw them in the wastepaper basket like you do with junk mail at your front door. The mail on your computer screen can keep you busy for hours on end.

We as Christians must beware of getting so busy with trivialities (unimportant small stuff) that we do not have time for God or for one another. We should set aside time to think about God, read the Bible and pray. We should also set aside time to help people who are in need.

Read the important laws that Jesus gave His followers in Matthew 22:37-40.

31 October

NOVEMBER

The Sabbath

Amy woke up with soft music in her ears. "Where am I?" she was wondering and then she remembered that she was with her grandparents for the weekend. She walked to the kitchen in a daze. Grandma was already dressed for church and was wearing a white apron. There was breakfast on the table and Grandma was arranging a few daisies in a vase. "It's the day of the Lord," she said with zest. "We should rejoice and be glad in it!"

Amy couldn't help thinking about Sunday mornings in her own home. Usually everyone was in a bad mood, because they had been up late the previous night. It was always a scramble to be in time for church.

Later on, when they were on their way to church, Grandpa gave Amy money for the collection. She wondered what he would think if he knew how often she forgot about that on a Sunday.

When the minister read the Ten Commandments from Deuteronomy 5, he repeated verse 12, *"Observe the Sabbath day by keeping it holy, as the Lord your God has commanded you."* Then he read Ezekiel 20:20 to go with it, *"Keep my Sabbaths holy, that they may be a sign between us. Then you will know that I am the Lord your God."*

"Oh dear!" Amy thought. "If the way I keep the Sabbath was an indication of how much I love the Lord, people would think I was an unbeliever." When she came home that night and crept into her own bed again, she thought about ways in which she could change her Sundays into special days.

Paste a little heart or a star next to each Sunday on your family calendar to remind you that it is a very special day of the week.

1 November

Reading in the dark

One benefit of being blind is that you are able to read in the dark! You can have your braille book under the blankets and read with your fingers until you fall asleep. There is no need to read with a torch under the bed after lights out. No need to practice the bad habit of balancing a torch on your chest in order to read in bed when there's a power failure.

If you do not know braille, you need a light to read with. However, there is something else that you need when you are reading: insight! If you do not understand what you are reading you are wasting your time. Then you might as well be sitting in pitch darkness. That is why it is essential to ask God to explain His Word to you before you start to read from the Bible. He must cast His light on the words that we read, so that we can understand their meaning. Nobody, not even the cleverest person on earth, can understand the Bible if the Holy Spirit does not explain it to him. The Holy Spirit is like a light that puts everything into perspective.

2 Peter 1:19 says, *"And we have the word of the prophets made more certain, and you will do well to pay attention to it, as to a light shining in a dark place."* And in verse 20 we read, *"No prophecy of Scripture came about by the prophet's own interpretation."* This means that we need God's light to understand His Word.

Sometimes the Holy Spirit uses your parents or a teacher or a preacher to explain His Word to you. Therefore you can ask their advice if you still don't understand something.

Make a bookmark for your Bible with the words of Psalm 119:34 written on it.

2 November

It's raining from beneath!

Sometimes God uses very ordinary things to make people realize that He exists.

Whittaker Chambers, a well-known author, said that he had been an atheist for most of his life. (An atheist is someone who does not believe in God.) One day he was sitting in his home, watching his little baby girl eat. She was handling the porridge with unskilled fingers, smearing it across her face and letting some of it fall to the floor. While he was watching her, he thought: This little human being is definitely not a mere assembly of atoms brought together by coincidence! There must have been a magnificant Designer who invented her. He also realized that she must have a spirit or a soul. Fortunately he knew people he could ask about God. Eventually he became a Christian.

In faraway places, where people only believe in spirits and idols, God often reveals Himself through ordinary incidents. John Paton worked on the Hibridic islands for many years, but the people there did not believe his message about God. He did not give up and many Christians in his homeland prayed for a breakthrough. Then one day Chief Namakei was converted. How did it happen? There was a severe drought in that region and John dug a well and prayed for water. The islanders never knew that fresh water could come from underground sources. While John was digging, the people thought that "Missi" (as he was called) was mad. When he finished digging, he prayed and the well flooded with water. "It is raining from beneath! It is raining upward!" Namakei shouted in amazement. He then wanted to hear more about the God of John Paton and he and many of his tribesmen found the true God.

Read Psalm 145:1-7.

3 November

Sitting on God's lap

There once was a little girl who kept a diary of all the things that she learned about God. Isabelle Holland wrote a book about her called *Abbey's God Book*. Maybe you can find the book in your library, read it and start your own account of your experiences with God.

First of all she wrote down all the things that she reckoned God wouldn't be. She thought that "God is not like Santa Claus" and "He is not just make-believe" and "God is not like an angry policeman."

"What is He really like?" Abbey often wondered. When she was six years old, her parents showed her the statue of George Washington, sitting in front of the White House. It was enormous and the look on the president's face was strong, yet kind and sad. Each time she thought about God after that, this picture came to her mind. Often, when she was scared or lonely, she would imagine climbing on the lap of this man and then she would feel safe with God.

However, when she grew up, she realized that God was not like that statue at all! He was not like any person she knew and nobody could take a picture or make a drawing of Him. Some of Abbey's friends said that God was a woman and others said that He was just a presence. There were even some who did not believe that there is a God at all. But Abbey learnt the truth about God by studying the Bible bit by bit. God was real, but invisible.

There is nothing wrong with imagining that you can climb up on His lap. That is probably exactly how David felt one night when he wrote Psalm 4:8: *"I will lie down and sleep in peace, for you alone, O Lord, make me dwell in safety."*

Read how Elijah met God in 1 Kings 19:11-13.

4 November

Cruelty

Every year in England the 5ᵗʰ of November is time for fireworks. Then people commemorate the day when Guy Fawkes failed in his plans to blow up the Houses of Parliament. Most children aren't sure why the festivities take place, but they just love the firework displays that go with it. Some people spend vast amounts of money on crackers and rockets that burn out in seconds. To see all the lights against the night sky is of course a beautiful sight. Some people revel in the loudness of the noise that comes from crackers and they love to see people jump from fright.

But animals hate that. Every year hundreds of dogs get lost on Guy Fawkes day because they try to escape the noise of the crackers and then get completely lost. That is why the SPCA often asked the authorities to prohibit the sales of fireworks.

A dreadful story was published in one newspaper after one Guy Fawkes celebration. A group of young people took a dog and fastened a rocket to its tail. Then they lit the fuse and waited to see what would happen. Imagine being so cruel!

However, things worked out differently from what they had planned. As the little dog ran away in fright, the rocket came loose from his tail and rolled underneath these young people's car. Because there was an oil leakage, the car caught fire when the rocket went off. The car blew up before their very eyes. One could say, "It served them right," because cruelty like that should be punished. We should be kind to all of God's creatures, not only to human beings. In Psalm 37:27 David said, *"Turn from evil and do good."* Surely we all know that God doesn't want us to hurt any animal.

Read the warning in Romans 13:4.

5 November

An important happening

It was a big day in the Blairs' house. They had acquired a television set! All their relatives, friends and neighbors already had sets, but Mr. Blair always said that there were too many other things that had to be bought. The children were very glad that their dad had finally decided to buy a TV.

"No more than an hour a day," their dad said, "and don't let me find out that you are neglecting schoolwork or sports activities to watch TV." The kids studied the program guide in the newspaper and selected the shows that they wanted to watch during their first week of viewing.

That evening when the television was set up and tuned in, their father called all of them together. "Now we are first going to thank the Lord for this wonderful device," he said. "Heavenly Father, thank You that we can afford to buy this television set. How privileged we are. We will be able to sit in this room and laugh and relax together. We will see different parts of the world and we will see many people for whom we can pray. However, we know that the devil can use this medium to lure us away from You, O God. So we ask that You will always give us the courage to turn off the TV if there is any program that dishonors You. Please see to it that we do not spend so much time in front of this box that we won't have time for You or our friends."

When their dad said *Amen*, their mom was ready with a glass of grape juice for each of them. "Let's drink to a new experience in the Blair household," she said. "Happy viewing!" they all said as they clinked their glasses.

Read 1 Corinthians 6:12. What does this text say about watching TV?

6 November

The treasure hunt

One day the Radikids had a special type of treasure hunt. Miss July gave each group a map which they had to follow in order to get to the house where the treasure was hidden. They were to talk to the person they would meet there and then report back.

After following the instructions, Belinda and her friends reached 4 Union Street. They rang the bell and a lady in a wheelchair opened the door. She was expecting them and offered them cool drink and cupcakes. While they were enjoying this, she said, "Miss July asked me to tell you how I became a Christian." Then this kind lady told them how she realized, after a serious car accident, that she could not live without God. "So I asked Him to forgive my sins and to take over my life. From that day on I have been one of God's children and He has been looking after me in a most special way," she said.

The children asked her many questions and they were sad when they had to leave. But they had to be back at the church at 16:00. So they thanked their host and said goodbye.

One person from each of the groups had to tell what they had experienced at the houses they were sent to. At each destination there had been somebody who witnessed about their first meeting with God. It was very interesting to hear how God called different people in different ways. One woman said that it was her fear of hell that made her flee to Jesus. An old gentleman said that there was somebody at his workplace that lived such a remarkable life, that he asked him about the secret of his success. Then that man led him to Christ.

Miss July asked, "What did you learn today?" "That it is worthwhile to be a Christian," said Belinda. The others agreed.

Read Hebrews 10:35.

7 November

God's kingdom

"Mom, what's the meaning of *ancient*?" Clarence wanted to know. "It means *old*. Why do you ask?" "We have to make a list of the Seven Wonders of the ancient world for history. Will you help me with it, please," Clarence begged. "Oh dear, I'll have to do some surfing on the Internet for that!" his mother said. "The only ones I can remember are the pyramids and the hanging gardens of Babylon."

They soon found the other five. There were Mausolos's grave, the two statues of Apollo and Zeus, the temple of Artemis and King Ptolemy's lighthouse. They found some interesting facts about these man-made wonders, which unfortunately, except for the pyramids, have all been destroyed.

"The work of men will soon be past, only what's done for God will last," said Clarence's mom. "People erect the most awesome buildings, but wind and weather and earthquakes and wars destroy them. Take the World Trade Center as an example." Clarence remembered the awful events of 11 September 2001 when two planes crashed into the two tallest buildings in New York in order to destroy them. He had seen it over and over again on television.

The Sunday after that catastrophe their pastor read a passage from the Bible that made a lasting impression on Clarence. It was from 2 Peter 3. According to that Scripture the whole known world will one day be destroyed, but God's kingdom will last for ever. His kingdom consists of three groups of people: those who are already with God, those who are living today as God's children and those who must still be born and will become servants of God. Clarence was very glad that he was one of those who would one day live in God's new world that will never be destroyed.

Read 1 Peter 3:1-14. Make sure that you are in God's kingdom.

8 November

A real life drama

In the City of Damascus the Christians were waiting anxiously. They had heard that Saul of Tarsus was on his way to their city to kill the believers. What could they do? They prayed that God would stop this vicious man and that He would protect them. However, Saul was getting nearer and nearer to the city! As the hooves of his horse touched the ground, it sounded as if they were echoing: "Kill them! Kill them! Kill them!"

Saul couldn't wait to lay his hands on the members of the new sect. They were a threat to the Jewish faith. "I will put a stop to this madness," he thought. "These people who say that Jesus is the Son of God and that He rose from the grave must be silenced for ever."

But God had heard the anxious prayers of His children and Acts 9:3-6 tells how He answered their prayers. You can also read Paul's own version of the story in Acts 26:12-18. On that day Saul met the living Christ and it changed his life completely.

Jesus met him on the road to Damascus and asked him, "Saul, Saul, why do you persecute me? You are only hurting yourself by acting the way you do." Saul must have been surprised that Jesus did not scold or punish him. He just invited him to stop living a life that was exhausting, yet worthless. From that day onwards Saul only wanted to serve Jesus. He became Paul, the greatest missionary that ever lived.

If you have also met with Jesus Christ, you can sing this song: "Blessed assurance, Jesus is mine! O what a foretaste of glory divine! Heir of salvation, purchase of God; born of His spirit, washed in His blood!"

9 November

Be creative!

One Saturday morning Sheila complained to her mom, "Oh, how I wish that I could be more creative." Her brother started teasing her, "Little sister, I never even thought that you would know the meaning of such a big word," he said. He was very creative and made beautiful wooden toys which he sold at a craft-market on Saturday mornings. He was just about to leave with his toys for the market. Sheila's sister, on the other hand, had a gift for music. She could play the piano and the guitar without having had any lessons.

"I must have inherited Mom's genes," she said. "We can't paint or draw or sing like Dad and the rest of the family." At that moment her dad entered the kitchen. "And who laid out our garden so artistically? And who makes all your stylish outfits?" He gave her mom a hug. Sheila never thought that making a pretty garden and doing needlework were also creative.

Later she asked her mom, "Do you think that I can also be creative?" "You can make us a tasty salad for lunch," her mom suggested. "You can also write Grandma a kind letter for her birthday. In these ways you can be just as creative as any one of us."

Sheila took a tomato and a cucumber and started to cut them in slices. She arranged them in neat rows on a plate. "I'm making a creative salad!" she said. Then she laid the table for lunch. She folded the serviettes into little fans, like she had seen at a restaurant.

On Sunday she would now also have something to mention when her teacher asked who had been creative. She needn't be a painter or a musician, like some of the other kids, to be called creative!

God is the greatest Creator. Read Genesis 1:1-27 and list all the things He created.

10 November

Louis Pasteur

Almost 200 years ago a boy was born in France and his name is still seen in supermarkets today. Who was he and how did this come about?

The boy's name was Louis Pasteur and his parents were poor peasants who loved God. They taught him to serve the Lord and to be kind to everyone. Louis was an intelligent boy and one day his school teacher allowed him to look through his microscope. Louis was very excited about what he could see through this magnifying lens. He spent hours watching insects and plants through the microscope and he decided that he wanted to become a scientist one day so that he could learn more about God's wonderful creation.

Eventually his dream came true when he became a professor in science at a college in Paris. In those days people knew nothing about germs or bacteria. However, Professor Pasteur discovered that tiny living creatures, which were invisible to the eye, caused milk and food to go bad. He also discovered that many people in hospitals died as a result of these germs. All the scientists and doctors laughed at him when he shared this idea with them. But he kept on fighting a war against germs and ignorance. After a while people saw that he was right and doctors and nurses realized that hospitals and clinics had to be spotlessly clean and germ-free.

Today our milk is *Pasteur*ized. This process bears Louis Pasteur's name because he discovered the bacteria in milk and realized that it had to be killed.

Louis Pasteur used his talents to investigate God's creation and to help others. He loved God with his whole heart and his whole mind and he also loved his neighbors, as Jesus told us to.

Read Matthew 22:34-40.

11 November

Suffering for your faith

Somebody from *Open Doors Ministry* came to Mavis's church to tell them about countries where Christians are martyred for their faith. Some parents took their toddlers outside because the stories were too gruesome for little ears. Then the visitor read from Hebrews 11:36-37: *"Some faced jeers and flogging, while still others were chained and put in prison. They were stoned, they were sawn in two; they were put to death by the sword. They went about in sheepskins and goatskins, destitute, persecuted and mistreated."*

That night Mavis could not sleep. She walked to her parent's room and stood next to her father's side of the bed until he woke up. "What's the matter?" he asked. "I can't sleep," she said. He got up and carried her to her bedroom. Then he put her into bed and said, "Tell me what's bothering you." Mavis started to tell him about all her fears after the morning's service. She was really scared that the same kind of things could happen to her. "I'm afraid that I will not stay true to Jesus if they hurt me like that," she blurted out. Her father sat down on the bed.

"When do I usually give you your bus fare?" he asked. Mavis wasn't sure why her father wanted to know that, but she answered nevertheless, "Just in time for when I need it." "Well," her dad said, "maybe we will never be martyred for our faith like some Christians. But if it should happen, God will give us the strength to endure like many of His children have done in the past. He doesn't give us courage way in advance. Just in time for when we need it."

Read 2 Corinthians 11:24-29 to see what Paul had to endure and then read 2 Corinthians 12:9-10 to see what he had to say about it.

12 November

Getting ready

Mr. and Mrs. Lightfoot were planning to go overseas for a holiday. They already had their plane tickets and needed to get things ready for the trip. They bought cotton clothes, because the weather was hot in the places they wanted to visit. They bought a booklet with Thai and Japanese phrases so that they could understand a little bit of the foreign languages.

At the library they took out books and video tapes about the Far East. Just before they left, they would also exchange their money for baht and yen, which they would use in Thailand and Japan. They had to arrange for passports and visas, because without them they would not be allowed into those countries. Yes, there were a lot of things that had to be seen to before they could undertake their journey.

Jeanne and Harry would stay with their grandmother while their parents were away. "As soon as I'm grown-up, I'm also going overseas. It will be fun to prepare for a trip," Jeanne said. She paged through an atlas to see which countries she would like to visit.

That evening during devotions their father read Isaiah 65:17-18. Then he said, "I have read you a passage about a country everybody wants to go to." "And that's heaven!" Harry said. "Luckily our tickets have been paid for by Jesus." His dad added, "But we need to do some preparations. We should prepare for our trip by studying the Bible, our guide book." "We can also enjoy getting ready for heaven just as we are doing now," Mrs. Lightfoot agreed.

Afterwards the whole family sang the hymn: "Only a few more years, then an eternal song!"

What passport will you need before you can enter heaven? Read Revelation 22:14.

13 November

The lady with the lamp

Can you believe that there was a time when nursing wasn't an honorable calling? The girls who had to look after sick people in hospitals did not have a good reputation and were not trained for the job. But through Florence Nightingale nursing became a respectable profession. She was the daughter of wealthy and distinguished parents in England. When she told her parents that she wanted to be a nurse, they nearly had a fit. "Let us take her on a tour around the world so that she can get rid of these bad ideas," they said. So she accompanied her parents on a trip through Europe and Egypt. But wherever they went, Florence was only interested in the hospitals. Her parents could not change her great passion for sick people. So when they returned to England, she started her own hospital.

Shortly afterwards the Crimean war broke out between England and Russia. Florence heard that thousands of soldiers had been wounded and were in desperate need of help. She picked 38 good nurses to accompany her and they took food, blankets, medicines and bandages to Scutari, where there were more than 4 000 wounded soldiers in the most awful circumstances. With love and compassion she started looking after the sick even late into the night. With her lantern she made the rounds to see whether everyone had been cared for. When the war was over, the queen of England presented her with a golden brooch inscribed with the words, "Blessed are the merciful". The government gave her a large sum of money which she used to build a nurses's college.

For many years after that, whenever student nurses got their diplomas, they were given a small lamp to remind them of Florence Nightingale, the lady with the lamp.

Read Matthew 5:7.

14 November

An impossible prayer

Have you ever asked the Lord for something, thinking that it was impossible that your prayer could ever be granted, but then you got what you had asked for? Many Christians can tell about such things happening to them, because we serve a God who can do the impossible.

A man once kept a record of all the prayers that God granted him. He recorded 50 000 such prayers! His name was George Müller and he ran a large number of orphanages in England. He never asked anybody for money to care for the orphans. He simply prayed about their needs and the Lord provided.

One morning, for example, there was no food to give the children in the orphanage. Despite this, he rang the bell for breakfast and the children came in and took their seats. George Müller prayed and thanked God for the food that He was going to provide. When he finished praying, there was a short silence. Then suddenly there came a knock at the door. A child ran to open the door and in walked the baker with armloads of bread. He told them that he could not sleep during the night and that he started thinking about the orphans who might be without food. So he got up early and baked some extra bread.

When the bread was dished out, a second knock sounded on the door. This time it was a dairy farmer with cans full of milk. "My wagon broke down a short way from here," he said. "It will take some time to repair. Would you like to have the milk?"

The Lord had seen the great need of the children and so he answered George Müller's prayers.

Read David's words about God in Psalm 116:1-6.

15 November

The mediator

Francine was upset. In the current edition of the town's newspaper there was an article about children who had been taking drugs at a party, and now her mother didn't want her to go to her best friend's birthday party. Francine joined her eldest sister on the bed. "Beth, won't you please talk to Mom about Friday evening?" "What is it worth to you?" Beth asked. "I'll make your bed every morning," Francine offered, "for a month!" "Okay!" Beth replied.

Beth and Mom talked for a long time before Beth returned. "Mom wants to see you," she said without telling her the result of her conversation.

"You may go to the party on Friday night," her mother said. "But you must be back by 23:00. The person who brings you back, must have a driver's license and I want to know which videos you are going to watch."

Francine grabbed her mother around the waist. "Thanks, Mom!" she said. "Steady now," her mother called out when she took a short cut across the flower-bed to go and phone her friend. "Ask her whether her parents will be at home on Friday night," she called, "and who else will be at the party."

"It's amazing!" Francine said to Beth later. "How did you do it?" "Ah! I was a good mediator. Remember, I was your age once but I also know the things that are important to Mom and Dad."

Later that evening Francine was busy preparing her Sunday school lesson, when she came upon the following passage: *"Jesus is the perfect mediator between us and God, for He was a man and He knows best what the will of the Father is for our lives."* For the first time she understood the meaning of those words.

Read 1 Timothy 2:5-6.

16 November

Serves him right!

Fred had a most unpleasant experience. He had wanted to play a trick on Donald, but in the end he had to bear the brunt of it. This was how it happened. Fred and his uncle went fishing and their bait had a horrible smell. This made Fred think of a nasty plan. He wanted to play a trick on Donald, because he always teased Fred about his red hair and freckles. When they were packing up to go home, his uncle threw the left-over pieces of bait into the sea. But Fred kept a smelly morsel behind. He took it home in a plastic bag. He left it at the back-door and when he went to school the next day, he took it along in his book bag. At school he quickly put it in Donald's bag.

This caused havoc in the classroom. Everybody wanted to know where the horrible smell came from. Miss Small followed the odor and demanded that Donald open his book bag. She scolded him, in spite of Donald's plea that he knew nothing about it. She put his name down for detention and everyone teased him. "Stink!" they said. "You smell so bad, we can't think!"

However, to Fred's dismay, his own bag started to smell too. Donald's bag could be washed in the washing machine, but his was made of leather and the smell grew worse by the hour. Although he scrubbed and washed it as much as he could, the bad odor remained. He put it out in the sun. He tried a deodorant – all to no avail! According to Proverbs 26:27, *"If a man digs a pit, he will fall into it."* Fred discovered the truth of this in a very unpleasant way as he sat in detention with his smelly bag.

Mark this verse in your Bible with a colored pencil.

17 November

A true hero

Have you seen the movie *Chariots of Fire*? It is an inspiring story. It tells about the life of Eric Liddell, who won the gold medal for the 400 meter race at the Olympic Games after he refused to run the 100 meter sprint on a Sunday. Once you have seen this movie, you will agree that he was a true hero.

But few people know what happened to Eric Liddell later on in life. He became a missionary and worked among the Chinese people to tell them about Jesus. But then the Second World War started. Eric was put into a concentration camp with hundreds of other people. It was a dreadful place to be. There was not enough space or food, and they were plagued by flies and mosquitos. In a prison camp like that, tempers flare up easily and disagreements, gossiping and fighting occur often.

But everybody could see that Eric was different. He did everything he could to make the camp more pleasant for the people around him. He helped elderly people chop wood, visited sick people and played games with the children. Whenever a fight started, he tried his best to get the quarreling parties to become friends again.

Today, people who hear the name Eric Liddell will quickly tell you that he was the man who won the gold medal for the 400 meter race in the Olympic Games in 1924. But he achieved something even more noteworthy in the eyes of the Lord. He was a witness to God in the most difficult circumstances.

If you encounter difficulties in your life, see them as a chance to amaze people at the positive way you respond. This can bring great honor to the God whom we serve.

Read 1 Corinthians 9:24-27.

18 November

Mary Jones

Do you know how it came about that the Bible became so readily available that today anyone who wants to can buy one? It is all because of a little girl who lived in Wales 200 years ago. Her name was Mary Jones. From the moment she could read, she longed to have a Bible of her very own. But in those days, shops didn't keep Bibles. If you wanted one, you had to buy one from a minister. Moreover, a Bible in those days was very, very expensive! So Mary started things like baby-sitting, selling eggs and gathering firewood in order to earn enough money to buy a Bible. In the meantime she was allowed to read the Bible of a kind lady who lived near to her home. She could go there any time she liked and she often made use of this kind offer.

At last, after 6 long years, she had sufficient money for a Bible. She heard that there was a minister in a neighboring town who sold Bibles. To get there, however, she would have to follow a dangerous road, winding through thick forest and across mountains. After praying about this with her parents, Mary set out. When she reached the house of the reverend Charles, her feet were worn out and very sore. He had one Bible left to sell her.

Afterwards Reverend Charles told a gathering of ministers in London about this brave little girl, and so it came about that a new organization was founded: the Bible Society. They started printing Bibles in order to make it easy for people all over the world to obtain Bibles. That is why many people all over the world today can afford to buy a Bible: because of one little girl's love for the Lord.

Say thank you for your own Bible in the words of Psalm 50:1-6.

19 November

Good medicine

"**H**ave you taken your pills?" Annette's mother asked her one morning. "Do I still have to?" she asked. She had flu and the doctor had prescribed antibiotics. Her headache and sore throat were now better and she thought that taking the pills was unnecessary. "Remember, the doctor said you should finish the course," said her mom. "It might well be that some viruses are still lingering somewhere and could harm you if you don't give them the full dose of medicine."

That afternoon a friend came to visit Annette. They were chatting in the lounge. Annette's mother could hear them from the kitchen. "Mary made a mess of Corrie's book again! It was full of oily stains after she'd borrowed it. Their house must be like a pigsty," Marge commented. "Have you seen her shoes lately? They're so worn out." The rest of the conversation was also mainly about irritating habits of their classmates.

When Marge left, Annette's mother called her. "It seems as if you're not taking your medicine anymore," she said. "I have taken my tablets," she protested. "I'm talking about your New Year's resolution," her mom reminded her. Annette remembered that she had decided to learn verses from Proverbs by heart to help her not to gossip. For the first few weeks she had tried to memorize these Scriptures, but later she thought it was unnecessary. Suddenly she ·felt bad about what she had said about Mary. She knew that Mary's family were poor and that her dad was jobless. Making fun of her behind her back was most unkind. She realized that she would have to carry on with her medication against gossiping.

Read one of the texts that Annette had learned to guard her against gossip: Proverbs 11:12-13; Proverbs 12:18.

20 November

A winner for Christ

When the football team came onto the field, the crowd went mad. Today the inter-school match was being played and the reputation of two very good teams hung in the balance.

Ricky was fired up to win. He tried to remember all the instructions of their coach, "Bob will pass to you and you must keep your eyes on your opponent. When you get the ball, either break to the inside, or pass to Fred!" Suddenly Ricky got the ball. He could hear spectators alongside the field shouting his name. With difficulty he tried to remember all they had practiced. With all his might he kept the goalposts and his opponents in sight at the same time. He side-stepped the opponent's center and then went for the goal!

When he scored, everybody cheered, but Ricky only wanted to see the face of his coach. Mr. Dreyer's smile made him very happy.

On the bus going home there was much joy and singing. But suddenly Ricky realized that the bottle of cooldrink being passed around had been doctored. Someone passed the bottle to him, "Drrrrrink Ricky drrrrrink and score again!" one of his teammates shouted. Suddenly it was as if he was again caught up in a very hard game, so many voices edging him on! "Why not pretend that I am taking a swig from the bottle?" he thought. But then he remembered what his father once said to him, "Your witness is most effective when you can say NO to temptations!"

He handed back the bottle, "Come along!" said Fred. "Our captain won't mind." "But my Captain will!" said Ricky. In his mind's eye he saw the smiling face of his Master.

Read what Paul says about being a winner in 1 Corinthians 9:24-27.

21 November

The lady with the expensive perfume

What would you say if somebody opened a beautiful jar of expensive perfume before your very eyes and used it all in one batch? You would probably say, "Are you crazy?" and "What a waste."

In the Bible there's a story of someone who did exactly that! You can read about it in John 12:1-8. Jesus had been invited to eat with Martha, Mary and Lazarus. He and his friends had to walk a very long distance to get there and their feet must have been tired and sore. They reclined at a low table and Martha probably brought them water, bread, cheese, honey, raisins and almonds (typical delicacies in those days). Then Mary appeared. She had a jar of nard, a very expensive perfume. She broke the jar and poured the contents over Jesus' feet. Then she dried His feet with her hair. With this gesture she said, "Thank You, Lord!"

Jesus looked at her with gratitude. The whole place was filled with the fragrance of the perfume. However, not everyone liked the idea. Judas, one of the disciples, objected, "Why wasn't this perfume sold and the money given to the poor?" Jesus said, "She has done a beautiful thing for me. The poor you will always have with you, but you will not always have me. I tell you, wherever this gospel is preached throughout the world, what she has done, will also be told." That is exactly what happened. This story can be found in three of the gospels and is still as beautiful 2 000 years later.

Sometimes people say, "It is too expensive to send missionaries to faraway countries." They should read this passage in Scripture. Nothing that is done for Jesus, within God's will, is ever wasted!

Spend some time thanking the Lord for everything that He has given you. It will not be a waste of time.

22 November

Perhaps He's coming today!

A tourist took a detour from the usual mountain trail and came upon a well-built cabin with a beautiful garden. An old man, working in the garden, greeted him warmly. They started the following conversation: "You have a beautiful home!" "It's not mine, it belongs to my employer." "He must be very happy to live in such a gorgeous place." "No, he lives in the city." "Do you often see him?" "No!"

The kind gardener proudly showed the traveler around. The hedges had been trimmed, the rose trees had been pruned, the lawns were well-kept and the flower beds were neat. New seedlings had been planted in preparation for the coming spring.

The conversation between the two men continued, "How long have you been working for your employer?" "Twenty-four years." "How many times has your boss come visiting during this time?" "Only four times." "How long since his last visit?" "Twelve years."

"That's remarkable!" the tourist exclaimed. "You look after this garden as if your master will return tomorrow." "No," replied the gardener, "as if he will come today."

We should also be ready for Jesus' return every day. We do not know when He will come. But when He comes, our lives should be as beautiful and prepared as the garden on the mountainside.

The Bible says, *"Now, brothers, you know very well that the day of the Lord will come like a thief in the night … So then, let us not be like others, who are asleep, but let us be alert and self-controlled"* (1 Thessalonians 4:11, 5:6).

Why not tidy your room as you would want it to be when Jesus comes. See it as symbolic of how you want your life to be.

23 November

Burn it!

For the last few weeks Zelda hadn't felt like reading the Bible or praying. She wasn't keen on going to church either. However, her mother didn't allow her to stay at home on Sunday morning. At Sunday school her teacher gave each member of the class a piece of paper and a pencil. "Write down all the things that you have done this past week that bother you," she said.

The children started making lists. Zelda thought about the money she had taken from her mom's purse. She also remembered that she had been nasty to her younger brother. Oh yes, and she had told a lie to a friend who wanted to come and visit.

After ten minutes Miss Morris took in all the sheets of paper. She put them in a tin that she had brought along. She told them to pray silently about the stuff that they had written down. Zelda prayed, "Lord, I am sorry about the money that I stole. I will give it back to Mom. I also feel bad because I was mean to Jeremy. I will try to be extra kind to him in future. And if Molly wants to come and play with me, I will let her come. Please help me to like her more. Thank you Jesus. Amen."

Then Miss Morris took a box of matches from her handbag and set the papers alight. She read from Isaiah 43:16-25. To Zelda it seemed as if God's love was burning away all her sin. She took a deep breath and felt wonderfully relieved.

As she was walking home, she realized that it must have been sin that caused her lack of enthusiasm for the things of God. Now that she had been forgiven, she could make a new start!

You can also make a list of the sins that you have committed recently. You can talk to God about them and burn them in a metal container outside.

24 November

The fireman

There was a great commotion in Bridge Street. A woman had forgotten a pot of boiling oil on the stove and it had caught on fire. The curtains caught alight and eventually the whole building was on fire! All the people fled from their apartments, but a little girl got trapped on the fourth floor. She was standing at one of the windows and yelling at the top of her voice. A fireman saw her and leaned his ladder against the wall next to her.

A fresh breeze blew the flames towards the fireman as he was climbing up the ladder. The crowd that were watching saw that the fireman hesitated to go further. In unison they started to chant, "Save her! Save her! Save her!" This encouraged the man to go on with his quest. He was coughing and sneezing from the smoke that surrounded him and the heat was getting unbearable. But each time he considered giving up, he could hear the people shouting, "Save her! Save her!" and then he would climb further.

At last he reached the little girl and picked her up in his arms. Then he carried her to safety. If it was not for the people's support, the fireman would not have had the courage to complete his task.

There are many people who sometimes have to do challenging and difficult work. Often they also lack the courage to go through with things. We can help them by encouraging them. The Bible teaches us to do that. In Thessalonians 5:14 Paul said: *"Encourage the timid, help the weak."*

Make a card for a policeman, nurse, teacher or missionary to encourage that person. You can write the last part of Isaiah 49:5 on it.

25 November

The account

Bruce's friends each had a new scooter and he really wanted one too. But even if he added up all the money that he had received for Christmas and for his birthday, he still did not have enough to buy one.

"Where can I find enough money?" he wondered. Then he had a bright idea. He wrote down all the chores that he had done for his parents during the last week. Next to each task he put an amount of money. If his parents would pay him for these chores, he would soon have enough, he thought.

He made some calculations. In this way he could have the scooter by the end of April. He went to his parent's room and put the note on his mom's bed.

He waited all day for their reaction. But they acted as if nothing unusual had happened. However, when he went to his room that night, he found an envelope on his pillow. It was also an account. At the top was written: *"Services rendered"* and *"Debts"*.

Below was a long list: *washing your clothes: free of charge; preparing meals: free of charge; cleaning the house: free of charge; issuing love and advice: free of charge!*

Bruce was glad that his mom wasn't there to see how embarrassed he was. He sat down to write her a letter, *"Dear Mom, sorry for being so greedy. Thank you for all the things that you do for me every day."* He made a bright border on the letter with his coloring-pencils and put it next to the kettle in the kitchen. She would find it there when she made coffee early the next morning.

He would have to make another plan to earn enough money for a scooter!

Read Ephesians 6:1-3.

26 November

The Dead Sea

We all know about dead flowers, dead plants, dead animals and dead people. But did you know that one could get something like a dead sea? Yes, at the bottom-end of the Jordan River in Israel, there's a sea full of water, but the water is "dead". The water in the Dead Sea contains five times more salt than ordinary seawater and it tastes bitter. Nothing can live in that water and fish that come from the river into the sea die. People who visit Israel always like to see this place and some tourists even swim there. It's fun, because you can't really sink in that water, but nobody stays for too long. A nasty smell hangs over the whole area.

The sand on the beach is also salty. Nothing grows there and no birdsong is heard. Here and there you'll find a piece of driftwood. But apart from that, the beach is deserted.

How did the Dead Sea come about? The reason is that the sea receives thousands of liters of water every day, but it has no outflow. The countryside around it is barren, because the water from the river never reaches it. The water is caught up in this sea, so that the valley does not benefit from it. The sun bakes down on this expanse of water and the water evaporates so that only the salt stays behind.

People who are selfish and who keep everything for themselves, can learn a lesson from the Dead Sea. If you are always on the receiving end and never give anything to those around you, you will become bitter and unattractive like this sea.

It is also a disaster to your spiritual life to hear the Good News about Jesus Christ over and over again, without telling others about it!

Read Luke 6:38.

27 November

What are you doing?

A man was walking along the street. He came upon a building site where lots of people were working. He could see heaps of building sand and bricks lying around. Trucks, concrete-mixers, cranes and bulldozers were moving about. He asked one of the workers, who was busy with a trowel and cement, "What are you building?" "A wall," the man said grumpily. "It's going to be a church," another man said, a little friendlier. "We're building a house of prayer," a third man said with enthusiasm. Why did the last fellow enjoy his work so much and with which of these workmen would the Lord be the most satisfied?

In Colossians 3:23-24 we read, *"Whatever you do, work at it with all your heart, as working for the Lord, not for men, since you know that you will receive an inheritance from the Lord as a reward. It is the Lord Christ you are serving."*

Maybe the third builder knew this passage in Scripture. His boss was probably not only the contractor who paid him every Friday. He did his work for the Lord and that was why he enjoyed it so much. He felt that he was doing something worthwhile.

How does that compare with the way you do your schoolwork? Do you say, "I must finish my assignment so that I can go and play outside." Or do you think, "I must do these exercises so that I can get good results," Or do you say, "I want to do my homework as best I can to please my parents and God!"

If you do everything as best you can, as for the Lord, He will reward you greatly. It doesn't matter whether it is schoolwork, chores or sport, you will find lots of joy in everything you do!

Write the passage from Colossians quoted above on your homework book.

28 November

Count your blessings!

"There you are," Louisa said when the workers had left. "Now I can start fixing up this place!" They had put a new carpet in her bedroom and now she was keen to redecorate the whole room. She could have new bedding, new curtains and a new bedside lamp to match the new color-scheme.

"Who wants to go with me?" her dad shouted down the passage. Louisa ran outside and jumped into the truck. "Where are we going?" she asked as her dad moved in behind the wheel. "We're taking Uncle John home," her dad answered. "He asked whether he could get the old carpet from your bedroom." Only then did Louisa notice that Uncle John was sitting at the back of the truck smiling from ear to ear, his arm resting on the roll of carpet. He was a gardener who worked at their house every Thursday.

John had to show the way along windy roads between the squatter homes. At last he stood proudly in front of his home. The front door was made from the boot of an old car. The windows must have come from a scrapyard too. They were cleverly built into the sink wall. A whole gang of children came to watch as the carpet was offloaded. John's wife came out carrying her baby. "Thank you, Sir. May God bless you!" John said gratefully. His wife looked as if she already knew where this piece of luxury from the rich people's home would fit into her shack.

Louisa and her dad didn't talk much on their way home. Louisa had put all thoughts of redecorating her room from her mind. She was thinking which of her toys she could give to Uncle John's children when he came to work next Thursday.

Which Bible verse matches this story best: Psalm 69:33 or Proverbs 14:21?

29 November

Looking for fruit

"**M**om, the gardener is cutting the peach tree down!" Pierre announced with dismay as he entered the kitchen. "Don't worry," his mom said. "I told him to do it." "But why?" Pierre asked. "Because it didn't produce anything," his mother said. "We have spent so much money and effort on that tree already. We watered it regularly, we applied fertilizer, we pruned it, but to no avail. Now we can chop it down and plant something else in its place."

Pierre had a glass of water before he went outside to see what the garden would look like without the huge peach tree. "Remember, there's a story in the Bible about a fruit tree that was chopped down because it didn't bear fruit," his mom reminded him. This casual remark of his mom disturbed Pierre more than he thought it would. He remembered how Jesus ordered His disciples to cut down a fig tree because it had no fruit on it. He also thought about the text that was on the wall in his mom's office. It was Galatians 5:22-23 which said: *"The fruit of the Spirit is love, joy, peace, patience, kindness, goodness, faithfulness, gentleness and self-control."* The Lord had already invested so much in him and he still lacked some of these fruit! Did it mean that God would remove him from His garden because he was often impatient and unkind? He watched in awe as the gardener set the tree-stump on fire.

That evening he had a long conversation with his mom. She read Philippians 3:12-13 to him. It made him feel better. Because he belonged to Christ, he would never be destroyed like the peach tree. However, like Paul, he would have to strive towards reaching the goal that was put before him, to be more and more like Jesus.

Read the verses that made Pierre feel better.

30 November

DECEMBER

God's plan

In Micah 5:2 you will find these words, *"But you, Bethlehem Ephrathah, though you are small among the clans of Judah, out of you will come for me one who will be ruler over Israel."*

When Micah had spoken those words, the people who listened to him said to each other, "Christ, the Savior, the Man who God will send to come and help us, will one day be born in Bethlehem."

And then, when Jesus was already grown up and was teaching the people about God, some of them said, "Just listen to Him and look at the miracles that He performs. Isn't He perhaps the Christ?" "Oh no!" the learned men replied. "He comes from Nazareth. Out of that little village nothing worthwhile can ever come." But what they did not know, was that Jesus was actually born in Bethlehem.

Now how did it come about that a mother and father from Nazareth went all the way to Bethlehem for the birth of their baby son? God organized it that way! He gave the governor the idea to have all the people counted. "Everybody must go to the place where his forefathers came from," he said. "There their names will be recorded in a book."

That is why Joseph and Mary had to travel all the way from Nazareth to Bethlehem. Because the grandparents of their grandparents came from that city. They had to travel for four days to get there. And you probably know what happened in a stable in Bethlehem on the night of their arrival. Jesus, the Savior was born! Exactly as the prophet Micah predicted 700 years before.

God knows what is going to happen and He can influence people to do the things that fit into His plans.

Read what the learned people told King Herod in Matthew 2:1-6 when he inquired about the birth of Christ.

1 December

Your own Psalm

The Sunday school teacher had asked each of the children in Matt's class to write his own version of Psalm 23. Matt went home and tried several versions before he came up with this one, which he wrote in his diary:

The Lord looks after me like a good shepherd would. He knows my name and He sees everything I do. He gives me all I need. When I'm tired of being outside, I can come home to my family. I get enough to eat and to drink. When the sun sets, I have a place to sleep. And when the sun comes up, I am eager to start the new day.

He does not allow me to do what I want. He stops me when I want to wander away from Him. He punishes me if I do not listen to Him, because He does not want me to get lost.

Although I am frightened of the dark, I know that this is unnecessary. Because, even if I get sick or am threatened by danger, He never leaves me alone. He deals with all the frightening things around me.

I am very grateful for all the fun I have. My Shepherd sees to it that I have time to laugh and play.

It is a wonderful thought that He will always be there for me. When I grow up and have lots of responsibilities or when I grow old and need lots of help, He will be there to care for me. His love will carry me through. And when I die, they will burn or bury my body, but my soul will go to be with God in a place where there will be great festivity, for ever and ever!

Try to write your own version of Psalm 23.

2 December

Use your weapons!

Is there somebody you regard as an enemy? Perhaps a kid at school who bullies you? Or a teacher who is unfair? Yes, there might be people around who make life difficult for you. But they are not your biggest enemies. Satan and his evil forces are. The Bible says that our struggle is not against flesh and blood, but against the powers of this dark world. You can read about this in Ephesians 6:12.

The devil is a very dangerous enemy, because he can disguise himself very effectively. He will never come to you, saying, "Hello, I'm Satan!" He prefers that people do not even believe that he exists. He wants to enter our lives stealthily and poison our thought life bit by bit. That is why he says, "The Bible isn't quite true!" He wants to take away our enthusiasm for Bible study. Or he says, "Sin doesn't matter, because God is a God of mercy." That is because he wants us to be disobedient to God. He says, "As long as you believe in something, you're okay." That's because he does not want you to acknowledge Jesus as your Savior.

Fortunately the Bible teaches us how to fight against this dangerous enemy. In Ephesians 6:12-17 you will find a list of the weapons with which you can conquer the devil. When Satan tried to mislead Jesus in the desert, Jesus also used these weapons. He used the sword of the Spirit, which is the Word of God. Each time Satan attacked Him, He quoted a verse from the Bible. That is why we should know our Bibles thoroughly, to be able to chase the devil away!

Look at the three lies of Satan: Read Revelation 22:18-19, Revelation 20:15 and Acts 4:12. You will find good answers in these verses to drive Satan away.

3 December

Beware of the seducer!

Do you know what a seducer is? It is someone who wants you to do what is wrong. First he infiltrates your thought life and then he causes you to stumble. The devil is a real slanderer and seducer. First he will make you dissatisfied with what you have, because then he can easily seduce you to sin. He will tell you, "Your mom loves your brother more than you." Or, "The teacher's favorite always gets the highest marks." If the devil ever comes to you with lies like this, send him away immediately. Just say, "Go away" as Jesus did when He was tempted.

In the Bible we find the sad story of David and Bathsheba. There we see how David fell for Satan's suggestions and had to bear the terrible consequences. Do you know the story?

One evening David was on the roof of his palace when he saw a beautiful woman. "Who is she?" he asked his servants. "She is Uriah's wife," they said. Satan took his chance, "Why should Uriah have such a beautiful wife? You are the king. She should have been your wife!" Then David forgot God's command which says, "You shall not covet your neighbor's wife." God gave that command because He knew that when we envy others, more sin soon follows. And so it happened to David. He was so jealous of Uriah, that he had him killed, so that he could marry Bathsheba.

But God had seen everything and He was very unhappy with David's behavior. Therefore he sent the prophet Nathan to reprimand him. After that David realized the seriousness of his sin and he asked God to forgive him.

God pardoned him, but he had to live with the terrible consequences of his deed. So, beware of the seducer!

You can read this story in 2 Samuel 11 and 12.

4 December

God knows everything

"René, where are you?" her mother called. René did not answer. She was lying under the bed, not making a sound. She had done a terrible thing. She had accidentally dropped the fish-bowl and it had smashed into tiny pieces. That was exactly what her mom had predicted, "Never pick up the fish-bowl, René," her mom had warned. "You might drop it."

René lay dead still, but she did not realize that her feet were sticking out at the bottom of the bed. When her mother entered the room, she immediately knew where her little girl was hiding. "Come out from under the bed," her mom said. René was quite embarrassed. She did not look her mother in the eyes. Her mom was serious when she spoke, "You were disobedient!" she said. "You will have to contribute towards a new bowl for the fish. You will also have to clean up everything. Fortunately I could still save the fish."

While she was picking up the pieces of glass, her mom came to sit on a chair near her. "René," she said softly, "always remember that it is no use trying to hide when you have done something wrong. Even if I did not see you, God would have known exactly where you were hiding. The best plan of action is to admit if you have done something wrong." "I'm sorry, Mom," said René. Her mother gave her a hug. Now she could look her in the eyes again.

Yes, God sees everything we do. According to Ezekiel 11:5 He even knows what we are thinking! Nothing happens without His knowing about it and nothing can be hidden from Him. That should be a warning to us, but it is also a comforting thought. What we don't know, God knows and He can protect us from unknown dangers.

Read Job 36:21.

5 December

The name of Jesus

Do you know the meaning of your name? You should try to find out. Maybe you will feel that your name doesn't suit you at all, or maybe you like the meaning and it can be an inspiration to you!

You probably know that Peter means "rock". "Theo" and "John" both mean "gift of God". "Anne" means "grace" and "Sonia" means "wisdom". These names can be a real encouragement to those who are called by them.

In Luke 1:31 we read that the angel told Mary to give her baby the name "Jesus", which means "Savior". Jesus really lived up to His name. Throughout His life He saved people, some from illnesses, some from evil spirits, others from a life without meaning. Think about the poor man at the pool of Bethesda who had been sick for 38 years and Jesus healed him in the blink of an eye. Then there was the mad man from the region of Gadarenes who had to be tied up because he acted so wildly. Jesus delivered him from the evil forces that were ruining his life. Remember Zacchaeus, who only lived for money and possessions? Jesus saved him from his lust for money. After his encounter with Jesus, he turned his back on sin and started to give most of his money away.

Is there something that you would also like to be delivered from? Maybe a quick temper? Or laziness, or a lack of love? Jesus' name is Savior, and He can truly save you from whatever is preventing you from having a full and happy life.

Jesus took His work as Savior very seriously. He was prepared to die for it. After He was crucified, He could say to Satan, "You can never again keep My children in your power, for I have paid the price for them to be saved."

Read what people said about Jesus in John 4:42.

6 December

Houses

Uncle Jack, who had traveled extensively, brought a video to Chris's house to show them all the places that he had seen. He was especially interested in the homes of different people groups. First Uncle Jack showed them a hut in central Africa. It looked like a basket that had been turned upside down. The home had no windows and the door was very low. "The people try to keep out as much of the sun as possible," he said.

Then they visited a place in Morocco where people lived in tents. The Bedouins are forever moving from one place to the other, therefore they do not build houses. In a town in Italy the people also do not build houses because they live in grottos. The hills where they stay look like beehives.

Uncle Jack also visited Greenland, where the Eskimos live in igloos made from blocks of ice. "It must be freezing inside," Chris said. "No," his uncle replied. "They burn oil-lamps inside, which keep them warm." Chris couldn't believe that their houses did not melt away. The cutest homes are the tree houses in South America. The inhabitants climb to their front door with a rope ladder. Babies are fastened with a rope so that they don't fall to the ground.

At the end of the video Uncle Jack's camera scanned a deserted field in Australia. All that was visible were heaps of soil. But apparently, beneath the soil there was a hive of activity as people lived in old underground mines.

"I like our type of housing best," Chris said. "I think the best is yet to come," Uncle Jack said as he took the video out. "Our home in heaven will outshine all the houses on earth."

Read 2 Corinthians 5:1-9.

7 December

No laughing matter

Miss Linde was shocked when she heard a group of seventh grade boys telling dirty stories in the library. They didn't realize that she was behind one of the bookshelves. They were supposed to be working together on a project, but they used their time to tell obscene jokes instead.

Suddenly she appeared next to them. They immediately kept quiet and acted as if they were busy with research.

"Boys, I'm very disappointed about what I've just heard from you. I'm sure that you all feel quite ashamed about the filthy stories that you've been sharing with each other," she said. Their eyes were downcast. "I want you to come here after school and draw up a list of reasons why this type of conversation is abominable," Miss Linde said before she walked away.

Later she found the boys around a table in the library. "Miss, we found six reasons why we shouldn't tell dirty jokes," said William. "What are they?" Miss Linde asked. William read what they had written, "One, it brings out the worst in us. Two, we were not brought up that way. Three, it encourages us to have unclean thoughts. Four, it will cause a loss of respect for each other. Five, it'll make us forget that you can have fun without being smutty. Six, it can make our favorite teacher cross with us." The children watched to see what her reaction would be.

Miss Linde said earnestly, "Your displeased teacher is pleased that you put some thought into this matter. And she wants to give each one of you a Scripture verse to learn by heart." All four boys put out their hands to take the written cards from her.

Read the verse that Miss Linde wrote on the cards: Hebrews 4:13.

8 December

Poor frogs!

On Friday night at the Youth Club one of the youth leaders told a story that left a mark on many of the children's minds.

There was once a frog who jumped into a pot of water on a stove. The frog swam vigorously around in the pot, enjoying the cool water.

But what he didn't know was that the pot was slowly heating up as the stove plate got warmer. The frog started feeling lazier and lazier and swam more and more slowly. Without his realizing, his body was adjusting to the rising temperature of the water.

Eventually the frog stopped moving and gave his last kick. He was dead. If the frog had been put into the hot water straight away, he would have jumped out, but because the water was heated gradually, he didn't object. He could not survive in the water that had slowly became too hot for his body to adapt to.

The youth leader went on to explain what happened to the frog can also happen to us. He said, "The devil changes our world-view bit by bit. Things that we at first knew to be sin, later seem innocent. We do not shy away from them like before. We adjust to a sinful world. Later on we capitulate completely and live like others in the sinful world around us. So we become spiritually dead."

Then the leader read from 1 John 2:15-17 and each person had a chance to pray. They asked God to help them to stay true to His Word, and not to forget about His commandments bit by bit.

Also read Romans 12:2.

9 December

Masks

A minister once used this story to illustrate the necessity of being an honest Christian.

Once there was a little boy who wanted to go for a swim in the sea. On the beach he saw a lady with an enormous umbrella. He went to her and asked, "Excuse me Ma'am, are you a Christian?" "Yes," she replied. "And do you read the Bible?" he asked again. "Yes," was her answer. "And do you do what the Bible teaches?" he continued. "I try," she said. "Why would the little fellow ask all these questions?" she must've thought. "Will you please keep my money for me while I go swimming?" he asked, handing her his wallet.

The boy was lucky to get his money back, because unfortunately there are many people who say that they are Christians, but who are not real followers of Christ. They might go to church, they might write "Christian" on their CVs, they might even put a Scripture verse in their car window. These people know how Christians are supposed to behave, but they do not love Jesus at all!

On the surface they appear to be Christian. However, when you get to know them, you find that they are not really God's children. They are only wearing religious masks. In 2 Corinthians 11:13-15 Paul warns us against these false "Christians". We should not trust everybody who parades as a Christian. When we choose our best friends or when we need advice or when we have to choose our leaders, we have to be very careful and discerning. Ask God to show you if somebody is merely wearing a religious mask without truly loving the Lord.

2 Timothy 3:1-5 lists the kinds of people we should be wary of. Make a list of ten of these and write at the top: "Beware of ... " Keep it in your Bible.

10 December

A spoilt brat

Owen Bacon was a real spoilt brat. He could get anything he wanted from his mother. All he had to do was to whimper or cry, and then she would give him whatever he wished.

On his birthday his mom made a special breakfast. A bunch of balloons was tied to his chair and when he came out of his bedroom, the whole family sang "Happy Birthday". They expected Owen to be surprised and happy, but instead he said, "Why didn't anybody tell me what was going on!" When he opened his gifts, he said, "This isn't what I wanted!" They started to eat and Owen said, "Why is there no ice-cream? You know that's my favorite!"

Then his dad got really mad at him. "Come here, young man! Enough is enough," he said. "You go on with your breakfast," he told the rest of the family. "Owen and I are going for a drive." They got into the car and drove off to a township on the other side of the railway line. They stopped outside Mrs. James's door. She came regularly to clean their windows and tidy up their home.

"Good morning, Mrs. James!" Mr. Bacon said when she opened the front door. "Where're David and Cathy?" The two kids came to the door, each with a piece of bread. Owen's father whispered something in their mother's ear and then she wiped their hands and faces and said, "Mr. Bacon wants you to go with him." The two kids jumped into the back of the car. "Come inside!" Owen's father said when they reached the Bacon's house. "There's lots of food on the table. Eat as much as you like." He didn't have to ask them twice. When last had they had such a feast?

Owen went quietly to his room. He had learned a lesson that he would not easily forget.

Read 1 Thessalonians 5:18.

11 December

The best gift of all

The world-famous author O. Henry wrote this beautiful story.

There once lived a husband and wife who were happily married, even though they were very poor. One night they went window-shopping. In a jewelry shop John saw a magnificant strap for his watch. "I wish we had enough money to buy that strap," he said. He owned a gold watch that he had inherited from his grandfather, but the strap was broken. A little bit further on they saw a lovely comb made of real tortoise shell. Delia thought how she would fasten her hair with that comb and she said, "I wish we had enough money to buy that comb."

As Christmas drew nearer, they were both making plans. Delia went to a place that made wigs and asked the owner how much he would pay for her hair. She was thrilled when she heard that she could receive enough money to buy Jim the strap for his watch. Jim went to a pawn-shop and asked the owner how much he would pay for the gold watch. He was delighted to hear that he could receive enough money to buy Delia the comb for her hair.

When Jim came home on the night before Christmas, Delia was waiting for him with a neatly wrapped parcel in her hands. But he hardly noticed it. "Where's your beautiful hair?" he asked. "I sold it so that I could buy you this gift," she said. He opened the parcel and found the expensive strap inside. "Here is your gift," he said softly. She opened the parcel that he gave her. And what did she find inside? The lovely decoration for her hair! "I sold my watch to buy you the comb," he said. They had both given each other their most precious possessions!

Make a beautiful Christmas card for someone that you love and write John 3:16 inside.

12 December

The days before Christmas

Do you find December to be very different from all the other months? The days before Christmas pass away so slowly, much more slowly than any other days! You see Christmas cards, Christmas trees and Santa Clauses everywhere and you hear "Silent Night" over and over again. But it usually feels as if Christmas will never come.

But the people who waited for the very first Christmas had a much longer wait. They waited for hundreds of years. Right at the beginning of the world God made a promise. He said that one day a child would be born who would make right all the wrongs that Adam and Eve caused by their disobedience. But many years came and went and this promise of God did not come to pass. God told His messengers, the prophets, not to get discouraged because the Savior was on His way. But there was no sign of Him anywhere.

If you look at the last book in the Old Testament, you will see that Malachi also mentions God's promise. In Chapter 3:1 he said, *"See, I will send my messenger, who will prepare the way before me. Then suddenly the Lord you are seeking will come to his temple."* The people waited and waited. But the Savior did not appear.

More than three hundred years passed after Malachi had given his message. Still nothing happened. But then, one night in Bethlehem, Jesus the Savior was born! God's promise did come true at last!

God always keeps His promises. To us it might seem like ages before He does what He promised. But He knows when it is the right time for things to happen.

Is there something that you have been waiting for for a very long time? Read Psalm 37:7. It is a message especially for you.

13 December

Speechless

Do you know what the word "speechless" means? It is used when someone is so surprised about something that he cannot speak a word. In the Bible a story is told about one of the priests at the temple who was speechless for ten whole months! The name of the priest was Zechariah and on that memorable day, it was his turn to go to the holy part of the temple where the incense was burnt on the altar.

Then something wonderful happened! An angel of the Lord suddenly stood next to the altar. Zechariah was scared, but the angel comforted him, "Don't be afraid," the angel said. "Your prayers have been answered. You and your wife Elizabeth are going to have a little boy and he will prepare the way for the Savior that is going to be born."

Zechariah did not believe it. He and his wife were both old and could not have children any more. "Because you did not believe God's message, you will not be able to speak again until the baby is born," the angel said.

Everything happened exactly as the angel said it would. Zechariah was not able to speak until Elizabeth gave birth to the baby.

Did God make Zechariah dumb to punish him? No, God wanted to teach him a lesson. He would come to understand that what seems impossible to man is possible for God. God can suddenly make a person speechless and He can also make someone who can't speak before, speak again. He can also enable an elderly man and his wife to have a baby if it is in His will. Indeed, nothing is impossible for Him.

Learn Luke 1:37 by heart and repeat it to yourself.

14 December

The message

Her name was Mary and she wasn't much older than you, about fourteen years of age. She lived with her parents in an ordinary house in the small town of Nazareth.

Often, when she was alone, making bread or doing some weaving, she must have wondered when God would answer her prayers. She and her people, the Israelites, were praying that God would send a Savior, because their country was under the rule of the Romans. Ages before, God's messengers, the prophets, had predicted that Somebody would come along to help them. The words of the prophets were written down on scrolls and kept safely in the temple. People would never tire of listening to them and then they would pray that God would do what He had promised.

One day Mary was alone in the house. Suddenly a stranger stood in front of her. It was an angel. His name was Gabriel and she realized that he had brought a message from God. He told her that she was going to have a very special baby. "You must call Him Jesus," the angel said, "because He will be the Son of God."

Can you imagine how surprised Mary must have been? To think that she was going to be the mother of the Savior for whose arrival she had been praying all along. She knelt down and said, "I am the Lord's servant. May it be with me as you have said."

None of us will ever get a similar message from God. But He might sometimes use us to answer our own prayers, like He did with Mary. Maybe you have been praying for somebody who is suffering a lot. Have you ever thought of doing something loving and kind for that person?

Read Mary's song in Luke 1:46-55. See how glad she was to be used by God to fulfill His promises.

15 December

Advent

Excitement was building up in the Warner home. Four candles were glowing on the dining room table, Christmas day was on its way!

The family were singing Christmas carols along with the choir on TV. At the end of the program, Mr. Warner turned off the TV set and asked, "Anybody want to share some Christmas plans?" Marilyn, the youngest, responded quickly, "I've sent my wish list to Santa Claus!" The other children giggled softly and remembered with glee how they also went through that stage.

"But Dad," the little girl asked, "why do we get presents when it is Jesus' birthday?" "That's a good question," her father said. "It's because we want to remind each other of the wonderful gift that was given to us when God sent Jesus to the world."

Now their mom spoke up, "I suggest that this year we all give Jesus a birthday gift." Her words made everybody think. Gerald spoke first, "I will give my soccer ball to the gardener, whose children badly want one. In Matthew 25 it says that if we do anything for people in need, it is just as if we have done it for Jesus." "That's a good idea," Mary said. "I am going to bake some cookies for poor Aunt Margaret in the frail-care center. If Mom says it's all right, of course!" "That's fine with me," her mom smiled. "I was thinking of taking flowers to a few lonely people that I know." "And I will make a birthday card for Jesus," Marilyn volunteered.

"I will obviously have to be a taxi-driver to get all of you to your different destinations," Mr. Warner said smilingly. "I will also send an extra offering to our missionary in Mozambique," he added.

You can also think of something special that you can do for Jesus on His birthday.

16 December

The nativity

Disaster on the night of the play! At first Chris didn't even want to think back on it. But later he smiled when people mentioned it. And luckily Pastor Williams knew how to handle the awkward situation.

This is what happened. When the rehearsals started, Chris was given the part of Joseph. But because his friends teased him about it, he asked Miss Moore whether he could rather be one of the wise men. "If any of them will be willing to change roles, it's okay," she said. Manuel volunteered to give up his role as a wise man. He didn't mind the teasing. "Manuel must hold his wife's hand," the boys cheered. But Manuel felt proud to play the part of Joseph, the husband of Mary, the mother of Jesus.

But because Chris didn't know his role as one of the wise men very well, he caused an upheaval on the night of the play. He left his prop in the dressing room. It was only when the three of them knelt in front of the manger, that he realized his mistake. The other two wise men had their gold and frankincense with them, but he had forgotten the myrrh. What could he do? He got up and sprinted past the angels, past the shepherds and vanished behind the curtains, only to reappear a little later with the treasure that he was to bring to the crib for the Baby. Eventually he could offer it with the other gifts, while the audience was laughing and cheering. Miss Moore wasn't impressed at all. The atmosphere of reverence was gone. But luckily the pastor saved the day with a beautiful prayer of devotion and said, "Lord, thank You that You understand our fallibility and that You always accept our gifts, even if they sometimes arrive a little late!"

Read the story about the wise men in Matthew 2:1-12.

17 December

The party

Have you heard about the two friends who wanted to give a surprise party to one of the students in their class? They invited guests, bought cold drinks and cake, decorated the venue with balloons and organized a band to play music. But on the evening of the party, they couldn't find the birthday boy anywhere!

When the guests arrived, they decided to have the party anyway. They all had a good time singing and laughing and chatting away. They even lit the candles on the birthday cake and sang the birthday song. Then they burst eighteen balloons to celebrate the eighteen years of John's life on earth. But John himself was nowhere to be seen! The next day the friends discovered that John had been to a movie with his parents. The organizers of the party had forgotten to invite the guest of honor! It was a big joke and the talk of the town for quite a while afterwards.

But do you know that something similar happens every year at Christmas time in many homes? Christmas is Jesus' birthday, but people tend to forget that. Often Jesus is completely left out of all the celebrations. You should think of ways in which He can be honored in your home. What about songs of praise around the Christmas tree together with a reading from Scripture and a prayer?

In Luke 2:7 you can read about the birth of Jesus, " ... *and she gave birth to her firstborn, a son. She wrapped him in cloths and placed him in a manger, because there was no room for them in the inn.*" Let's make sure that there is room for Christ at our family festivities on Christmas day.

Make a place card for everybody who comes for Christmas dinner and write a suitable verse on each one. (What about John 10:10.)

18 December

The wise men

"**L**ong, long ago, in a faraway land, there lived a group of people who studied the stars and who knew their movements very well. They believed that these lights of heaven could convey certain messages to human beings."

That was how Granddad started the story about the wise men one Christmas Eve. The children were listening in awe and even their parents, who had heard this story many times before, sat quietly while they marveled again at the wonder of it all. To think that God used a group of stargazers to let the world know that the Savior had been born!

We believe that God planned it that way, so that it could be known all over the world that Jesus did not only come for the Jews, but for the whole of mankind.

"*Eventually the wise men came to Bethlehem and found Joseph and Mary and the baby, Jesus. They knelt before him in adoration and presented him with precious gifts: gold and frankincense and myrrh.*" That was how Granddad ended his story. Then the children waited anxiously to see what their grandmother would get out of the manger that was put under the tree. Every year she had a surprise for each child in the family. She put her hand between the blankets and took out a beautiful silver star for each one. It could be tied around their necks with a blue ribbon that was fastened to it. And then they all sang, "Brightly beams our Father's mercy from His lighthouse evermore; but to us He gives the keeping of the lights along the shore!"

Make a star for your Christmas tree and write Matthew 2:10 on it.

19 December

One of us

There was once a man who did not believe the Christmas story. "Why would God come to earth as a baby?" he asked.

One evening, while his family was attending the Christmas celebrations at the church on their own, it started to snow outside, as it often does in December in Europe. The man was sitting in front of the fire, reading a book. Suddenly he heard a sound against the window pane. It sounded as if a snowball had crashed against it. It happened again and again. He got up to investigate and saw a flock of birds sitting in the snow on their lawn, looking miserable. A snowstorm was raging outside and these birds flew into the window of the lounge in a desperate attempt to escape the storm.

The man felt sorry for the birds, so he put his coat on and walked to the garage. He decided to attract them to the shelter of the carport, so that they would not get frostbitten and die. He opened the door of the garage and put the light on. But the birds didn't move. Then he went to the kitchen, took a piece of bread, and dropped crumbs all along the pathway up to the garage door. But the birds weren't interested.

Eventually he realized that the birds were scared of him. How could he gain their confidence? "Maybe I would've been able to rescue them if I could become a bird myself," he thought. "Then I would've been able to tell them in their own language how to get to safety."

At that very moment the church bells started to ring out a Christmas tune and the man suddenly realized why Jesus had to come to earth as a baby. He had to become one of us so that He could lead us to the safety of His Father's house.

Read the name the angel gave Jesus in Matthew 1:23.

20 December

Christmas around the world

Christmas is a very special time almost everywhere in the world. It is quite interesting to read about the Christmas traditions in different countries.

In Holland, St. Nicholas does the rounds early in December. Children put out their clogs (wooden shoes) at the front door at night, hoping to find a gift there in the morning. This is a very good custom, because on 25 December, Jesus can be the center of attention. Elsewhere Father Christmas often steals the limelight.

In the homes of Indian Christians, there is usually meat on the table on Christmas day. It is a luxury that few people in India can normally afford. The children often have a Christmas pageant outside in the street for everyone to see.

In the Philippines there's a procession through the streets on the day before Christmas. The five most important people in town are visited and from each house they are escorted to the church, which is in the middle of the town. There's a nativity scene inside the church which everyone gathers around while they listen to a reading from Scripture. After that, people walk home through the streets with lanterns while they sing hymns of praise. It must be a beautiful parade! When they get home, they eat fried pork and fried pic-pacs (pig's ears).

In most homes in England there will be a Christmas pudding on the table and in America there will be turkey and pumpkin pie. Yes, in many different cultures Christmas is joyfully celebrated every year. And yet there are still people in some regions of the world who have never heard about the birth of Jesus. We must pray that they will also hear the Good News!

Read the Christmas story in Luke 2:1-20.

21 December

When God came as a baby

According to Exodus 19:10-12 the Lord said to Moses, *"Go to the people and consecrate them today and tomorrow. Have them wash their clothes and be ready by the third day, because on that day the Lord will come down on Mount Sinai in the sight of all the people. Put limits for the people around the mountain and tell them: 'Be careful that you do not go up the mountain or touch the foot of it. Whoever touches the mountain shall surely be put to death.'"*

God said this because He is holy and He wanted people to realize that sinful people were not allowed to come near a Holy God.

So the people washed themselves and their clothes and stood a little way off at the foot of the mountain. Then God spoke to Moses from the top of the mountain amidst thunder and lightning and smoke. A trumpet sounded, the earth shook and the people shivered with fear. That is how God came to His people in the Old Testament.

But when Jesus came in the New Testament, a different scene was set. On a quiet night He came as a baby. A beautiful star shone in the heavens and angels sang to announce His arrival. Shepherds visited Him, and they could touch His little hands and feet if they wanted to. When He was grown-up, people could talk to Him and laugh with Him and little children could sit on His lap. They were not scared of Him, because He was a human being like them. The only difference was that He never committed any sin. That is why He can stand between us and a Holy God and ward off all the lightning and thunder of God's wrath. We should thank God for sending His Son, Jesus.

First read Exodus 20:18 and then Matthew 1:23. Can you see the difference?

22 December

King of kings

Recently the queen of a well-known country visited the United States of America. In a weekend paper there was an article about the amount of baggage that she took along for her visit. A special plane was hired to take her there. Apart from her personal body-guards, servants, counselors, doctor and hairdresser, she also took along forty suitcases of clothing. In case the weather wasn't right, she had two outfits for each function that she had to attend. She also had twenty liters of blood with her in case of an emergency. When she landed at John F. Kennedy aiport, a military band and thousands of people were there to welcome her.

It was a completely different scene when Jesus came to visit our planet. He did not come by plane, but he was born from the body of a woman. He did not have any designer clothes to wear and there were no angels to dress Him or to fan Him with their wings. His parents, Joseph and Mary, had to put him in a manger to sleep.

In John 1:1-3 we read, *"In the beginning was the Word and the Word was with God and the Word was God. He was with God in the beginning. Through him all things were made; without him nothing was made that has been made."* Do you know of whom this was written? Yes, it was written about Jesus! And this same Jesus who was the One who had created everything together with God right at the beginning of time, came to earth as a baby who had to be fed and cared for.

He was the King of kings, but He came without any baggage while the rest of the world was fast asleep.

Say thank You to King Jesus who was prepared to become an ordinary human being so that He could come and teach us about God's love.

23 December

A feast of peace

"O little town of Bethlehem … O Morning Stars together, proclaim the holy birth, And praises sing to God the King and peace to men on earth." Maureen had been humming this song all day. The choir had sung it in church the previous day. But something bothered her. When they came home after the service and watched the news on television, there was no peace on earth. War in the Middle East, bombs in Afghanistan, crime in South Africa, riots in the Philippines … did God's plan for peace go horribly wrong somewhere along the line?

Maureen decided to ask her grandmother about it. Granny Riley knew her Bible very well and she would perhaps know what the angels meant when they said that Jesus would bring peace to the world. Her grandma lived in a cottage at the back of their house. She was always glad to see Maureen.

"Oh no, my dear," she said in her soft, calm voice. "The peace you were singing about did not mean there would be no more war and fighting after Jesus' birth. It meant that there would be peace in the hearts of God's people. The angel said, 'On earth peace to men on whom His favor rests.' People cannot have real peace without Jesus. That is why so many people are restless and dissatisfied. They do not love or care about others and they are jealous of each other. Jesus came to bring peace between God and man and when we have that, there's also peace in our hearts and love towards other people."

Now Maureen understood the words the angels spoke to the shepherds.

Maureen wrote out the words of the angels in Luke 2:14 and stuck them on her door. You can do the same.

24 December

The crib and the cross

"Mom, why do you always cry when we sing *Silent Night, Holy Night*?" Patricia asked her mother as they were walking home from church. "I'm not sure," her mom said. "I think about my childhood and all the Christmasses I've had with my family and I miss the people who have passed away since then."

"Well, at least the first Christmas was without any tears," Patricia said. "Oh, not at all!" her mom replied. "There was much crying and many tears that first Christmas. Have you forgotten what King Herod did when he heard from the wise men about the new King that had been born? 'Kill all the little boys in the vicinity,' he told his soldiers. He wanted to make sure that there would be no competition for the throne when his own children came of age. Can you imagine the grief and sorrow that the murder of the baby boys brought to the people of Judea? Thankfully an angel warned Joseph, so that their family could flee to Egypt. However, thirty-three years later, Jesus was murdered by envious people. One can never forget the cross while you are standing at the crib. The two go together."

Patricia and her mom walked in silence now. Patricia also felt sad. She thought about her dad who was not with them any longer and about all the scary things that were going on in the world. A deep longing took hold of her. She wished that Jesus would come again soon to put an end to all the tears and suffering on earth.

When they arrived at their front door, Patricia's face lit up. "Mom," she said, "now I understand why you always write Maranatha beneath the Christmas wreath on our front door." "Yes," said her mom. "It means, 'Come, Lord Jesus, come!'"

Read the last four verses in your Bible.

Maranatha

25 December

A turkey for Christmas

Focus on the Family magazine tells the story of how a certain woman became a Christian.

Mrs. Powers said that she had believed that there was a God, but she did not take Him seriously. Then something happened that changed her life completely. It all started with a turkey.

As a Christmas bonus Mr. Powers received a turkey at his workplace. However, Mrs. Powers had already bought one at the supermarket. She decided to give away the extra turkey. "To whom should I give it?" she wondered. She thought of a family living down the street. They had a lot of children and she could see that they weren't rich.

The day before Christmas she phoned them and asked whether they were interested in having the turkey. The mother of the family said, "Yes, thank you!" She sent the eldest daughter to fetch the gift. "Madam," the girl said when she arrived, "my mom has been praying for a turkey for our Christmas dinner for more than a week. She said I must tell you that God used you to answer her prayers." Mrs. Powers had never before realized that the Lord was personally involved with the prayer requests of His children. Shortly after that she became a Christian.

That Christmas God delivered a gift to each of the two homes in that street, not through the chimney, but through the channel of His love. He moved Mrs. Power to give a turkey to people who had been praying for it. And He moved a neighbor to witness to her benefactor. In that way an indifferent woman could receive in her heart the greatest gift of all, Jesus Christ, the Savior!

Make a colorful card to put amongst your Christmas decorations. Write 2 Corinthians 9:15 on it.

26 December

A basket full of prayers

Miss Nell told a story at the youth camp:

"The Lord once sent two angels to go and fetch all the prayers that had been offered that day. The one had to bring all the requests and the other one had to bring all the praise. The angel who collected the requests soon came back with a load of prayers. However, the one who had to look for the thank yous, arrived late at night with only half a basket full of praise."

Miss Nell took a letter from her pocket. "Listen to one of the prayers from the first basket," she said. *Dear Lord, please give me a scooter for my birthday and let my friends be kind to me. Help me with my music exam, although I did not practice enough for it. Let me be chosen for the basketball team and please see to it that I don't sit next to Harry on the bus, I'm not very fond of him.*

The children smiled.

"Here is a letter from the second basket," said Miss Nell. *It is good to praise the Lord and make music to your name, O Most High, to proclaim your love in the morning and your faithfulness at night ... For you make me glad with your deeds, O Lord.* She added, "This is a prayer that David wrote in Psalm 92:1-3. One can easily make it your own prayer of praise."

Then Miss Nell gave the children the opportunity to write a "thank You" letter to God. Her husband opened his car and took out a helium-filled balloon for each of the children. "Let's fasten our 'thank You' notes to the balloons and let them go," he suggested. As the kids looked up at the sky full of colorful balloons, they sang, "Give thanks with a grateful heart, give thanks to the Holy One!"

Why don't you write a thank You letter to God?

27 December

Stress

"How do you handle stress?" Camilla asked her mother. Her mom came to sit next to her. The previous week a girl at her school had committed suicide. At the parent's meeting a medical doctor had addressed the parents and said that more and more children had recently been found to have stomach ulcers, which were the result of stress. Everybody was shocked to hear that young kids could contract sicknesses that were previously only common among grown-ups.

"What's made you so tense?" her mom asked. Camilla started to cry. "Everything!" she said. Her mother had noticed that she had been very quiet recently. "Let's talk about it," her mom said. "It's no good keeping everything to yourself." "I can't," said Camilla. Her mom remembered that the doctor had said if your child does not want to talk about his troubles, let him write them down. So Camilla's mom went to fetch a writing pad and a pencil and told her to go outside and write down all the things that were bothering her.

This is what Camilla wrote: 1. I miss my friend Darlene. 2. I can't do maths. 3. Nobody at school likes me. 4. I'm ugly 5. I'm scared of Uncle Donald.

"May I see your list?" her mom asked when she came inside. She gave it to her mom and went to her room. After a while her mom followed.

"Thanks for sharing these things with me. When you are ready, we can discuss it. But now I first want you to talk to Jesus about it." She put the list on Camilla's lap and kissed her on her forehead. Then she quietly walked out of the room.

Camilla prayed and felt much better afterwards.

Make your own stress-list and then read Psalm 55:22.

28 December

Oil crisis

"Wait for me!" Colby said as he ran to keep up with the rest of the family. They were on holiday at Pearly Beach and were going to a place where penguins were being cleaned. A week earlier an oil-tanker had sunk nearby and tons of oil had been spilled into the sea. The coats of all the penguins in the vicinity had been covered by the thick oily substance. Fortunately a lot of considerate people immediately started cleaning the cute little birds.

At a house on the beach-front a crowd of helpers were busy. Some people were scrubbing the birds, others were feeding them or giving them water to drink. Colby was too young to help with the operation, but he stood outside the fence and watched all the activity. He laughed to see a penguin swallow a whole fish at a time.

"Why must the penguins be scrubbed, Mom?" asked Nerina when one of them bit her on her finger. "If we don't do it, they will die," her mom said. "They will get sick. The oil on their coats causes the feathers to stick together. Then they can't keep the cold water from their bodies. If somebody doesn't help them, fifty thousand penguins will die right here on the beach." Nerina scrubbed with renewed energy.

The family was dead tired and very dirty when they went home that evening. Their dad said, "I know that God is glad about what we've been doing today." When they had all taken a shower and were sitting down for supper, he read Proverbs 12:10. It said, *"A righteous man cares for the needs of his animal, but the kindest acts of the wicked are cruel."*

"We're not cruel!" said Colby as he clapped his little hands.

Write Proverbs 12:10 on a card and put it up near the place where you keep your pet's food.

29 December

Jesus is coming again!

Ray's father had promised to tell him more about Christ's second coming on New Year's Eve. Ray had been curious about it for a long time. Before his parents left for the midnight service that evening, his dad came to sit at the foot of his bed. "When Jesus came to earth for the first time, He came silently and unobtrusively," he said, "but it will be completely different when He comes for the second time." Ray's father was talking with great enthusiasm. "A trumpet will sound which will even wake the dead in their graves. Crowds of angels will announce His coming and then He will be seen on the clouds where He will be visible to everyone!"

"Won't people be scared?" Ray asked. "People who ignored Jesus during their lifetime, will be very scared indeed. But all His followers will be extremely glad, because He is coming to fetch them. We don't know when this day will be and we don't know for sure how it will happen, but we should trust God about it. Christians have been looking forward to this day for more than two thousand years. Jesus Himself gave us a word of consolation about His second coming. You can read it in John 14:1-3." After his dad had left, Ray looked up the passage and read out loud, *"Do not let your hearts be troubled. Trust in God, trust also in me. In my Father's house are many rooms; if it were not so, I would have told you. I am going there to prepare a place for you. And if I go and prepare a place for you, I will come back and take you to be with me that you also may be where I am."*

"Thank You, Jesus!" Ray said as the church bells started to ring in the new year.

Read Matthew 25:31-46.

30 December

The stone

It was New Year's Eve. Everywhere people were getting ready for New Year parties. However, at 74 Gray Street everything was way too chaotic for any type of celebration. The Osbornes had moved in that day. They had left their previous home at daybreak and arrived at their destination just ahead of the furniture removal lorry.

Douglas and Emma sat with their parents in the kitchen. Their father had bought take-aways and they were eating straight from the polystyrene containers. "I'll miss the farm," Douglas said. He loved farm-life. "I'll miss my friends," Emma said. She had been very happy in the boarding school where she had to stay during the week. "Yes, all of us will have to adjust to life in the city," their mom said. She was thinking of the kind neighbors that she had left behind. Their dad didn't say a word. Moving from the farm was exceptionally hard for him. The drought had forced him to sell the farm and now he had to start a new job in the city. He went outside.

After a while he called the whole family to come to him on the veranda. They clambered over the boxes and bits of furniture in the passage to get to him. Mr. Osborne had put up a stone on the garden wall. On it was painted EBENEZER. 'What does that mean?" Emma wanted to know. "It means: 'Thus far has the Lord helped us.' It is the name for our new home. God, who had been looking after us up till now, will also do so in future!"

"Where did you get that from?" Douglas asked. "In the Bible," said their dad. "The Israelites also put up a stone like that to remind them of the fact that God listens to His children when they call on Him for help."

Read 1 Samuel 7:9-12 and make a similar little stone to put on your desk for the new year.

31 December

Index of topics

Prayer:	19 April; 26 April; 27 April; 13 May; 23 May; 26 May; 9 June; 26 June; 10 July; 14 July; 12 August; 10 September; 29 September; 4 October; 15 November; 27 December.
Purity:	13 October.
Quiet time:	1 January; 6 June; 19 June; 17 July.
Responsibility:	2 March; 28 November.
Salvation:	7 January; 3 March; 10 May; 11 May; 21 May; 5 June; 14 June; 26 August; 9 September; 27 September; 30 October; 9 November.
Self-esteem:	22 February; 29 April; 27 May; 10 June; 27 June; 19 August; 26 October; 10 November.
Senior citizens:	9 June; 30 July.
Sin:	5 April; 8 April; 1 June; 3 June; 18 June; 2 July; 29 July; 31 July; 20 September; 17 November; 5 December.
Spiritual growth:	20 August; 2 September; 27 November; 30 November.
Suffering:	10 June; 7 July; 21 July; 24 July; 28 July; 28 December.
Superstition:	19 April; 9 May; 5 September.
Swearing:	29 January; 9 February; 1 July; 6 August.
The Bible:	19 February; 16 March; 15 April; 22 April; 24 April; 6 June; 29 June; 12 July; 15 July; 16 September; 14 October; 2 November; 19 November.
The future:	18 February; 20 February; 15 September; 8 November; 13 November; 30 December.
War:	11 February; 24 December.
Witnessing:	9 March; 13 March; 18 April; 25 April; 30 June; 1 August; 2 August; 14 September; 24 September; 5 October; 11 October; 15 October; 7 November; 12 November; 18 November; 27 November.